Montaigne's

Travel Journal

*Translated and with an Introduction
by Donald M. Frame*

Foreword by Guy Davenport

*North Point Press
San Francisco
1983*

CONTENTS

FOREWORD BY GUY DAVENPORT

When, in the good September weather of 1580, Michel Eyquem de Montaigne's medicine-and-book-laden coach set out for Rome by way of Austria and Switzerland and all the sights and spas along the road, Shakespeare was a loud sixteen (given to making speeches in a high style, Aubrey records) in the country town of Stratford, and Ben Jonson was a cunning little schoolboy of seven in London, learning Latin and Greek. Michelangelo had died the year Shakespeare was born. The springtime of the Renaissance was over. It was in its high summer, and its energies were moving outward from the Mediterranean. Raleigh and Drake were on the seas, copies of North's Plutarch on their cabin tables. Elizabeth, the Protestant queen of the English, who was the same age as Montaigne, had translated Boethius. A few months before his journey Montaigne had seen the first edition of the *Essais* through the press in Bordeaux.

With the *Essais* the Renaissance leaves its long period of fervent rediscovery and invention and enters the moment when Classical attitudes have become an habitual climate for the arts and education. Montaigne's first language was Latin. His mind was speculative in the manner of the Hellenistic age: eclectic in philosophy, skeptical in religion, Stoic in the conduct of life. Montaigne's emulator in the eighteenth century, the Danish Humanist Ludvig Holberg, would write, "If a man learns theology before he learns to be a human being, he will never become a human being." In the *Travel Journal* we see Montaigne again and again trying to find the man beneath the theology, the human reality beneath the trappings of office and position. He admires the affable humility of an innkeeper who is also a town councilman and who abandons his civic duties to wait at table, while finding a grand duke a snob. In Ferrara he may have seen Tasso insane, and in the next edition of the *Essais* speculated on how ambition and genius can destroy the mind.

The account of a journey by a wide-awake traveller rarely fails to make good reading. In his ability to convey a sense of place with a few deft details (a topiary garden, an historical site, local anecdotes) Montaigne can be compared to Basho, whose *Journey to the Far North* is the ideal form of all journeys of passionate pilgrims to shrines and to places which they have already visited in their imagination. Other than the meditations of his contemporaries Pierre Ronsard and Joachim du Bellay on the ruins of Rome and the remoteness in time of the Golden Age, Montaigne had no Romanticism to color his response to Italy. His eye is practical, curious, ironic.

He is, in a surprisingly modern sense, a tourist, with a tourist's interest in the amenities of the table and the bedroom. He is also, as we are never allowed to forget, a man in pain looking for a cure. His body cannot use certain minerals, probably calcium, which accumulate as pellets in his kidneys and bladder. The pain of a kidney stone is fierce, and in a male can be as sharp as birth pangs. The frequent "colic" in this journal (assuming that to be Montaigne's word for an attack of the stone) is a severe nausea in combination with the feeling that one's back is broken and that one's bowels are about to move. Montaigne was fortunate in being able to pass his kidney stones. Another sufferer, Sir Walter Scott, could not, and abided pain of excruciating intensity for as long as two weeks at a time, helplessly screaming and hearing the New Testament read to him. Montaigne's constant scrutiny of his urine in a chamber pot, his colics and dizzy spells, his ability to drink heroic amounts of hot sulfurous water, locate his journal in a time when the body was still part of personality. Later, it would disappear. Dickens' characters, for instance, have no kidney stones because they have no kidneys. From Smollett to *Ulysses*, there is not a kidney in English literature.

With the occlusion of the body there is an anaesthesia of sensibilities. Montaigne's curiosity is omnidirectional. An aristocrat with inbred self-assurance, he is unhampered by the timidities that bedevil the modern tourist. With what cool aplomb does Montaigne arrange a beauty contest and a dance for young folk at a spa, inquire vigorously of Protestants their differences sect by sect, kiss the Pope's slipper, master the social ins and outs of the Roman *ricorso*, and talk with people in every level of society, from children to cardinals.

A lively conversation with a craftsman in Pisa causes an invisible event which we read over in innocence unless alerted to what's happening. When, on Saturday, 8 July 1581, Montaigne in Pisa learned "that all trees bear as many circles and rings as they have lasted years" he is recording that fact for the second time in history. Until recently, we thought it was the first time.

On this particular day he was, like any tourist, shopping for things he would probably have other thoughts about back in Bordeaux. He bought a little cask of tamarisk wood with silver hoops, a walking stick "from India," a small vase, a walnut goblet also "from India." The man who sold him these things made mathematical instruments and fine cabinets. He knew wood. We can imagine the conversation between the craftsman and the polite foreigner with such curiosity about everything. Did the French gentleman know that in a cross-section of a tree trunk the number of concentric rings gives the age of the tree?

He did not, but was careful to make note of the fact. And there it is, in the essayist's journal, between a passage about a gift of fish to an acting company in Pisa and a passage about a laxative for his debilitating constipation, seemingly the first notation of a fact we might have supposed that everyone had always known. Historians of science used to assure us that until this nameless woodworker imparted the fact to Montaigne we had no evidence of it before.

Ninety-two years afterwards, in one of those collisions that seem to plague scientific discoveries, the secretary of the Royal Society in London received two manuscripts of botanical studies. One was from the Italian anatomist and botanist Marcello Malpighi, the founder of modern physiology. The other was from an Englishman with the wonderful name of Nehemiah Grew. The advantage that these two Renaissance botanists had over the ancients was the microscope, and between them they added as much to information too minute for the eye as their contemporary wielders of the telescope added to information too remote. And in both their manuscripts was the fact that the rings of trees in a cross-section of tree trunk tell us the tree's age.

Montaigne's recording of this fact would not be published until 1774, when the manuscript of the journal was found in a chest at the chateau. So Malpighi and Grew, neck and neck, beat Montaigne into print. Let's, briefly, follow this one detail of the journal into its reverberations, if only to show how Montaigne's acute and voracious attentiveness can steer us along a current of the times. Malpighi had been a professor at the University of Pisa, where he was a friend of the mathematician Giovanni Borelli. Now, earlier in the century Borelli's professorship had been held by one Luca Pacioli (he invented double-entry bookkeeping, if you want something to remember him by), a friend and associate of Leonardo da Vinci. Leonardo drew the illustrations for Pacioli's geometric study *De Divina Proportione*. Leonardo's best-known drawing, that of a man with his arms and legs in two positions inside a circle and a square, derives from his work with Pacioli.

When, in 1771, subscribers to the first *Encyclopaedia Britannica* could read, in the article "Agriculture," that "annual rings, which are distinctly visible in most trees when cut through, serve as natural marks to distinguish their age," they were being given a fact culled from Nehemiah Grew's *Anatomy of Plants*, one of Johnson's authorities for the *Dictionary*. Only recently have scholars knuckled down to sorting out everything in Leonardo's extensive notebooks, new volumes of which keep turning up. The Italian scholar Antonio Baldacci noticed that Leonardo recorded, and most probably discovered, some eighty years before Montaigne had his conversation at Pisa with the maker of mathematical instruments, that a tree's age can be told from its annual rings. It would seem, as Pisa keeps bobbing up in the history of this fact, that Pacioli learned it from Leonardo, Borelli from Pacioli. Did Malpighi learn it at Pisa, or discover it on his own? Montaigne's woodworker would have learned it from a Pisan professor or a Pisan professor from him.

Thus we can trace Leonardo's "obstinate rigor of attention" (the phrase is Paul Valéry's) to one fine detail of nature as it caught the sharp eye of Montaigne. Just as we have to be alerted age after age by our own new concerns to go back to Leonardo to see if he wasn't there first, so must we reread Montaigne, the *Travel Journal* along with the inexhaustible *Essays*, with fresh eyes every generation. Fernand Braudel found a mine of information in the journal for his studies of everyday life in the sixteenth century. The historian of religion, of Renaissance Italy, of medicine, of economics—Montaigne's obstinate rigor of attention serves them all.

The emotional center of gravity of the journal is, I like to think, the day in the Vatican library when Montaigne, having gazed lovingly at a manuscript Vergil and other treasures, falls into a conversation with scholars and gentlemen about Plutarch. It was his opinion that Amyot's recent translation of the *Parallel Lives of Noble Greeks and Romans* (1559) and of the *Moralia* (1572) had "taught us all how to write." Plutarch had indeed taught Montaigne how to write. It is a common error to say that Montaigne invented the essay. Plutarch invented the essay, and wrote seventy-eight of them; Montaigne invented its name in French and English.

Renaissance, rebirth. But most of the rebirths were also transformations. Phidias is not reborn in Michelangelo, nor Ovid in Poliziano. For accuracy of regeneration we have to turn to Plutarch and Montaigne. There is an uncanny resemblance between the mayor of Chaeronia in the first century and the mayor of Bordeaux in the sixteenth. Both retired early from public life after a thorough formal education and a taste of metropolitan business and court intrigue. In his life of Demosthenes, Plutarch notes that Greek opinion held that "the first requisite of a man's happiness is birth in a famous city." Virtue, however, can flourish anywhere, Plutarch says, and as for him, "I live in a small city, and I prefer to dwell there that it may not become smaller still." So the *Lives* and *Moralia* were written by a family man in a small town in Boiotia, and the *Essays* were written on a wine-growing estate outside Bordeaux, both by men of the most honest introspection in the history of letters, both skeptics with stoic minds and well-tempered good natures. It has been said of Montaigne, and can be said of Plutarch, that in reading him we read ourselves.

We all lead a moral inner life of the spirit, on which religion, philosophy, and tacit opinion have many claims. To reflect on this inner life rationally is a skill no longer taught, though successful introspection, if it can make us at peace with ourselves, is sanity itself. The surest teachers of such reflection, certainly the wittiest and most forgiving, are Plutarch and Montaigne.

Montaigne's stately tomb (with effigy in marble, his *Essays* on his chest, and with the inscription in Greek, a Latin translation being provided beneath for the illiterate) is in the Municipal Building at the junction of the rue Pasteur and the Cours Victor Hugo in Bordeaux. Montaigne's even temperament and habitual affection for life in all its forms was shaped by the ancient, even prehistoric, spirit of Bordeaux, one of the most cultivated provincial towns of the Roman Empire. In its first distinguished literary figure, Ausonius (4th century A.D.) we can make out affinities with Montaigne. He was half pagan, less than half Christian. He read everything, quoted everybody, and sported an erudition that clearly had for its message that although he lived at a great remove from Rome, Alexandria, and Athens, nevertheless we Bordelais are right up with everything. We read books. We have a university. We have travelled. We are witty and well-mannered.

Bordeaux is still a gracious, very beautiful provincial city, which has been chosen down through history to be the city to which the government in Paris retires in time of trouble. It therefore considers Paris imprudent and a bit vulgar, looking to London through ancient allegiances as its spiritual capital.

A Roman tombstone in the Museum of Aquitania states the persistent theme of Bordeaux: a society of people and animals. This stele is a sculpture of a child holding a rooster whose tail a puppy is pulling. An hour's drive brings you to the prehistoric caves in the Val Dordogne with their murals of thousands of animals painted and engraved. A city bus takes you to Montaigne's chateau, where he wondered if he played with his cat or his cat with him. Bordeaux is the birthplace of Rosa Bonheur. Did she know that she was continuing the business of the painters of Lascaux? Goya died here, having restated in *The Bulls of Bordeaux* a subject native to the region for thirty thousand years. Every Bordelais has a dog for a companion. The local strays have evolved a breed over the years, the Bordeaux Dog, an affable boulevardier of considerable charm and friendliness. Every restaurant and café has its cat (even the bar at the Théâtre, where John Adams saw his first play). It is wonderful that Montaigne lies at the corner of the rue Pasteur (doctor of men and animals) and the Cours Victor Hugo, whose favorite dog was named Senate. The nostalgia we feel in reading Montaigne, the sense that he was more comfortable in his world than we can ever be in ours, is in part that he knew without embarrasment the animal body in which the human spirit lives. In Switzerland we watch him listening to the doctrines of Zwingli as if he were a very intelligent horse, his common sense as unassailable by Zwingli as a mountain by a snowflake.

It is his poor animal body whose urine is full of painful sand that he takes from spa to spa on his journey. It is with a tame animal's willingness to play his master's games (sit up, roll over, heel) that he kisses the Pope's foot (thinking God know what in the inviolable privacy of his mind). He thought for himself, Monsieur Montaigne of Bordeaux. And thought so well, so searchingly, with such wit and intelligence, that he remains for us the best example of the sane mind and liberal spirit.

INTRODUCTION BY DONALD M. FRAME

Montaigne's *Travel Journal* has long been read less for itself than for light on its author, Michel de Montaigne (1533–1592; in his lifetime pronounced, and often spelled, Montagne), and on the vigorous *Essays* (*Essais*: 1580–1588–1595) that have kept him freshly alive for four centuries with no sign yet of decline. Next to these the *Travel Journal* seems an unwanted and unhonored child beset with handicaps: written only in part (about half) by Montaigne himself (and with half of that not in his native French but in Italian), the other half (to be sure, from Montaigne's dictation) by a secretary about whom we infer much but know little, unpublished in his lifetime and not even intended for publication, it is an orphan lucky to be alive at all. Apparently forgotten, unmissed, and unsought for two centuries after Montaigne's death, it was discovered on the eve of the French Revolution by a regional historian simply in quest of new documents, Abbé Prunis, and haphazardly published by an unscholarly bellettrist, Meusnier de Querlon, who outmaneuvered Prunis for that honor. Querlon first brought out three simultaneous editions in 1774, in Paris and Rome, then two more in that year and the next; but all five are unsatisfactory and incompatible, giving us much of the time a garbled text and little recourse in our quest of a good one. Clearly two of the manuscript's 180 pages were missing from the start; then soon after its publication the manuscript itself disappeared and has not been recovered. Some help has come just lately with the discovery by Professor François Moureau of a new source, the "Copie Leydet," copied in 1771 from Prunis's original manuscript and now published by him and Dr. René Bernoulli in their valuable book entitled *Autour du Journal de Voyage de Montaigne/1580–1980/Actes des Journées Montaigne/Mulhouse, Bâle, Octobre 1980/Avec une copie inédite du Journal de Voyage*, Geneva-Paris: Slatkine, 1982, 187 pp. plus facsimile page. (Although my time has not allowed me a thorough comparison of my translation with this text, a swift but careful check convinces me that this would produce no really significant change.)

Michel de Montaigne came from a prosperous old Bordeaux family, the Eyquems, for generations exporters of important regional commodities—the dyestuff woad, cod from the Newfoundland banks, and the fine local wines—a family ennobled in 1476 when Michel's greatgrandfather Raymond Eyquem brought the "noble house" of Montaigne, the château (with surrounding land) where Montaigne was born and that stands little changed today, on a hill just north of the river Dordogne where Périgord borders Guienne about thirty miles due east of Bordeaux. It is a tawny, red-roofed manor whose buildings and walls surround an unfinished courtyard about fifty yards square and include the famous tower that houses his study, the workplace and lair that he calls his backshop. Once ennobled, the family moved steadily out of trade into more prestigious careers in the Church and public service. Montaigne's uncle Pierre Eyquem de Gaujac was an abbot, a curate, and a councillor in a tax court. His older brother, Pierre Eyquem de Montaigne (1495–1568), in Michel's eyes "the best father there ever was" (2.12.320a and *passim*),[1] fought in Francis I's army in Italy before marrying in 1529 and then serving his city in several high offices, culminating in the mayoralty of Bordeaux (1554–1556), a charge whose onerous demands, added to the agonies of the kidney stone, sapped his health and peace of mind and brought him to the grave in 1568. He counted as much as his wife did little in the life of his oldest son and heir Michel, Micheau to his father even in his thirties. Michel's mother, born Antoinette de Louppes (Lopez) of Toulouse, probably of a family who were once Spanish Jews, was also of prosperous merchant stock but not ennobled. She bore Pierre Eyquem de Montaigne ten children, of whom the first two died very young, leaving Michel the oldest of the eight survivors. Two of these, a sister and a brother, became Protestants, while the other six and the parents remained Catholic; yet in a time of bitterly divisive religious strife the family retained its unity. Clearly Pierre de Montaigne set freedom of conscience far above sect.

It was father Pierre who arranged for Michel's upbringing: peasant neighbors for godparents and for his nursing (to bring him close to those who later on would need him); back home, gentle rearing, always waking him to the sound of music, and until age six having him taught Latin (but no French) by the direct, Erasmian method as his native tongue. Next he sent him to the admirable new school, staffed with several topnotch Latinists, which Pierre as mayor had helped found and foster in Bordeaux, the Collège de Guienne. Here Michel, whose native Latin made

---

[1]All references to Montaigne's works are to my translation of his *Complete Essays* and *Complete Works* published in 1957 and 1958 (plus paperback *Essays*, 1965). I have regularly used the initials CW to designate the *Complete Works*. In both texts the *Essays* occupy pp. 1–857 and paging is identical. References to the *Essays* provide book number, chapter number, and page number, in that order, usually with the strata indicator (a, b, or c) appended to the page number; thus the reference here is to Book II, chapter 12, page 320. The strata indicators, showing in which stratum of composition the following passage first appeared in print, before 1588 (a), in 1588 (b), or after 1588, in 1595 (c), are explained in CW, p. xvi.

him a child prodigy, daunted some teachers by his fluency and starred in several Latin tragedies by others (George Buchanan, Guillaume Guérente, Marc-Antoine Muret), while completing the twelve-year course in six; but he later looked back on those as unpleasant years, wasted "without any benefit that I can place in evidence now" (1.26.130). In the same later retrospect, he saw his schoolboy self as healthy, docile, rather mature in judgment, but in mind and character lazy and inert. "No one," he wrote, "predicted that I should become wicked, but only useless. They foresaw loafing, not knavery."

For the next eleven years, from schoolboy at thirteen to fledgling magistrate at twenty-four, we lose sight of Montaigne; hence about these years conjectures abound. He probably spent some time at the French court in Paris; much in study, perhaps at a law school (Toulouse?), probably at the prestigious new College of the Royal Lecturers, the future Collège de France, hearing such great scholars as Adrianus Turnebus, for whom his praise is unstinting.

In 1554 uncle Pierre de Gaujac bought a councillor's post in a new tax court, the Cour des Aides, or Cour des Généraux, of Périgueux, established by King Henry II precisely to raise money by such sales. Three years later, under heavy pressure from competing jurisdictions, he abolished it, but ordered its members to be incorporated into the major rival, the Parlement of Bordeaux, which received them with predictable hostility. Among these involuntary intruders was Gaujac's favorite nephew, Michel de Montaigne, in whose favor he had resigned his post; but whether Michel had served in Périgueux we do not know. We know he was under the normal minimum age for a councillor, but that his Périgueux colleagues chose him to speak for their rights at least once; and we may surmise that then, as in a different intervention two years later, he expressed himself, in the words of the official court reporter, "with all the vivacity of his character."[2]

Not a legislative body, the Bordeaux Parlement was one of the eight high courts of justice constituting *the* Parlement of France, the king's right arm in these matters (often supplanting local officials and nobles), and also a force in administration through its right to register royal edicts, hence to delay their promulgation and even at times add conditions. The Bordeaux branch was a learned and hard-working body, normally sitting from early morning until late afternoon.

It contained several chambers: Requests; Inquests; Tournelle for criminal cases; and Grand' Chambre or Great Chamber, seat of the interest and the power. Having close relatives in the upper chambers, from first to last Montaigne was denied entry to them and remained in a lesser chamber with limited jurisdiction mainly over minor cases. He spent thirteen years there, a conscientious magistrate but quite without zest

[2]See my *Montaigne: A Biography* (hereafter *Biography*; New York: Harcourt Brace & World, 1965), p. 54.

or illusion, before selling his post to retire to his château and his tower—years brightened only by the closest bond he ever formed, his deep friendship with his fellow councillor Etienne de la Boétie (1530–1563; now pronounced La Bo-ay-see, then La Bwettie), formed at their first meeting soon after his arrival and lasting four to six years (Montaigne's figures are conflicting) until La Boétie's brief illness and death at age thirty-two.

Montaigne in his late twenties was an attractive young hedonist, though in many ways thoughtful and judicious beyond his years. His friend, two years older but seeming more so, a homely man, married, with a stepson and an adolescent stepdaughter, was an accomplished though unpublished writer and a trusted negotiator for the Parlement, settled, disciplined, a pious Christian idealist drawn to the attitudes of stoical humanism, sure of his standards and aims. Different as they were, they shared an ardent reverence for the ancient Greek and Roman heroes and a desire to emulate them. From their first encounter, together they formed a friendship that both men pronounced unique and ineffable, perhaps heaven-sent; its reason, in Montaigne's memorable words, "Because it was he, because it was I" (1.28.139c). Their mutual use of the term "brother" may be a clue: Montaigne, an oldest child, may have sought an older brother's steadying hand, while his friend, orphaned early, welcomed this brilliant but still rudderless elective younger one.

La Boétie's sudden illness (dysentery) and death were a cruel blow to his friend, who never replaced him or ceased to mourn him. For a year or so he sought diversion in various amours; then at age thirty-two, on his father's arranging and urging (which he approved), in 1565 he let himself be married, to Françoise de La Chassaigne, twenty, of a Catholic Bordeaux family long prominent in the Parlement. She bore him six children, all girls, of whom only one, Leonor, lived past infancy, growing up to marry twice and continue the line. Theirs was apparently a dutiful union, but except for occasional child-getting not of the closest.

No doubt well aware of Michel's unfulfillment in the Parlement, father Pierre gave him another nudge, a year or two later, in a new direction, by asking him to translate into French a long (almost a thousand pages), plodding, but popular Latin theological treatise, the *Book of the Creatures* (or, *of the Creation*) or *Natural Theology* of the Spanish polymath Raymond Sebond,[3] written shortly before the author's death in Toulouse in 1436 and published in 1484, an instant success in Germany and Holland and from 1509 on in France. Sebond tries to prove all the Christian dogmas by the evidence of the creation, the book of nature, calling this more convincing than Scripture, and aiming thus to combat nominalist fideism, which opposes faith to reason. His "Prologue" abounds

---

[3]Many spellings of the last name appear, including Sabaude, Sabonde, Sabunde, Sabiende, Sabieude, Sebon, Sebonde, Sebeyde, Sibiude. I use the form Montaigne used, but write him as Raymond Sebond instead of Raimond Sebond.

in extravagant claims of success; his main argument is the analogy of man's superiority over the lower orders of creation, which he compares to the infinite superiority of God over man and the rest of the created world. Probably for this liminary presumption, in 1559 the work was placed on the Church's Index of Forbidden Books, then in 1564 the text proper was removed but the Prologue retained. Montaigne translated its nine hundred-odd pedestrian pages at his father's request, and presumably (despite 2.12.320a) needed a year or two to do it. Was Pierre de Montaigne's youthful Latin too rusty to let him enjoy the original, or was this a pretext for setting his gifted son to a suitable task—or both? We do not know; but the accuracy and sprightliness of his version suggest some satisfaction in the making of it, and the neophyte showed genuine flair, hewing to the sense of the original but opening up the style to let in light and air. He is accurate only in the body of the text, however; for in the censured Prologue Montaigne systematically cut down Sebond's excessive claims for the book from "necessary" to "useful," thus showing much the same reservations about the Spaniard's intellectual stature that so strongly mark his "Apology for Raymond Sebond" (2.12) about eight years later. Neither his own translation nor its Prologue was ever censured.

Pierre de Montaigne lay dying at home while Michel was in Paris preparing the translation for publication, even dating his dedication to his father—presumably to explain his absence from the deathbed—on the very day his father died (June 18, 1568).

Now Lord of Montaigne and head of the family, married and before long to have a child on the way, Montaigne late in 1569 applied to rise to a higher chamber in the Parlement, met the inevitable refusal, and chose to resign rather than seek the usual royal dispensation, selling his post to his friend Florimond de Raemond. Much of summer 1570 he spent in Paris publishing the five minor works of La Boétie that he had preserved, each one with his own dedication, one to his wife, the rest to friendly notables whom he wished to enlist as champions of his friend's memory. Not six months after completing this pious duty, on his thirty-eighth birthday (February 28, 1571), he had a Latin inscription painted on a wall near his study to commemorate his retirement from the cares and duties of Court and Parlement to the bosom of the learned Muses, there to invite his soul—and, we judge, do some writing of his own and find out what he had to say and wanted to write. His new leisure was to be neither uninterrupted nor an unmixed blessing; but out of it were to come his *Essays*.

A devotee of history and memoirs, he started many chapters with observations on current or past events, only later, and then gradually, turning more and more for his main matter to himself, his thoughts, and his experience. For the previous eight years especially, from the death of his dearest friend (1563) to that of his father, a younger brother, and his first infant child (1568–1570), besides his own closest brush with it

in a horseback collision right near home in 1569 or 1570 (see 2.6), death
had been all around and had repeatedly struck close. In these circumstances, and in a France all too often drenched with human blood, as
from the Massacre of Saint Bartholomew's Day (October, 1572), Montaigne's near obsession with death in his early *Essays* (1.19–20, 2.13,
etc.) is hardly surprising: after all, death has always been the surest fact
of human life. Nor is his nearly equal concern with pain: it too was all
around, and he had witnessed his dear father's long suffering that led to
his death, and this from a malady, the kidney stone, that he might well
inherit—as indeed he later did. To Montaigne around age forty, adjust-
ing to retirement, life and the human condition looked bleak: the condition frail, ignorant, and presumptuous; the life holding less to hope for
than to fear (2.12.363–364a). His pessimistic outlook resembles that of
his late friend as we glimpse this in Montaigne's account of his death (CW
pp. 1046–1056, especially 1048–1054).

   And so, predictably, does Montaigne's early stance, apprehensive
and defensive. Against the two great threats to man's life and happiness,
what better preparation than premeditation of death (1.20.56a and *passim*) and tensing the will to resist pain when it comes (1.14.39 and *passim*)? In his early retirement and essays Montaigne's solution to life's
main problems, much like La Boétie's before him, is that of an apprehensive stoical humanist.

   While his friend lived, Montaigne had not always fully agreed with
him on all matters nor been fully won over to his stoical sympathies; but
after witnessing his death, braver than Montaigne had thought possible,
as he says (CW, p. 1050), "I praised God that this had been in a person
by whom I had been so loved and whom I loved so dearly; and . . . this
would serve me as an example, to play the same part in my turn." This
he had said to his dying friend; it was in effect a sacred promise. Now in
his early retirement at thirty-eight, it may have struck him that for someone his age with his advantages in birth, station, native gifts, and upbringing, someone who was soon to write that "our souls are as devel-
oped at twenty as they are ever to be" (1.57.237a), he had not
accomplished much nor was likely to in future. He had paid one pious
tribute to his friend's memory by publishing, as advantageously as he
could, his minor works; he planned to publish his masterpiece, the *Dis-
course on Voluntary Servitude*, in his own chapter on friendship at the
heart of his first book of *Essays*. The one thing he still must do was live
up to his promise and his friend's memory by trying to live and die as
bravely as he—or as bravely as possible. He might have failed in much
else; in this he must not fail.

   When we consider how much Montaigne's *Essays* are themselves
(among other things of course) a compensation for the loss of La Boétie,[4]
we need not wonder that even more than before, for ten years after his

<hr />

[4]*Biography*, pp. 81–84.

death, Montaigne was under his spell, almost under his shadow, as he sought above all to be the guardian of his friend's shrine. La Boétie had taught him that death could be met bravely and that our studies must aim at this. Now in his earliest chapters, full of the subject, he writes in the same vein: "I leave it to death to test the fruit of my studies. We shall see then whether my reasonings come from my mouth or from my heart" (1.18.55a). There are of course bookish influences also at work here— Seneca, Cicero, Lucretius among others—for both friends were bookish, La Boétie unashamedly so. But the major role in changing Montaigne in his thirties from a blithe though reflective young hedonist into an apprehensive stoical humanist was played, in life and even more in death, by La Boétie.

Whereas in his earliest chapters (about 1572–74), relying largely on his books, Montaigne had preached resistance to pain and premeditation for death, by a little bit later (1573 or so) his own experience and his reflection on it had taught him a more relaxed attitude toward both adversaries (2.6.267–268a), and, more important, what vast resources experience and reflection offer us all through self-study. In the next few years (1573–1575), to follow Pierre Villey's dating,[5] he comes more and more to look critically at stoical humanism, finding it unfit for mankind, unnatural, impractical, and unsound. At first he had looked to the stoical hero Cato the Younger (of Utica) as a model of consistency as well as of heroism (2.1.241a); but now, in the very next chapter (2.2.251a), he finds consistency incompatible precisely with the heroic actions he had most admired; and after beginning the chapter after that with a barrage of stoically colored slogans from Seneca and others favoring suicide as man's ultimate resource against the woes of life, he abruptly turns about (2.3.253a) with the remark "this does not pass without contradiction," and condemns suicide as cowardly, unnatural, and un-Christian. In short, in the few chapters datable to 1573–1575 Montaigne attacks stoical humanism, mainly in its heroic extremes, as unfit for himself and for man in general, un-Christian, cowardly, comically histrionic (2.2.249a), and presumptuous. He is well on his way toward his next major step, which fills the enormous "Apology for Raymond Sebond" (2.12): a devastating critique of human reason and its vanity, and indeed of all dogmatic philosophy, toward which he sums up man's only appropriate attitude in his famous question "Que sçay-je?" ("What do I know?" 2.12.393b). The dominant theme of this chapter is Pyrrhonian skepticism; and this is rightly considered one of the important aspects of Montaigne's thought.

The sweeping skepticism of the "Apology," however, is not at all a commitment or a conviction, but rather a temper of mind and a tool of argument, which Montaigne uses deftly to deflate man's vanity and pre-

[5]Pierre Villey worked out a remarkably satisfactory dating of the individual chapters of the *Essays* in that milestone of Montaigne scholarship, his dissertation *Les Sources et l'évolution des Essais de Montaigne* (Paris: Hachette, 1908, 2 vols.) I follow it here.

sumption. Even the original version shows his distance from any commitment by his story (2.12.430a) of the newfangled physicist who found the ancients mistaken about wind directions, prompting Montaigne's reply that he would rather follow facts than reason—and then his note that "the Pyrrhonians use their arguments and their reason only to ruin the apparent facts of experience," and his wonder at the plausibility of their arguments. More important are two vital facts about the chapter as a whole. Montaigne's skeptical arguments apply almost solely to knowledge of externals, not of self (and mainly to perfect knowledge, not the imperfect practical kind available to man). Moreover, one of his strongest proofs of our universal ignorance is our ignorance of ourselves; and he draws the moral of what should be done when he writes: "he who understands nothing about himself, what can he understand?" (2.12.418c) and later on, with the same problem in mind, "At least we must become wise at our own expense" (2.12.423a).

In short, one key idea of the "Apology" from the very first (though most clearly stated in a late addition, 2.12.418c) is that knowledge of self is basic to all human knowledge and wisdom, and is presumably not inaccessible to man. (At least nothing suggests that it is, and much implies that it is not.)

From this point on (perhaps around 1577–1578) Montaigne sets himself to make the *Essays* the "book of the self" that they have since been called, and that in his 1580 notice to the reader he seems to imply they have been all along: the self-portrait produced by his self-study. His chapter "Of Presumption" (2.17), probably composed in 1578–1580, offers his first sketch of a self-portrait; and in the chapters of this period, the late 1570s, he speaks readily of himself and uses himself as example, often as proof. After 1580, in Book III and in all the *b* and *c* additions, he will do so even more.

This is not to say that in 1578 self-study and self-portrayal were new ideas to Montaigne, unexplored before the composition of the "Apology for Raymond Sebond"; far from it. The first clear trace and praise of self-study, at the very end of the original version of "Practice" (2.6.272a), dates probably from 1573–1575; and there, curiously, he says nothing about self-portrayal. That, I am convinced, he had in mind from the appalling moment (presumably between 1574 and 1578) when he saw to his consternation his dead friend's masterpiece, the *Voluntary Servitude*, published twice, once in part and later in full, in two collections of seditious pro-Protestant pamphlets.[6] Therefore he abandoned his cherished plan to publish it at the center of his chapter on friendship and thus of his first book of *Essays* (see 1.28.135, 144), recognized the vulnerability of his own memory to complete misrepresentation (which no be-

---

[6]See my article "Specific Motivation for Montaigne's Self-Portrait" in *Columbia Montaigne Conference Papers*, pp. 60–69 (eds. Donald M. Frame and Mary B. McKinley, Lexington, Ky.: French Forum Monographs 27, 1981).

reaved friend would correct for him as he had done for La Boétie), and so undertook his self-portrait (which therefore had to be lifelike; see 3.5.677) as his best, perhaps his only, protection against this: as he says (3.9.752n), "That is why I myself decipher myself so painstakingly."

Insofar as one can arrange such matters chronologically, I believe that Montaigne's plans for self-study and self-portrayal generally went hand in hand in his planning and thinking; but that probably the value of self-study was the first to emerge clearly. His horseback accident must date from some time in 1567–1570; it was four years later that he wrote it up; and clearly it was the writing up, not the event, that taught him most—and led him to the generalization about the value of self-study ("spying on oneself from close up") that ends the original chapter (2.6.272a). His immediate and specific motivation for the self-portrait, I am convinced, is one or both of the two traitorous publications noted above, the *Réveille-Matin des François* of March 1574 and Volume III of the *Mémoires de l'Estat de France* of 1577. Of course Montaigne may possibly have known, or known of, either or both before publication; but in any case the critical date for his decision (unknown to us now, perhaps forever) is of course the one when he first learned of either of these, hence probably in or soon after March, 1574; while the first actual sketch of a self-portrait, in "Presumption" (2.17), was probably composed in 1578–80, thus not long before the *Essays* first appeared. In short, I believe that his thinking about self-knowledge as our basic knowledge in the "Apology" did not engender, but rather strongly confirmed, his decision to study and portray himself; for surely that decision—or those decisions, if that is the truer term—was (or were) not made with a snap of a finger or turn of a card, but reached slowly, along with that of the essay form, as Montaigne wrote and thought his way into his lifework and into the subject, title, and medium of his book.

By about 1578 these three had all taken clear shape for him, and he had also completed the first half of his general mission, the critique of man's knowledge, reason, and capacity for either one, the demonstration of human frailties and limitations, that he deemed the necessary prelude to any constructive views. He made his point well; for the next two centuries and more, from Descartes and Pascal to Emerson and countless others since, he was to be primarily Montaigne the skeptic. Never a melancholic, he was now ready to examine the other side of the coin and show man his capacities and resources for happy living, through self-study, according to the human condition and God's laws for it. In short, he is now fully ready to move ahead—or to build on solid ground; either metaphor will serve—but he still needs one more thing first. His constant depreciation of his book and his plan (of which more shortly) in the last few years before publication (1578–1580), I believe, though of course less than candid, is yet more than the "modest-author" version of the threadbare "Unaccustomed as I am . . . " of the public speaker, *de rigueur* today and possibly already stale when Socrates used it (perhaps rashly) to his prospective judges in ancient Athens. I think that Montaigne in 1578–1580 felt about his intensely personal book something akin to stage fright. By his own account at least (though it may have been a Gascon *boutade*, 3.2.614c, that he bought printers in Guienne, elsewhere they bought him), he presumably subsidized that first 1580 edition. And I read his later statement (3.9.736b, first published in 1588) that "the favor of the public has given me a little more boldness than I expected," as a serious comment, on his state of mind before publication as well as after. I believe, that is, that he still needed assurance *from someone else* that what he was up to made sense: that there was more to his self-portrait than the self-indulgent anecdotage of a well-read eccentric. He did not lack all confidence: his translation had done well, and indeed would soon require a second edition; he probably had at least some wind of this before his own debut, when he dated March 1, 1580 the offhand farewell that ends his salute to the reader of his new book, the *Essays*, even while in it warning that reader—prematurely, for this was as yet only partly true—that he himself was the matter of his book, which therefore scarcely merited attention. In using this variant, then still relatively new, on the familiar topos of the modest author, he rightly foresaw readers who would be disarmed not dissuaded by this quip to the wise, even as by his relentless depreciation of the book and the plan—the "stupid enterprise" and "wild and eccentric plan" (2.6.278a) that spawned these "mean and trivial remarks" and "stupid things" (2.17.495–496a), or, in short, "these absurdities" (1.26.108a). Well and good. But it is one thing to anticipate an understanding "gentle reader" (or better, many of them), quite another that for this book so personal as to be a second self there should be many such readers out there, and buying the book. Death might be the test of his studies and his philosophy; publication would be the test of his plan and work, of the very writer that he had become. So let the *Essays* essay their destiny; he too, their alter ego, would be essaying his. He must have known well, though he refrains from quoting it (too hackneyed, perhaps?), the one memorable phrase of Terentianus Maurus on the subject (*De Syllabis*, line 1008): "Pro captu lectoris habent sua fata libelli." So let the printer Simon Millanges do his best, and "vogue la galère!" Now at least and at last, for better or for worse, he would find out where he stood. Indeed (and why not?) he might pay another visit to Paris and the court, this time to present his book to His Most Christian Majesty, Henry III of France, whom for years he had served as a gentleman of his chamber, and who, for all his notorious dissoluteness, his devotion to transvestitism and to his *mignons*, was a cultivated connoisseur of letters. Such a visit might even be the start of the long leisurely trip he was now planning with a few close relatives and friends. Lacking any confidence in his own durability, he presumably made no attempt to plan far ahead or peer far into the future—those ever-fruitless exercises that would have made no sense at all in the France of his time. His own future, both in life and on earth after, would no doubt have surprised and perhaps gratified him. He would surely have shaken his head—or, as he likes to say, with a donkey in mind, his ears (3.8.721c)—at the notion that today, four hundred years later, in that New World then frequented, one gathers, by his friends the cannibals, men sprung from his "neighbors and former cousins" the English (2.12.436a) and still using that tongue, had displaced the cannibals and would now be seriously discussing, even translating and publishing, not only his other self the *Essays* but even that most casual of documents his *Travel Journal*. Lacking documentary proof, he would surely have relegated any such cock-and-bull story to a conspicuous place among the fables he derides in "Cripples" (3.11). Credible but still amazing is how I suspect he might have found much of the honor and recognition that later came his way in life; but since he did experience them, one may hope he would not have dismissed them like posthumous honors as "mustard after dinner" (3.10.772c).

Many and varied, his honors in life were to include, in roughly chronological order, his bull of Roman citizenship, obtained not easily although with Papal help while in Rome (*Travel Journal*, hereafter TJ, p. 98; *Essays* 3.9.764–766b); his election, unsought, unwanted, and apparently unexpected, to a two-year term (1581–1583) as mayor of Bordeaux (3.10.768–770b, 781–784b; TJ, pp. 155–156; *Biography*, pp. 223–245); the second term (1583–1585), far more demanding, that he sought and won (3.10.768b and CW, pp. 1068–1088); the considerable success of his *Essays* from the start, attested by compliments from Henry III and the Papal Censor, the need for a second edition within two years, the many borrowings, the high praise from current literature reviewers La Croix du Maine and Antoine du Verdier in 1584, the enthusiasm of a literary pundit and future friend, the eminent Belgian Latinist and man of letters Justus Lipsius (1547–1606), who reveled in the *Essays* and crowned Montaigne as an "Eighth Sage" by calling him the "French Thales" (*Biography*, p. 249); and the continuing ready acceptance of the *Essays* attested by their appearance in three or four editions[7] leading up to the first one in three books, by the topnotch Paris publisher Abel L'Angelier in 1588, and then leading Montaigne, in view of a sixth edition that would offer no new books or new chapters (for he must have sensed that he had little time left), to continue for his last four years of life carefully rereading what he had written, often revising it (to make his final message as true as he could), and adding to it, in his own hand, about a thousand passages that in total length make up about one quarter of his complete final text on a copy (mainly in the margins) of his 1588 edition now preserved in the Municipal Library of Bordeaux and hence known as the "Bordeaux Copy," which is the basis for the first posthu-

---

[7]That 1588 L'Angelier edition is the fourth we know of (after those of 1580, 1582, and 1587) and probably the fourth that existed; but it is issued as the fifth, and the revised and augmented copy of it is marked "sixth."

mous edition (1595) by Marie de Gournay, and, with that 1595 edition, for most texts of the *Essays* ever since.

So the *Essays* came out in Bordeaux, and soon after, apparently, Montaigne rode north to Paris and the court to present a copy to the king, who may have received a copy already, since we are told that he complimented him on it and that Montaigne replied that if his Majesty liked his book he should like him too, since it was simply an account of his life and actions (see *Biography*, p. 208). Montaigne followed this state visit by serving as a volunteer in the king's army, under his future co-worker, leader, and mainstay in the region of Bordeaux during the four years of Montaigne's mayoralty (1581–1585), Jacques II de Goyon, comte de Matignon (1525–1597), marshal of France, at the long-drawn-out siege of Protestant-held La Fère in Normandy, where he saw a friend, Philibert de Gramont, husband of Diane d'Andoins and one of the king's *mignons*, mortally wounded by a cannon shot, and rode with the funeral cortège as far as Soissons.

Next on his agenda was a seventeen-month trip (June 22, 1580 to November 30, 1581) which would have been longer had he not been called back to France—a trip to Rome and a long stay there, going via mineral baths and other points of interest in France, Switzerland, Germany, Austria, and especially Italy. He had five strong reasons for the trip: ill health, heartsickness over the state of France, weariness of domesticity, eagerness to see Venice and especially his spiritual homeland Rome, and sheer love of travel.

After enjoying health he called ebullient for his first forty-odd years, for two years he had been a prey to the agonizing attacks of the kidney stone, which had tormented and finally killed his father. Advisedly mistrusting the empty pretensions of medicine and convinced that each man could, and should, be his own best doctor, he viewed the use of mineral waters (for both drinking and bathing) as harmless, since natural, and possibly offering some slight relief, and had found some relief himself, in France, at the spas of Aigues-Caudes and Bagnères. Now he proposes to try some others there and abroad, in neighboring countries; he starts, still in France, with Plombières; but La Villa, near Lucca, will be his favorite. He went about his study seriously and clinically, assessing each spa; thus his Journal is in part a record of treatment and effect, waters drunk and voided, stones passed (and circumstances), and reactions resulting; so that at times he sounds rather like his neighbor who made his life known, he says, "only by the workings of his belly. You would see on display at his home a row of chamber pots, seven or eight days' worth. That was his study, his conversation; all other talk stank in his nostrils" (3.9.721b). His journal, however, is no mere case history; and we sense a wry smile when Montaigne remarks: "It is a stupid habit to keep count of what you piss" (TJ, p. 124).

Montaigne's revulsion and horror at the depravity of the civil wars in France fill much of the *Essays*, especially the parts written late: the last four chapters of Book Three and many of the final (*c*) additions (e.g., 2.12.323–325c; 3.9–13, especially 3.9.722b, 725, 730–733, 741–744, 754–760; 3.10.774, 777–783; 3.11.785–790; 3.12.796–801, 811–814; 3.13, 815, 819–821, 825–826). "I ordinarily reply," he writes (3.9.743c), "to those who ask me the reason for my travels, that I know well what I am fleeing from, not what I am looking for. . . . It is always a gain to change a bad state for an uncertain one. . . . The troubles of others should not sting us like our own."

So weary is he of domesticity that much of the chapter ("Of Vanity") where he talks the most about travel is much concerned with that too: he states and explains his feeling early in it (3.9.723–729); and parts of it further on read almost like a debate with his wife over travel, with Michel pro and Françoise con (3.9.743–748, 750–756).

While Rome was understandably his main destination and objective, Venice was a good second. For many freedom-loving western Europeans in Montaigne's time its prestige was great on several counts: as a center of political intelligence and power, as a seat of learning that rivaled the best, and as a genuinely democratic republic stoutly preserving freedom of thought and expression. La Boétie had used it as a symbol of liberty in his *Voluntary Servitude*; Montaigne had written that his friend would rather have been born there than in Sarlat; and after the trip he added: "and with reason" (1.28.144a) Montaigne was later to try to persuade a friend to accept the ambassadorship there, offering, if he should, to keep him company there as much as he might wish (*Biography*, p. 206). And on the trip the secretary notes "his extreme hunger to see that city" (TJ, p. 58) and his saying that he could not have stayed peacefully anywhere in Italy, even in Rome, without having had a look at Venice. As for Rome, going there was a sort of first homecoming at age forty-seven; early training, favorite reading, bond with La Boétie, awe at its greatness, all conspired to make it his obvious destination. He had known its affairs long before those of his own house, the Capitol before the Louvre, the Tiber before the Seine; he started (as a youngster, we may assume) a hundred quarrels, he says, in defense of Pompey and of Brutus (3.9.762–763); and all this just about the ancient city, besides its importance to a Catholic as the seat of his Church. No wonder this was where he headed for, stayed the longest, and came back to once more when recalled to Bordeaux before returning expeditiously to France and home; no wonder the secretary writes that the night before he first arrived there (November 29, 1580, TJ, p. 71) he got his whole company up and off three hours before daybreak, "so eager was he to see the pavement of Rome."

The love of travel is a recurrent theme especially of the chapter "Of Vanity." Perhaps it betokens restlessness and irresolution, he admits. If so, so be it: "these are our ruling and predominant qualities." And he goes on in the same vein: "A single cord never keeps me in place. 'There is vanity,' you say, 'in this amusement.' But where is there not? And these fine precepts are vanity, and all wisdom is vanity" (3.9.756b; see also 766b). The most striking evidence of it, however, is the secretary's long account of it in the *Travel Journal* (CW, p. 915), written at Rovereto in late October after over four months of travel with the essayist, and written as a sort of early taking stock or summing up, perhaps shortly after a talk with his master, noting "the pleasure he took in visiting unknown countries, which he found so sweet as to make him forget the weakness of his age and of his health," and "that after spending a restless night, he would get up with desire and alacrity in the morning when he remembered that he had a new town or region to see" (CW, p. 915); so that "I never saw him less tired or complaining less of his pains." Had he been alone, he says further of Montaigne, "he would rather have gone to Cracow or toward Greece by land than make the turn toward Italy"; but he could not win over the rest of his party to his mind in this. Montaigne felt, says the secretary, "rather like people who are reading some very pleasing story . . . or any fine book" and come to fear "that soon it will come to an end"; for likewise "he took such pleasure in traveling that he hated to be nearing each place where he was to rest. . . . "

A secret motive, such as a diplomatic mission, has been suggested for the trip, but on scanty evidence; and the five clear reasons listed were quite enough.

Because of the missing manuscript pages at the start of the *Journal*, we do not know just when and where the trip started: apparently in or very near Paris in early September, 1580; but at all events September 5 finds the party just north of Paris at Beaumont-sur-Oise, where young Charles d'Estissac joins the others—that is to say, besides Montaigne and a number of servants, Michel's youngest brother, Bertrand de Mattecoulon, aged twenty, who went to learn fencing in Rome and was to become involved (and nearly condemned to death or long imprisonment for his role) in a deadly duel in which, as a second, he killed his man, then had to assist his principal in finally killing the latter's adversary as well (see 2.27.526b and *Biography*, pp. 33–35, 118), Bernard (also sometimes called Bertrand) de Cazalis, widowed husband of Michel's youngest sister Marie, and a certain Monsieur du Hautoy, from the Barrois region.

On the trip as a whole Montaigne spent 451 days (228 in long stays, 154 in Rome and 74 in La Villa) and covered between 2500 and 3000 miles in about 120 days of travel (all of course on his favorite horseback), at a pace between 20 and 25 miles per day; and he visited five countries in all (in modern terms): Switzerland, Germany, Austria, Italy, and his native France. It may be viewed for convenience as divided into eleven stages, as follows: (1) Across France toward Switzerland (9/5–28/1580), about 225 miles SE by S from Beaumont through Meaux, Bar-le-Duc, Domrémy, etc., to the baths of Plombières for an eleven-day stay. (2) Switzerland (9/28–10/7/1580), about 75 miles E, from Mulhouse to

Schaffhausen, with two days at Basel and five at the baths in Baden. (3) Germany, Austria, and the Alps (10/8–27/1580), going E from Constance beyond Kempten, N to Augsburg for four days, then S through Munich, Innsbruck, and the Brenner Pass to Bolzano. (4) Italy on the road to Rome (10/28–11/30/1580), about 350 miles S, via Trent, Lake Garda, Verona, Vicenza, Padua, Venice (one week), Ferrara, Bologna (three days), Florence, and Siena. Stage 5 is nearly five months in Rome (11/30/1580–4/19/1581). Stage 6 (4/19–5/7/1581) took Montaigne about 125 miles NE to Loreto (three days), thence NW to Sinigaglia, W about 115 miles via Urbino and Florence to Lucca (three days) and the nearby baths of La Villa for his first stay (Stage 7, 5/7/1581–6/21/1581). For over half the summer (Stage 8, 6/21/1581–8/14/1581) he traveled, E to Florence (ten days), W to Pisa for twenty-four and Lucca for seventeen, then returned for his second stay (Stage 9, 8/14/1581–9/12/1581) at La Villa, which he left when summoned back to Bordeaux to take up his new duties as mayor. He first went back to Rome (Stage 10, 9/12/1581–10/1/1581), about 170 miles S, spending eight days in Lucca, three in Siena, and three in Viterbo; and after two weeks in Rome winding up his affairs, he returned rapidly home to Montaigne (Stage 11, 10/5/1581–11/30/1581; about 750 miles N, NW, and W) via Siena, Lucca, Piacenza, Pavia, Milan, Chambéry, Lyons (eight days), Clermont-Ferrand, Limoges, and Périgueux.

One final statistic to complete the cycle of our remarks on the *Travel Journal* and come out where we went in: of Montaigne's 451 days on the trip, he spent just over one-fifth (95 in all, at Baden, Plombières, and primarily La Villa) at mineral spas seeking relief from his stone.

But there is far more to the *Travel Journal* than the clinical record of Montaigne's illness and treatment of it. True, it is neither polished nor profound, neither markedly skeptical nor—as most of its first readers had hoped—daringly irreligious. Also true, it offers almost none of the rich Latin lore, often directly quoted, that fills the *Essays*, nor the inexhaustible abundance of concrete metaphor that gives each page of the *Essays* its fresh and enduring life; it simply is not a classic like his masterwork. But as a complement to the *Essays* it tells us much about Montaigne that the *Essays* do not. This is of various sorts and degrees of interest, ranging from the merely corroborative up through the complementary and that which modifies or qualifies what the *Essays* or other sources say or suggest to that which is in actual contradiction, explicit or implicit, with it, such as his failure to mention in the *Journal* seeing the poet Tasso insane and presumably in a madhouse in Ferrara, as the *Essays* speak so movingly of his doing (2.12.363a—a passage added in 1582) that painters found the scene an irresistible one to set their brushes and imaginations to.

About accommodations Montaigne is surprisingly informative, and concerned with meals and prices as well as living quarters. But he knows how little a tourist can rapidly learn in depth of a town or region, and some of these are for him brush strokes in a kind of portrait. From the many details he records in Basel, for example (TJ, pp. 13–14), of churches and houses, inside and out, furniture, clocks, spotless polished woodwork and floors, meals of several hours at groaning tables, we come to know a tidy, hard-working people, fond of food and comfort. Most revealing in this respect is his note on the Inn of the Rose at Innsbruck (TJ, p. 42): "Around some of the beds there were curtains; and to show the character of the nation, they were beautiful and rich. . . , for the rest short and narrow, in short no use for what we use them for."

Yet more surprising is his interest in machines, even in gadgets. He describes in detail water supply systems at Neufchâteau, Constance, and Augsburg (TJ, pp. 7, 24–25, 35), a clipped and trained tree at Schaffhausen, the complicated postern gate in Augsburg to screen late travelers seeking admission to the city; and the pleasure houses of the Fuggers there and of a duke and a cardinal elsewhere (at Pratolino, Castello, and Tivoli—the Villa d'Este). He is fascinated by all signs of human ingenuity. He favors those landscapes cultivated against odds, as is one near Thann and another near Foligno. A love of natural scenery shows in the latter and in his choice of a room on his first arrival at La Villa (TJ, pp. 119–120), influenced by the lovely view and confirmed by the gentle sound of the river below at night. Likewise, when the party approached Narni, a bad bout of the stone did not keep him from enjoying the beauty of the place.

His fondness for theological discussion is surprising but understandable. In his published work, the Sebond translation and his *Essays*, he is naturally cautious: for he fully accepts the Church's doctrines as true and knows that his own merely human views (or "fancies") may, without his knowledge or will, be heterodox and false; so when his personal convictions lead him into theological matters he is quick to disclaim any expertise. But he knows why he believes the Protestants are wrong, and loves to seek out the local dominie in Protestant regions or towns: so much so that in Mulhouse the secretary writes: "Monsieur de Montaigne went to see the church; for they are not Catholics there." Other faiths fascinate him. In Verona he visited a synagogue and reported the service as he later did a circumcision he witnessed in Rome, objectively but with a friend's eye rather for similarities to Christian ritual than for differences from it. A good Catholic, naturally he attends their services most often.[8] He is dismayed at Italian casualness at these, noting it at a High Mass in Verona, and even more in Rome at the Pope's Mass on Christmas Day, on the part of the prelates, even the Cardinals present and the Pope himself. In these services he finds more magnificence than devoutness, and less of the latter in general than in France—in which his Jesuit friend Father Juan Maldonado fully concurs. He reports what he sees that

---

[8]On the basis of the same evidence, Henri Busson found Montaigne's Catholic practice mediocre, while Canon Maturin Dreano found it distinctly good. Each has a case.

strikes him, edifying or not: the perplexing conduct of the flagellant Penitents, an ugly squabble among friars, a bizarre exorcism, a miraculous cure. Generally he seems well impressed by Catholic practice; much enjoyed hearing many fine sermons in Lent by preachers who included one "renegade rabbi" and two Jesuits who preached, one to his fellow Jesuits, the other to the Pope and Cardinals. He has the highest admiration for this order (the Society of Jesus) and marvels at its rapid rise to be a nursery of great men and bulwark of the Church against the heretics. He enjoyed two good meetings and talks with Maldonado (one at Epernay, one in Rome) and seems to have followed him as his spiritual director; at least a younger friend of Montaigne's says that "Maldonado was the heart and soul of the sieur de Montaigne," who "rested his own belief entirely on Maldonado's opinions" (*Biography*, p. 215). (An outstanding scholar-teacher of theology, it was Maldonado who managed the first, forced conversion of Henry of Navarre to Catholicism in 1572, and whom Navarre, then Henry IV for France, asked for in 1593 for his second and final one, only to learn of his death.) Maldonado, incidentally, is never mentioned in the *Essays*, only in the *Travel Journal*.)

Interesting to any reader of Montaigne are his report of his audience with the Pope, Gregory XIII (Ugo Buoncompagno, 1572–1585), who had held a public celebration of the Massacre of Saint Bartholomew's Day, and his comments on the pontiff. He notes his long white beard, his Bolognese language ("the worst idiom in Italy") and halting speech, but in the main is simply respectful, finding him very handsome and vigorous for his eighty-odd years (read, seventy-nine), majestic, a great builder and almoner and especially proselytizer, loving his son with a frenzy but still just, gentle in nature, generous with audiences but brooking no discussion. Montaigne tells us that the Pope helped him get his bull of Roman citizenship, and thinks that in the audience he raised his slipper slightly when it was time for Montaigne to kiss it.

Yet more interesting is his account (our only one) of his interviews with the official Papal Censor, Father Sisto Fabri, O.S.D. (1541–1594), Master of the Sacred Palace, professor of theology at the University of Rome, and soon (1583) to be general of the Dominican Order. What happened was this. On reaching Rome (November 30, 1580), Montaigne was surprised to have his books taken from him at the customs for inspection, as was the practice; then dismayed to learn how strict and knowledgeable their examiners could be, but relieved that he had no condemned books with him. When they returned his *Essays* four months later, their praise was gratifying, the criticism mild, and the interview a duel in politeness. Knowing no French at all, Father Fabri had had to depend entirely on the report of an unidentified French friar on his staff, a man evidently far less learned, cultivated, and sophisticated than himself whose judgment he did not fully trust. The Frenchman had criticized six items, all but one minor: using the term "fortune" rather than "Providence," praising certain heretics as good poets, finding the emperor Julian ("the Apostate") no apostate but a pagan who "came out of the closet" and a man of many virtues as well as one damning vice, saying that a believer should be free from evil impulses when praying, condemning as cruelty anything beyond plain death, and urging that a child be brought up able to do anything but loving to do only the good. The fideism of the "Apology for Raymond Sebond" was tacitly accepted. Montaigne admitted writing these things as his opinions, not thinking they were errors; but on other matters (unspecified) he denied that his corrector had understood his thought. His account continues thus: "The said Master, who is an able man, was full of excuses for me, and . . . not very sympathetic to these revisions; and he pleaded very ingeniously for me, in my presence, against another man, also an Italian, who was opposing me" (TJ, pp. 91–92). This first interview was on March 20, 1580. Of his second, April 15, when he went to say good-bye to Father Fabri as he prepared to leave Rome, he writes in part: "The Master of the Sacred Palace . . . urged me not to make use of the censorship of my book, in which censorship some other Frenchmen had informed them there were many stupid things; . . . they honored both my intention and affection for the Church and my ability, and left it to myself to cut out of my book, when I wanted to republish it, whatever I found too licentious in it, and among other things the uses of the word "fortune." It seemed o me that I left them well pleased with me." They added some courteous formulas urging his continued support of the Church, he lastly tells us. And here his account ends.

Montaigne made no changes because of these criticisms, presumably in order not to falsify his self-portrait. He does twice allude to his "errors" (to defend them) later in the *Essays*, however (use of the term "fortune," 1.56.234bc; praise of heretic poets, 3.10.775b). He does add two disclaimers of authority or will to convince in theological matters (1.56.234c, 3.2.612b), since he is but "an ignorant inquirer" offering "notions that are human and my own, . . . what I reason out according to me, not what I believe according to God; as children set forth their essays to be instructed, not to instruct . . . referring the decision purely and simply to the common and authorized beliefs."

The *Journal* alone reveals fully Montaigne's desire to live the life of the people he visits, which the secretary finds notable enough to mention more than once. "Monsieur de Montaigne," he notes in Baden after about a month on the road (TJ, p. 20), "to essay completely the diversity of manners and customs, let himself be served everywhere in the mode of each country, no matter what difficulty this caused him . . . in Switzerland he said he suffered no inconvenience," except for their tiny napkins, inadequate for a man who disdained the newfangled forks and preferred to use his fingers. In Augsburg two weeks later fortune turned on him. In chilly weather, plagued by a cold, in church he held his handkerchief to his nose, thinking to pass unnoticed since unattended and simply dressed; but this, he learns later, aroused comment: "At last he

had fallen into the fault he most avoided, that of making himself noticeable by some mannerism at variance with the taste of those who saw him;
for as far as in him lies, he conforms and falls in line with the ways of the
place where he happens to be, and in Augsburg he wore a fur cap around
the town" (TJ, p. 36). Especially noteworthy is his decision to write his
Travel Journal in Italian for the last six months of his stay in Italy (May
13–November 1, 1581). Fluent as he was, he could not express himself
fully and personally in that language (3.5.665b); and for a man bent on
expressiveness, this was a major sacrifice in order to try to "live Italian."

Finding much to enjoy and admire wherever he goes, Montaigne
resents the silly reports he has read of the wildness and discomfort of the
countries he visits, and likes the people and places he sees. He finds the
Swiss, for example (TJ, p. 20), "a very good nation, especially to those
who conform to them." Likewise the Lorrains around Plombières (TJ,
p. 19): "a good people, free, sensible, considerate." On leaving Germany and Austria, he wrote to François Hotman (whom he had seen in
Basel) from Bolzano how much he had enjoyed his stay and how sorry he
was to go. He finds the Roman upper classes "as courteous and gracious
as possible, whatever the common run of Frenchmen say, who cannot
call people gracious who find it hard to endure their excesses and their
ordinary insolence" (TJ, p. 83). And on his third visit to Florence (TJ, p.
142) he admits that it is rightly called "the beautiful"; and a little later in
Lucca, that he has been well lodged in Italy and lacks only a friend (TJ,
p. 150).

And Montaigne's friendliness is returned in kind. He gains ready
access to the Vatican Library, though the French ambassador does not.
The Papal censor treats him with cordial respect. Whether or not he
raised his slipper, the Pope greeted him graciously and helped him become a Roman citizen. He relished being called on more than once to
arbitrate in medical matters between doctors as on one important decision for young Signor Paolo Cesi, nephew of Cardinal Cesi (TJ, pp.
135–136), who asked him to "be good enough to hear their opinions and
arguments, because he was resolved to rely wholly on my judgment."
This gave Montaigne a contented chuckle, for the same thing had happened several times before.

When he left the baths of La Villa after his first stay, it was "after
receiving . . . all the indications of friendliness that I could desire" (TJ,
p. 139); and when he returned just under two months later, "I received
a warm welcome and greetings from all those people. In truth it seemed
that I had come back to my own home" (TJ, p. 142). In his month and a
half there before, the man who had feared that La Boétie had spoiled
him for ordinary acquaintanceships had shown himself an excellent
mixer. Besides making many friends as he went along, he had given two
parties. In the first and smaller one, for the peasant girls (May 14, 1581;
TJ, p. 127), he "danced in it [himself] so as not to appear too reserved."
A week later, wanting to give the first of these of the season, he offered a

big dance, had it announced several days ahead, sent to Lucca for the customary prizes (two for the men, nineteen for the women; six crowns' worth), hired five fife players (a crown and a day's food for the lot: a bargain), and invited all the adult guests at the baths to the dance and supper after. Though at first he feared he would have few takers, over a hundred guests came, besides the natives. When the time came to present the prizes, he cut his way deftly and amiably through ceremony, persuading the most important ladies to distribute them to the winners, but consenting to play the main role in selecting them. His enjoyment and thorough satisfaction with the whole affair shows clearly in his circumstantial account of it (TJ, pp. 129–131), about a thousand words long; and all in all, it seems clear that host and guests had a delightful time.

Not all the trip was pleasant; the *Travel Journal* also lets us glimpse the suffering Montaigne. At times great pain lasted for weeks without respite. He endured one of his worst attacks ever on August 24, 1581 at La Villa. After ten anguished days when the stone, with stomach trouble, headaches, and toothaches, gave him pain that rose to agony, at last the stone descended; but it stopped in the passage. He went without urinating from morning until dinnertime (midday) to strengthen his resolve to push it out, which at last he did with much pain and bleeding, before and after. It was much the largest he had ever passed, the size of a pine nut and in the shape of the male member. He had guessed the trouble from his urines for some time, and feels he was lucky to get this one out. As he says, "I shall see what is to follow."

"There would be too much weakness and cowardice on my part if, finding myself every day in a position to die in this manner, and with every hour bringing death nearer, I did not make every effort toward being able to bear death lightly as soon as it surprises me. And in the meantime it will be wise to accept joyously the good that it pleases God to send us. There is no other medicine, no other rule or science, for avoiding the ills . . . that besiege men from all sides and at every hour, than to make up our minds to suffer them humanly, or to end them courageously and promptly" (TJ, p. 154).

Here we have already Montaigne's final philosophy, balanced and receptive. Accept God's gifts joyously; prepare to bear death lightly; if the pain grows excessive, end it promptly—or better, suffer it humanly (*umanamente*). The adverb is significant; for henceforth "human" is in Montaigne an expression of high praise.

Imbrie Buffum several decades ago showed the influence of the trip on Montaigne's thought, finding this in five main areas: the role of experience; pain, pleasure, and virtue; solitude and society; custom; and unity and diversity. In each of these the *Essays* of 1588 reveal a considerable change, already prepared in 1578–1580, from those published in 1580; and the *Journal* shows an important step in that change. Already before it he had come a long way from the solitary shell he had recommended at first; the trip drew him much farther still. Originally he had presented custom as mainly tyrannical and absurd; on the trip he finds conforming to it well worthwhile; hereafter he will emphasize its utility more and more. His greatest change between the *Essays* of 1580 and of 1588 concerns unity and diversity. The trip made him more aware than ever of his own particularity, yet at the same time of the basic human nature underlying the various patterns of man's behavior.

Thus the trip, and the play of his mind on it, brought him further along the meditative journey of his life, farther from books and theory alone into his own convictions learned from life.

His major gain is heightened confidence in himself and in other men. Once worried about the eccentricity of his *Essays*, he had now found them accepted and successful. He had lost his one true friend and would always mourn him; yet everywhere he made cordial contacts easily, and not only with Frenchmen and Catholics but with Swiss, Germans, Italians, Calvinists, Lutherans, and Jews; and these, ordinary people and not just nobles, authors, or scholars. The earlier *Essays* do not foreshadow such liking as he shows for such ordinary people; but he shows it, and unabashedly. Coming to know others and their ways enhances his confidence in them and his sense of human solidarity.

The trip helped make him a citizen, not only of Rome, but in the fullest sense, of the world, a representative man, aware of this, confident and ready to speak to and for all men.

ANALYTICAL TABLE OF THE TRIP

Since the reader has an even harder time finding a particular passage in the *Journal* than in the *Essays,* I have introduced into the text the divisions shown in the following table. Montaigne bears no responsibility for any of these.

ACROSS FRANCE TOWARD SWITZERLAND (1580)

SWITZERLAND (1580)

GERMANY, AUSTRIA, AND THE ALPS (1580)

ITALY: THE ROAD TO ROME (1580)

ITALY: ROME (1580–1581)

ITALY: FROM ROME TO LORETO AND LA VILLA (1581)

ITALY: FIRST STAY AT LA VILLA (1581)

ITALY: FLORENCE—PISA—LUCCA (1581)

ITALY: SECOND STAY AT LA VILLA (1581)

ITALY: RETURN TO ROME (1581)

ITALY AND FRANCE: THE RETURN HOME (1581)

TABLE OF MONEY VALUES

FRENCH MONEY OF ACCOUNT

12 deniers = 1 sou   20 sous = 1 livre

The values of the money of account are not related to any metallic equivalents. There are two systems, that of Tours (tournois) and that of Paris (parisis). Parisis money is worth 125 per cent of tournois at each level: 4 parisis (deniers, sous, livres) = 5 tournois (deniers, sous, livres). The reckoning here is in tournois, which was internationally current, as the parisis system was not.

True equivalents in modern money are impossible to establish; but a very rough equivalence in buying power, for simple items such as food and lodging, with 1957 United States money would be this: 1 denier = about 1.5 cents, 1 sou = about 15 cents, 1 livre = about 3 dollars, 1 crown (French) = about 10 dollars.

OTHER COINS MENTIONED IN THE JOURNAL

baiocco (Roman) = about 6 deniers or 0.5 sou
batz, batzen (German) = about 2.3 sous
carolus (French) = 10 deniers or 0.83 sou
crown (écu) (French) = 3 livres or a little more
crown (scudo) (Italian) = 50 sous or 2.5 livres
gold crown, sun-crown (French) = 1 French crown
florin (German) = about 2 livres
franc (French) = 1 livre
giulio (Roman) = about 5 sous, 10 baiocchi
lira (Italian) = about 8.5 sous
pistolet or demi-pistole (Spanish) = about 1.1 crowns
quattrino (Roman) = 1.2 deniers or 0.1 sou
real (Spanish) = about 4 or 5 sous
teston (French and Roman) = about 14.5 sous
thaler (German and other) = about 9 sous

Montaigne's Travel Journal

Across France toward Switzerland
(September 4-28, 1580)

[THE JOURNAL BY THE SECRETARY, IN FRENCH]

Monsieur de Montaigne dispatched Monsieur de Mattecoulon[1] post-haste with the said groom to visit the said count,[2] and found that his wounds were not mortal. At the said BEAUMONT,[3] Monsieur d'Estissac[4] joined the group to make the same trip, accompanied by a gentleman, a valet, a mule, and on foot a muleteer and two lackeys. He was returning to our party to go halves on the expense.

On Monday, September 5th, 1580, we left the said Beaumont after dinner and came without stopping to sup at

MEAUX, which is a small town, beautiful, situated on the river Marne. It is in three parts; the town and the suburb are on this side of the river, toward Paris.

Across the bridges there is another big place called the Market, surrounded on all sides by the river and a very handsome moat, where there is a great multitude of inhabitants and houses. This place was formerly very well fortified with great strong walls and towers; but in our second Huguenot troubles, because most of the inhabitants of this place were of that party, all those fortifications were demolished. This part of the town withstood the attack of the English[5] when all the rest was lost; and as a reward, all the inhabitants of the said locality are still exempt from the taille and other taxes. They show on the river Marne an island two or three hundred paces long, which they say was an earthwork erected in the water by the English to batter the said Market with their engines and which with time has taken this permanent shape.

In the suburb we saw the Abbey of Saint-Faron, a very old building where they show the dwelling of Ogier the Dane and his hall. There is an ancient refectory, with great long stone tables of unusual size,

---

[1] Bertrand-Charles de Montaigne, sieur de Mattecoulon, Montaigne's youngest brother, then aged twenty.

[2] Unidentified. The first two manuscript pages of the *Journal* were missing when the rest of it was found.

[3] Beaumont-sur-Oise.

[4] Charles d'Estissac (c. 1563–86), son of Louise d'Estissac, to whom Montaigne dedicated Chapter 8 of Book II of the *Essays*, "Of the Affection of Fathers for Their Children."

[5] Under Henry V in 1421.

in the middle of which, before our civil wars, there welled up a spring of fresh water which served for their meals. Most of the monks still are noblemen. Among other things there is a very old and honorable tomb, on which there are the stone figures of two outstretched knights, of extraordinary size. They maintain that these are the bodies of Ogier the Dane and some other one of those paladins. There is neither an inscription nor any coat of arms; there are only these words in Latin, which an abbot had placed there about a hundred years ago, that "these are two unknown heroes who are buried here." Among their treasures they show some bones of these knights. The arm bone, from the shoulder to the elbow, is about the length of the whole arm of an ordinary-sized man of our time, and a little longer than that of Monsieur de Montaigne. They also show two of their swords, which are about the length of one of our two-handed swords, and are very much hacked by blows on the edge.

At the said place of Meaux Monsieur de Montaigne went to visit the treasurer of the Church of Saint Stephen, a man named Juste Ter-relle, known among the savants of France; a little man, sixty years old, who has traveled to Egypt and Jerusalem and spent seven years in Constantinople, and who showed him his library and the curiosities of his garden. The most curious thing we saw there was a box-tree spreading its branches in a circle, so thick and so artfully clipped that it seems to be a very polished and very massive ball, of the height of a man.

From Meaux, where we dined on Tuesday, we came to sleep at

CHARLY, seven leagues. On Wednesday after dinner we came to sleep at

DORMANS, seven leagues. The next day, which was Thursday morning, we came to dine at

EPERNAY, five leagues. On arriving there, Messieurs d'Estissac and de Montaigne went off to Mass, as was their custom, in the Church of Our Lady. And because the said seigneur de Montaigne had once read that when Marshal Strozzi was killed at the siege of Thionville his body was brought to the said church, he inquired about his sepulture and found that he was buried there, without any indication in the form of a stone, or coat of arms, or epitaph, opposite the high altar. And we were told that the queen had had him buried thus without pomp or ceremony because that was the will of the said marshal. The bishop of Rennes, of the Hennequin family in Paris, was then officiating in the said church, of which he is abbot; for it was also the day of the Festival of Our Lady of September.

In the said church after Mass, Monsieur de Montaigne spoke to Monsieur Maldonado,[6] a Jesuit whose name is very famous because of his erudition in theology and philosophy, and they had several talks together on learned matters, both then and after dinner, at the said Monsieur de Montaigne's lodgings, where the said Maldonado came

---

[6] Juan Maldonado (1533–84), eminent Spanish professor of philosophy and theology, especially exegesis. Montaigne was to see him again in Rome.

to see him. And among other things, because Maldonado had just come from the baths of Spa, which are at Liége, where he had been with Monsieur de Nevers, he told him that those were extremely cold waters and that the people there maintained that the colder you could take them, the better. They are so cold that some who drink them start to shiver and shudder; but soon after one feels a great warmth in the stomach. For his part he used to take a hundred ounces; for there are people who furnish glasses that hold their measure, according to what each person wants. The waters are drunk not only on an empty stomach but also after meals. Their operation, which he told us about, is like that of the waters of Gascony. As for himself, he said that he had noted their power by the harm that they had not done him, for he had drunk of them several times while all sweating and stirred up. He has observed by experience that frogs and other little animals that are thrown into these waters die immediately; and he said that a handkerchief placed over a glass full of the said water will turn yellow immediately. They drink it for at least two or three weeks. That is a place where one is very well accommodated and lodged, and it is recommended for any kind of obstruction and gravel. However, neither Monsieur de Nevers nor he had got much healthier for his stay.

He had with him a steward of Monsieur de Nevers, and they gave Monsieur de Montaigne a printed paper on the subject of the dispute between the dukes of Montpensier and of Nevers, so that he might be informed about it and be able to inform gentlemen who might inquire about it.

We left there Friday morning and came to

CHÂLONS, seven leagues. We stayed there at the Crown, a handsome lodging; and they serve you on silver plate, and most of the bedding and coverlets are of silk. The common buildings of this whole part of the country are of chalkstone, cut into little square pieces of half a foot or thereabouts; and others of turf of the same shape. The next day we left there after dinner and came to sleep at

VITRY-LE-FRANÇOIS, seven leagues. This is a small town situated on the river Marne, built thirty-five or forty years ago in place of the other Vitry, which was burned.[7] It still has its original form, well-proportioned and pleasant, and the center of it is a large square, one of the handsomest in France.

Here we learned three memorable stories. One, that the dowager duchess of Guise de Bourbon, eighty-seven years old, was still alive, and still could do a quarter of a league on foot.

The second, that a few days before there had been a hanging at a place called Montier-en-Der, near here, upon this occasion: Seven or eight girls around Chaumont-en-Bassigni plotted together a few years ago to dress up as males and thus continue their life in the world. One of them came to this place under the name Mary, earning her living

---

[7] In 1545, a year after Charles V had burned Vitry-en-Perthois, Francis I founded Vitry-le-François on the same spot.

as a weaver, a well-disposed young man who made friends with everybody. At the said Vitry he became engaged to a woman who is still alive, but because of some disagreement that arose between them, their compact went no further. Later he went to the said Montier-en-Der, still earning his living at the said trade, and fell in love with a woman, whom he married and with whom he lived for four or five months, to her satisfaction, so they say. But she was recognized by someone from the said Chaumont, the matter was brought before justice, and she was condemned to be hanged, which she said she would rather undergo than return to a girl's status; and she was hanged for using illicit devices to supply her defect in sex.

The other story is of a man still alive named Germain, of low condition, without any trade or position, who was a girl up to the age of twenty-two, seen and known by all the inhabitants of the town, and noticed because she had a little more hair about her chin than the other girls; and they called her Bearded Mary.[8] One day when she made an effort in jumping, her virile instruments came out, and Cardinal de Lenoncourt, then bishop of Châlons, gave her the name Germain. Germain has not married, however; he has a big, very thick beard. We were not able to see him because he was in the village. In this town there is still a song commonly in the girls' mouths, in which they warn one another not to stretch their legs too wide for fear of becoming males, like Marie Germain. They say that Ambroise Paré has put this story into his book on surgery. The story is very certain, and was attested to Monsieur de Montaigne by the most eminent officials of the town.

From here we set out Sunday morning after breakfast and came without stopping to

BAR-LE-DUC, nine leagues, where Monsieur de Montaigne had been before.[9] He now found nothing remarkable and new but the extraordinary expense that a private priest, dean of the place, had put into public works, and continues to put in every day. His name is Gilles de Trèves. He has built the most sumptuous chapel, in regard to marble, paintings, and decorations, that there is in France; and has also built and almost finished furnishing the most beautiful town house that there is in France, of the most beautiful construction, the best proportioned and upholstered, the most elaborately and richly decorated, and the best to live in. He wants to make a college of it, and is in the process of endowing it and setting it in operation at his own expense.

From Bar-le-Duc, where we dined Monday morning, we came to sleep at

MAUVAGES, four leagues, a little village where Monsieur de Montaigne was stopped by reason of his colic, which was also the reason why he abandoned the plan he had made to see Toul, Metz, Nancy, Joinville, and Saint-Dizier, which are towns scattered around this route,

---

[8] Montaigne tells this story in the *Essays*, I:21.
[9] With the court in 1559. See *Essays* II: 17, p. 496.

as he had intended, in order to reach the baths of Plombières in all haste.

From Mauvages we set out Tuesday in the morning and came to dine at

VAUCOULEURS, one league from there; and we passed along the river Meuse to a village called

DOMRÉMY, on the Meuse, three leagues from the said Vaucouleurs, the native village of the famous Maid of Orleans, whose name was Jeanne Darc or Dallis. Her descendants were ennobled by the favor of the king, and they showed us the arms that the king gave them, which are azure, a straight sword crowned and with a hilt of gold, and two gold fleurs-de-lys at the side of the said sword. A receiver of Vaucouleurs gave an escutcheon thus painted to Monsieur de Cazalis.[10] The front of the little house where she was born is all painted with her exploits; but age has greatly damaged the painting. There is also a tree beside a vineyard which they call the Maid's Tree, which has nothing else remarkable about it.

We came this evening to sleep at

NEUFCHÂTEAU, five leagues. Here, in the church of the Cordeliers, there are many tombs, three or four hundred years old, of the nobility of the region, on which all the inscriptions are in this form: *Here lies So-and-so, who was dead when time was passing through the year twelve hundred, etc.* Monsieur de Montaigne saw their library, in which there are many books, but nothing rare, and a well from which water is drawn in very big buckets by working with the feet a wooden pedal, supported on a pivot, to which is connected a round piece of wood to which the rope of the well is attached. He had seen others like it elsewhere. Next to the well is a big stone vessel raised five or six feet above the brim, up to which the bucket mounts; and without anyone touching it, the water is poured into the said vessel, and the bucket goes down again when it is empty. This vessel is of such a height that from it, by means of lead pipes, the well water is led to their refectory and kitchen and bakery, and spouts out of raised stone outlets in the form of natural springs.

From Neufchâteau, where we breakfasted in the morning, we came to sup at

MIRECOURT, six leagues, a beautiful little town where Monsieur de Montaigne heard news of Monsieur and Madame de Bourbonne, who live in the near vicinity.

The next day after breakfast he went a quarter of a league from here, out of his way, to see the "nuns of Poussay." These are religious houses, of which there are several in these parts, established for the education of girls of good family. Each girl has a benefice, for her main-

---

[10] This member of Montaigne's party is presumably Bernard de Cazalis, who a year before had married Montaigne's youngest sister, Marie; or it may be a brother of Bernard.

tenance, of a hundred, two hundred, or three hundred crowns,[11] some
worse, some better, and a private habitation in which she lives apart.
Girls at nurse are received. There is no obligation of virginity, except
for the officers, such as the abbess, prioress, and others. They are
dressed in all freedom, like other young ladies, except for a white veil
on their head, and in church, during the service, a great cloak, which
they leave in their seat in the choir. Company is received in all freedom
in the rooms of the individual girls, whom people go to see, whether
to pay suit to them for marriage or for other reasons. Those who leave
may resign and sell their benefice to anyone they choose, provided she
is of the requisite rank; for there are lords of the region who are formally
responsible (and they affirm their responsibility by oath) for testifying
to the lineage of the girls who are presented. It is not improper for one
single nun to have three or four benefices. Moreover, they perform the
divine service, as elsewhere. Most of them end their days here and do
not want to change their condition.

From here we came to sup at

EPINAL, five leagues. This is a beautiful little town on the river
Moselle, where we were refused entry because we had passed through
Neufchâteau, where the plague had been not long before.

The next morning we came to dine at

PLOMBIÈRES, four leagues. From Bar-le-Duc on, the leagues resume
the standard of Gascony, and grow longer as you come toward Germany, until they are finally doubled or tripled.

We entered on Friday, September 16th, 1580, at two in the afternoon.
This place is situated on the confines of Lorraine and Germany in a
deep valley between several high, steep hills which close it in on all
sides. At the bottom of this valley there issue several springs, some
naturally cold, some hot. The hot water has no smell or taste, and is
as hot as one can stand it for drinking, so that Monsieur de Montaigne
was forced to pour it from one glass to another. There are only two
springs from which people drink. The one that issues from the eastern
slopes and produces the bath which they call the Queen's Bath leaves
a sort of sweet taste in the mouth like licorice, without aftertaste; but
it seemed to Monsieur de Montaigne that if you paid special attention
to it, you could detect a faint taste of iron. The other, which springs
from the foot of the mountain opposite, of which Monsieur de Montaigne drank for only one day, is a little more bitter, and one may detect
in it the flavor of alum.

The custom of the place is only to bathe, and to bathe two or three
times a day. Some take their meals in the bath, where they commonly
have themselves cupped and scarified; and they use it only after being
purged. If they drink, it is a glass or two in the bath. The people here
considered Monsieur de Montaigne's practice strange, for without previous medicine he would drink nine glasses of the water, which came

---

[11] A French crown (écu) is about three livres. See Table of Money Values,
p. 866.

to about one pot, every morning at seven, and dine at noon; and on the days when he bathed, which was every other day, he did so about four o'clock, staying in the bath only about an hour. And those days he was apt to go without supper.

Here we saw men who had been cured of ulcers, and others of red spots on the body. The custom is to be here for at least a month. They recommend much more highly the spring season, in May. They hardly use the baths after the month of August, because of the coldness of the climate; but we still found company here, because the dryness and the heat had been greater and lasted longer than usual.

Among other friendships, Monsieur de Montaigne formed an intimate one with the seigneur d'Andelot, of Franche-Comté, whose father was grand equerry to the Emperor Charles V. He himself was first field marshal in the army of Don John of Austria, and was the man who remained as governor of Saint-Quentin when we lost it. One part of his beard was all white, and part of one eyebrow; and he told Monsieur de Montaigne that this change had come upon him in an instant, one day when he was at home full of grief for the loss of a brother of his whom the duke of Alva had put to death as an accomplice of the counts of Egmont and Horn; and that this part of his face had been resting on his hand, so that those present thought it was some flour that by chance had fallen on him just there. He has remained like that ever since.

This bath was formerly frequented by the Germans only; but for a few years now people of Franche-Comté and many Frenchmen have been arriving here in great crowds. There are several baths, but one great and principal one, built in an oval shape, of ancient construction. It is thirty-five paces long and fifteen wide. The hot water issues from underneath in several springs, and cold water is made to flow in from above to temper the bath according to the wish of those who are using it. The places are divided off on the sides by bars, suspended like those in our stables; and they throw boards over the top to keep out the sun and rain. All around the baths there are three or four rows of stone steps in the manner of a theater, on which those who are bathing can sit or lean. Singular modesty is observed here; and yet it is indecent for the men to go in otherwise than quite naked except for a little pair of drawers, and the women except for a shift.

We lodged at the Angel, which is the best inn, since it communicates with both baths. Our whole lodgings, in which there were several rooms, cost only fifteen sous a day. The landlords in all the places supply wood into the bargain; but the country round about is so full of it that it costs them only the price of cutting. The landladies are very good cooks. In the very crowded season these lodgings would have cost a crown a day, which is cheap. The feed for the horses was seven sous; all other kinds of expense equally reasonable. The quarters here are not sumptuous, but very convenient; for by the use of many galleries they make each room independent of the others. The wine and bread are bad.

They are a good people, free, sensible, considerate. All the laws of the country are religiously observed. Every year they renew on a tablet, in front of the great bath, in the German and French languages, the laws written below:

"Claude de Rynach, Knight, Lord of Saint-Balesmont, Montureulz en Ferrette, Lendacourt, etc., Councillor and Chamberlain to His Sovereign Lordship the Duke, etc., and his Bailiff for the Vosges:

"Be it known that in order to secure the repose and tranquillity of sundry ladies and other notable personages assembling from various regions and countries at these baths of Plombières, we have, pursuant to the intention of His Highness, instituted and ordained, and do institute and ordain, as follows:

"To wit, that the ancient corrective discipline for minor offenses will remain in the hands of the Germans, as of old; to whom it is enjoined that they see to the observance of the ceremonies, statutes, and rules which they have used to maintain the decorum of the said baths and to punish the offenses that shall be committed by the people of their nation, without exception of persons, by form of ransom, and without using any blasphemy or other irreverent language against the Catholic Church and the traditions thereof.

"All persons, of whatever quality, condition, region, and province they may be, are forbidden to provoke one another by insulting language tending to pick a quarrel, to bear arms in the said baths, to give the lie, or to lay hand to weapons, on pain of being severely punished as disturbers of the peace, rebels, and disobedient to His Highness.

"Also all prostitutes and shameless girls are forbidden to enter the said baths or to approach within five hundred paces of them, on pain of being whipped at the four corners of the said baths; and on pain, for the hosts who shall have received or harbored them, of imprisonment of their persons and arbitrary fine.

"Under the same penalty all persons are forbidden to use toward the ladies, gentlewomen, and other women and girls who are at the said baths, any lascivious or shameless language, to touch them dishonorably, or to enter or leave the said baths disrespectfully, contrary to public decency.

"And because, by the benefit of the said baths, God and nature procure us many cures and reliefs, and a decent cleanliness and purity is required to obviate many contagions and infections that might be engendered here; the Master of the said baths is expressly ordered to take pains to examine the persons of those who shall enter the baths, by day as well as by night, and to make them preserve modesty and silence during the night, without noise, scandal, or mockery. And if any person is not obedient to him in this matter, the Master shall promptly bring information against him to the magistrate, to have exemplary punishment inflicted on him.

"Moreover, it is prohibited and forbidden to all persons coming from infected places to enter or approach this place of Plombières, on pain of death; it is very expressly enjoined upon the mayors and officers of justice to take careful heed of this, and upon all the inhabitants of the said place to give us billets containing the names and surnames and residence of the persons whom they have received and lodged, on pain of imprisonment of their persons.

"All which ordinances above declared have this day been made public before the Great Bath of the said Plombières, and copies of them have been posted, in both the French and German languages, in the nearest and most conspicuous place to the Great Bath, and signed by us, Bailiff for the Vosges. Given at the said Plombières, the fourth day of the month of May in the year of grace of Our Lord, one thousand five hundred . . ."

(The name of the Bailiff)

We stopped at the said place from the said day, the 16th,[12] until the 27th of September. Monsieur de Montaigne drank of the said water eleven mornings, nine glasses each for eight days and seven glasses each for three days, and bathed five times. He found the water easy to drink and always passed it before dinner. He experienced no other effect from it than to urinate. His appetite was good. His sleep, his bowels, nothing of his ordinary condition was made worse by this drinking. On the sixth day he had a very violent attack of colic, worse than his ordinary ones, and had it in his right side, where he had never felt any pain except a very slight one at Arsac, without aftereffect. This one lasted him four hours, and he clearly felt the effect of it and the passage of the stone through the ureters and the lower abdomen. The first two days he passed two little stones that were in the bladder, and afterward at times some gravel. But he left the said baths judging that he still had in the bladder both the stone of the aforesaid colic and some other small ones whose descent he thought he had felt. He considers the effect of these waters and their quality, as regards himself, very like that of the high spring at Bagnères, where the bath is. As for the bath, he finds it very mild in temperature; and in truth children six months or a year old are ordinarily seen playing in it like frogs. He sweated abundantly and gently. He ordered me, as a favor to his hostess, according to the humor of the nation, to leave a wooden escutcheon of his arms,[13] which a painter of the said place made for a crown, and the hostess had it carefully attached to the wall on the outside.

On the said day, September 27th, after dinner, we left and passed through a mountainous country, which everywhere resounded under our horses' feet as if we were riding over a vault, and it seemed as though drums were drumming all around us; and we came to sleep at

REMIREMONT, two leagues, a beautiful little town, and a good lodging at the Unicorn; for all the towns of Lorraine (this is the last) have

[12] The text reads "18th."

[13] Montaigne describes his coat of arms (*Essays* I: 46, p. 203) as follows: "I bear azure powdered with trefoils or, with a lion's paw of the same, armed gules in fesse."

hostelries as comfortable and entertainment as good as any place in
France.

Here is that most famous abbey of nuns, of the same kind as those
I spoke of at Poussay. They claim, against the duke of Lorraine, the sov-
ereignty and principality of this town. Messieurs d'Estissac and de
Montaigne went to see them immediately after arriving, and visited
several private lodgings that are very handsome and very well furnished.
Their abbess, of the house of Dinteville, had died, and they were occupied in choosing another; one candidate was the sister of the count of
Salm. They went to see the deaconess, a member of the house of Ludre,
who had done Monsieur de Montaigne the honor of sending someone
to visit him at the baths of Plombières and bring him artichokes, partridges, and a barrel of wine. They learned here that certain neighboring villages owe the nuns as rent two basins of snow every Pentecost
day, or in default of that a wagon harnessed with four white oxen. It
is said that they never have failed to receive this rental of snow, yet in
the season when we passed there the heat was as great as it is in any season in Gascony. They wear only a white veil on their head, and above it a
wisp of crape. They wear black robes of whatever material and fashion
they please while they are on the premises, elsewhere colored ones;
petticoats as they please, and shoes and pattens; coifs over their veils.
Like the others, they must be descended from at least four noble houses
on the father's side and as many on the mother's. Our party took leave
of them when evening came.

The next day at daybreak we left. Just as we had mounted, the
deaconess sent a gentleman to Monsieur de Montaigne, requesting him
to go to her, which he did. This delayed us an hour. This society of
ladies gave him powers of attorney to handle their affairs at Rome. On
leaving here, for a long time we followed a very beautiful and very pleasant valley, skirting the Moselle river; and we came to dine at

BUSSANG, four leagues, a wretched little village, the last French-
speaking one, where Messieurs d'Estissac and de Montaigne, dressed
in linen smocks which were lent them, went to see some silver mines
that the duke of Lorraine has here, a good two thousand paces into the
hollow of a mountain. After dinner we followed along the mountains,
where we were shown, among other things, on inaccessible rocks, the
eyries where they catch goshawks (and these cost only three testons of
the money of the country), and the source of the Moselle; and we came
to sup at

THANN, four leagues, our first town in Germany, subject to the Emperor, very beautiful.

(September 29-October 7, 1580)

The next morning we found a very beautiful big plain, flanked on the left hand by hillsides covered with vineyards of the most beautiful and best cultivated sort and of such extent that the Gascons who were there said they had never seen so many in succession. The vintage was in progress. We came to dine at

MULHOUSE, two leagues, a beautiful little town of Switzerland,[1] in the canton of Basel. Monsieur de Montaigne went to see the church; for they are not Catholics here. He found it, like the churches throughout the country, in good condition; for there is almost nothing changed, except for the altars and images, whose absence was not found disfiguring. He took infinite pleasure in seeing the freedom and good government of this nation, and in seeing his host of the Sign of the Grapes return from a meeting of the Council of the said town, held in a very magnificent gilded palace, where he had been presiding, to serve his guests at table. And a man without retinue or authority, who served them with drink, had led four companies of foot into France against the king under Casimir, and had been a pensioner of the king at three hundred crowns a year for more than twenty years. This gentleman related to him at table, without ambition or affectation, his condition and his life; and told him among other things that they have no scruples on account of their religion about serving the king against the Huguenots themselves—which several others also told us as we went along; that at our siege of La Fère there were more than fifty from their town; and that they indiscriminately marry women of our religion before the priest, and do not force them to change.

From there, after dinner, we went through a beautiful, flat, very fertile country, adorned with many beautiful villages and hostelries, and came to sleep at

BASEL, three leagues, a beautiful city of the size of Blois or thereabouts, in two parts; for the Rhine goes through in the middle under a big and very wide wooden bridge.

The municipality did Messieurs d'Estissac and de Montaigne the honor of sending them, by one of their officers, some of their wine, with a long welcoming speech which was delivered to them while they were at table and to which Monsieur de Montaigne made a long reply, both parties being uncovered, in the presence of several Germans and Frenchmen who were in the common room with them. The host served them as interpreter. The wines here are very good.

A remarkable thing we saw here was the house of a doctor named Felix Platerus, the most painted and enriched with dainty adornments

---

[1] Mulhouse, now in Alsace, was not then in the canton of Basel or in Switzerland. It was a free Imperial city allied with the Swiss Confederation.

in the French style that it is possible to see; which the said doctor built very large, ample, and sumptuous. Among other things, he is preparing a book of simples, which is already well advanced; and whereas the others have the herbs painted according to their colors, he has discovered the art of pasting them in their natural state on the paper so perfectly that the tiniest leaves and fibers appear there just as in nature, and he turns the leaves of his book without anything dropping out; and he showed some simples that had been pasted there for more than twenty years. We also saw, both at his house and in the public school, some entire skeletons of men that stand up by themselves.

There is this, that their town clock, not the one in the *faubourg*,[2] always strikes the hours one hour ahead of time. If it strikes ten o'clock, that means it is only nine; because once, they say, just such an accidental error of their clock saved their town from an attack that had been planned against it.

Basilee is so called, not from the Greek word, but because *Base* means "passage" in German.

We saw a great many men of learning, such as Grynaeus, and the man who wrote the *Theatrum*, and the said doctor (Platerus) and François Hotman.[3] These last two came to sup with our party on the day after our arrival. Monsieur de Montaigne judged that they were not in agreement over their religion, from the answers he received: some calling themselves Zwinglians, others Calvinists, others Martinists;[4] and indeed he was informed that many still fostered the Roman religion in their heart. The form of giving the sacrament is generally into the mouth; however, anyone who wants may put out his hand for it, and the ministers do not dare to touch this chord in these differences in religion.

Their churches have inside the appearance I have told of elsewhere. On the outside they are covered with images, and the ancient tombs are still intact, on which there are prayers for the souls of the departed. The organs, the bells, the crosses of the belfries, and every sort of image in the stained-glass windows are intact, also the benches and seats in the choir. They put the baptismal fonts in the former place of the high altar, and they have another altar built at the head of the nave for the Lord's Supper; the one in Basel is on a very fine plan.

The church of the Carthusians, which is a very handsome building, is carefully preserved and kept up: even the ornaments and the furniture are there, which the Protestants allege as evidence of their fidelity, being obliged to this by the faith they pledged at the time of their agree-

---

[2] That is, the part of town across the river.

[3] The Grynaeus in question is variously identified as Samuel, professor of eloquence and jurisprudence, or Simon, author of an *Encomion medicinae*. The author of the *Theatrum vitae humanae* is Theodor Zwinger. Felix Plater is best known for a treatise on the parts of the human body. François Hotman, the famous French-born Protestant jurist who wrote the *Franco-Gallia*, took refuge in Switzerland after the Massacre of Saint Bartholomew's Day in 1572 and stayed on there.

[4] Lutherans.

ment. The bishop of the place, who is very hostile to them, resides outside the town within his diocese, and keeps most of the country people in the old religion; he enjoys a good 50,000 livres of income from the city, and the election of the bishop continues.

Several people complained to Monsieur de Montaigne about the dissoluteness of the women and the drunkenness of the inhabitants.

Here we saw a poor man's little boy cut open for rupture and treated very roughly by the surgeon. Here we saw a very handsome public library on the river and in a very beautiful site. We stayed all the next day, and the following day after dinner we took the road along the Rhine for two leagues or thereabouts; and then we left it on our left hand, going through a very fertile and rather flat country.

They have an infinite abundance of fountains in all this country; there is no village or crossroad where there are not very beautiful ones. They say there are more than three hundred in Basel by actual count.

They are so accustomed to balconies, even near Lorraine, that in all the houses, between the windows of the upstairs rooms, they leave doorways overlooking the street, looking forward to making balconies there some day. In all this part of the country, from Epinal on, there is no village house so small as not to have glass windows; and the good dwellings are greatly ornamented by being well equipped, both inside and out, with these and with panes of glass worked in many fashions. They also have plenty of iron, and good workmen in this material; they surpass us by far; and moreover, there is no church so small as not to have a magnificent clock and sundial. They are also excellent in making tiles, so that the housetops are greatly embellished with motley forms of tile, soldered with lead and variously worked, and also the floors of their rooms; and there is nothing more delicate than their stoves, which are of earthenware. They use a lot of pine, and have very good craftsmen in carpentry; for their casks are all carved and mostly varnished and painted.

Their *poêles*, that is to say common rooms for taking meals, are sumptuous. In each common room, which moreover is very well furnished, there are likely to be five or six tables equipped with benches, where all the guests dine together, each party at its own table. The smallest inns have two or three such rooms, very handsome; they are well lit by windows richly glazed. But it is very apparent that they have more care for their dinners than for anything else; for the bedrooms are just as wretched as the common rooms are fine. There are never any curtains for the beds, and always three or four beds in a room, right next to one another; no fireplace, and you get warm only in the common rooms and the dining rooms; for to have a fire anywhere else is unheard of, and they think it very bad if you go into their kitchens. They are not at all clean in their bedroom service; for lucky is the man who gets a white sheet, and it is their style never to cover the pillow with a case; and they rarely offer any other covering than that of a feather quilt, and that very dirty. However, they are excellent cooks, especially of fish. They have no protection from the night damp or the wind but the window alone, which is not protected by shutters; and their houses are full of windows and very light, both in the common rooms and in the bedrooms; and they hardly ever close the windows even at night.

Their service at table is very different from ours. They never mix water with their wine, and are almost right not to; for their wines are so small that our gentlemen found them even weaker than those of Gascony when these are well baptized; and yet for all that they are very delicate.

They have the menservants dine at the masters' table or at another near by at the same table with them; for it takes only one servant to wait on a big table, inasmuch as, everyone having his silver goblet or cup in front of his place, the man who serves takes care to fill this goblet as soon as it is empty, without moving it from its place, pouring wine into it from a distance with a pewter or wooden vessel with a long beak; and as for the meat, they serve only two or three dishes at each course. They mix together several well-prepared meats in combinations very different from ours, and serve them sometimes one on top of the other, using certain iron implements with long legs. On top of this implement there is one dish, and underneath another. Their tables are very wide, and either round or square, so that it is hard to place the serving dishes on them. The servant easily takes away all these dishes at once and serves two more, and there are up to six or seven such changes; for one dish is never served until the other is off. And as for the plates, when they want to serve the fruit, after the meat is taken away they put in the middle of the table a wicker basket or a big tray of painted wood, into which basket the most eminent person tosses his plate first, and then the others; for in this they observe a strict precedence of rank. This basket the servant easily takes off and then serves the fruit in two dishes like the rest, pell-mell; and they usually include radishes, just as they serve cooked pears with the roast.

Among other things they hold crayfish in great honor, and serve up a dish of them, always with a cover, as a privilege; and they offer them to one another, as they hardly do with any other viand. However, all this country is full of them, and they serve them every day, though they consider them delicacies. They do not give you water to wash with on sitting down and getting up; everyone goes to get some at a little water jug set in a corner of the room, as in our monasteries.

Most of them use wooden plates, yes, and wooden pots and chamber pots, and these as clean and white as possible. Others in addition place pewter plates on the wooden ones until the last course, the fruit, when there are never any but of wood. They use wood only out of custom; for even where they use it they give you silver goblets to drink from, and have an infinite quantity of them.

They clean and polish their wooden furniture scrupulously, even to the bedroom floors. Their beds are raised so high that commonly you climb into them by steps; and almost everywhere they have little beds under the big ones.

Since they are excellent workers in iron, almost all their spits are turned by springs or by means of weights, like clocks, or else by certain broad, light sails of pine that they place in the funnels of their chimneys, which turn with great speed in the draft caused by the smoke and steam of the fire; and they turn the roast slowly for a long time; for they dry out their meat a little too much. These windmills are used only in the large inns where there is a big fire, as at Baden. Their motion is very uniform and constant. Most of the chimneys between Lorraine and here are not in our style; they build up the hearth in the middle or the corner of a kitchen and use almost the whole width of this kitchen for the chimney flue. This is a great opening seven or eight paces square, which narrows as it goes up to the top of the house. This gives them room to place in one spot their big sail, which with us would occupy so much space in our flues that the passage of the smoke would be blocked.

The slightest meals last three or four hours because of the length of these servings; and in truth they also eat much less hastily and more healthily than we do. They have a great abundance of all sorts of food, both meat and fish, and they cover their tables very sumptuously—at least ours. On Friday they did not serve meat to anyone, and they say that on that day they generally do not eat any. The prices are like those in France around Paris. The horses ordinarily get more oats than they can eat.

We came to sleep at

HORN, four leagues, a little village belonging to the duke of Austria.

The next day, which was Sunday, we heard Mass here, and I noticed that the women all keep on the left side of the church and the men on the right, without mixing. They have several rows of cross-benches, one behind the other, of the right height for sitting down. The women kneel on these and not on the ground, and consequently look as though they were standing; the men have, besides these, wooden crossrails to lean on, and they too kneel only on the seats in front of them. Whereas we join our hands in prayer to God at the elevation of the host, they stretch them apart wide open, and hold them thus raised until the priest exhibits the pax. They gave Messieurs d'Estissac and de Montaigne the third bench of the men, and the other benches ahead of them were afterward taken by men of inferior appearance; as also on the women's side. It seemed to us that the most honored women were not in the first rows. The interpreter and guide we had taken at Basel, a sworn messenger of the town, came to Mass with us, and showed by his manner that he attended with great devoutness and zeal.

After dinner we passed over the river Aar at Brügg, a beautiful little town belonging to Their Excellencies of Bern, and on the other side came to see an abbey[5] which Queen Catherine of Hungary gave to their lordships of Bern in the year 1524, where are buried Leopold, archduke of Austria, and a great number of gentlemen who were killed with him by the Swiss in the year 1386.[6] Their arms and names are still inscribed

[5] Königsfelden.
[6] At Sempach.

here, and their spoils are carefully preserved. Monsieur de Montaigne here spoke to a gentleman of Bern who is in command, and he had them shown everything. In this abbey there are loaves of bread all ready, and soup, for travelers who ask for some; and, by the constitution of the abbey, no one is ever refused.

From here we crossed in a ferryboat which is worked by an iron pulley attached to a high cord that goes across the river Reuss, which flows from Lake Lucerne, and we came to

BADEN, four leagues, a small town, with a separate borough where the baths are. It is a Catholic town under the protection of the eight cantons of Switzerland, in which several great assemblies of princes have been held. We did not lodge in the town, but in the said borough, which is right at the foot of the mountain along a river, or rather a torrent, called the Limmat, which comes from the Lake of Zurich. There are two or three uncovered public baths, which only the poor people use. The others, in very great number, are enclosed in the houses, and are divided and separated into several little private cells, closed in and covered, which they rent with the rooms; the cells are as dainty and well-equipped as possible, and veins of hot water are drawn to them for each bath.

The inns are very magnificent. In the one where we lodged there have been as many as three hundred mouths to feed in one day. There was still much company when we were there, and fully a hundred and seventy beds serving the guests that were there. There are seventeen common rooms and eleven kitchens, and an inn next to ours has fifty furnished bedrooms. The walls of the inns are all covered with the escutcheons of the gentlemen who have lodged there.

The town is up above on the ridge, small and very beautiful, as they almost all are in this region. For besides the fact that they make their streets wider and more open than ours and their squares larger, and have so many windows everywhere richly glazed, they have the custom of painting nearly all the houses on the outside and loading them with mottoes, which make a very pleasant sight; and besides, there is no town in which there are not several fountains, flowing with streams of water, which have been erected sumptuously at the street corners, either of wood or of stone. This makes their towns appear much more beautiful than those of France.

The water of the baths gives off a smell of sulphur, like those of Aigues-Caudes and others. Its warmth is moderate, like that of Barbotan or Aigues-Caudes, and for this reason the baths are very mild and pleasant. If anyone has to escort ladies who want to bathe respectably and with delicacy, he may bring them here, for they are alone in the bath, which seems like a very rich cabinet, bright, with glazed windows, covered all around with painted wainscoting, and very neatly floored, with chairs and little tables to read or play on while in the bath if you want. The bather can empty and let in as much water as he pleases; and each bedroom is next to its bath. The walks along the river are fine, as well as the artificial walks of certain galleries.

These baths are situated in a valley commanded by the sides of mountains that are high but nevertheless for the most part fertile and cultivated. For drinking, the water is a little insipid and flat, as if it had been poured back and forth a lot; and as for the taste, it smacks of sulphur and has a sort of salty tang to it. The people of the region use it principally for bathing, during which they have themselves cupped and bled so heavily that I have sometimes seen the two public baths look like pure blood. Those who customarily drink take a glass or two at the most. People ordinarily stop here five or six weeks, and the baths are occupied almost all summer long. No other nation uses them, or very few, except the Germans; but they come here in very great crowds.

The use of them is very ancient, and Tacitus mentions it. Monsieur de Montaigne tried his best to find the main source, but could not learn anything about it; from all appearances, the sources are all very low and virtually on a level with the river. It is less clear than the other waters that we have seen elsewhere, and when you draw it, it carries certain very fine little filaments. It does not have those little sparkles that you see shining in other sulphurous waters when you take them into the glass, including, as the seigneur Maldonado said, those of Spa.

The day after we arrived, which was Monday, Monsieur de Montaigne drank seven little glasses of it, which amounted to one big chopin of his house; the next day five big glasses, which amounted to ten of the little ones and might make a pint. This same Tuesday morning at nine o'clock, while the others were dining, he got into the bath and after coming out sweated very hard in bed. He stayed in the bath only a half hour; for the people of the country who are in it all day long playing and drinking are in the water only up to the loins; he stayed in up to the neck, stretched out the full length of his bath.

This day there left the bath a Swiss lord, a very good servant of our crown, who had had a long talk with Monsieur de Montaigne all the preceding day about the affairs of the country of Switzerland, and showed him a letter which the French ambassador, son of the President de Harlay, had written him from Soleure, where he is staying, advising him to serve the king during his absence, for he had been summoned by the queen to meet her at Lyons, and to oppose the designs of Spain and Savoy. The duke of Savoy, who had just died, had made an alliance a year or two ago with certain cantons; which the king had openly resisted, alleging that they, being already allied with him, could not accept any new bonds without prejudice to him; some of the cantons had realized this, thanks especially to the mediation of the said Swiss lord, and had refused this alliance. In truth, in all these parts they receive the name of the king with reverence and friendship, and offer us all possible courtesies. The Spaniards are in bad odor.

This Swiss had a train of four horses: his son, who is already in the service of the king like his father, on one; a valet on another; a tall, beautiful daughter on another, with a cloth saddle cover and a woman's stirrup in the French fashion, a portmanteau behind her and a bonnet box at the saddlebow, without any woman with her (and yet they were two full days' journey from their home, which is a town where the said lord is governor); the goodman himself on the fourth.

The ordinary dress of the women seems to me as neat as our own, even the head-dress, which is a bonnet *à la coquarde*, turning up behind and with a slight projection in front, over the forehead; this is trimmed all around with tufts of silk or fur borders; the natural hair hangs down behind, all braided. If you take off this bonnet of theirs in play (for it does not stay on any better than ours), they are not offended, and you see their head quite bare. The younger ones, instead of a bonnet, wear merely a garland on their head. They do not have much difference in dress to distinguish their ranks. You salute them by kissing your hand to them and offering to touch theirs. Otherwise, if in passing you take off your hat and make them a bow, most of them stand still without any movement, and that is their ancient fashion. Some nod their head a little to return your salute. They are generally handsome women, tall and fair.

They are a very good nation, especially to those who conform to them. Monsieur de Montaigne, to essay completely the diversity of manners and customs, let himself be served everywhere in the mode of each country, no matter what difficulty this caused him. At all events, in Switzerland he said he suffered no inconvenience, except for having at table only a little cloth half a foot square for a napkin; and the same cloth the Swiss do not even unfold at their dinner, and yet they have plenty of sauces and many varieties of soups; but they always serve as many wooden spoons, with silver handles, as there are people. And never is a Swiss without a knife, with which they pick up everything; and they hardly ever put their hands into the dish.

Almost all their towns bear, above the particular arms of the town, those of the Emperor and the house of Austria; and indeed most of them have been dismembered from the said archduchy only by the bad management of that house. They say here that all the members of this house of Austria, except the Catholic King, are reduced to great poverty, especially the Emperor, who is held in small esteem in Germany.

The water that Monsieur de Montaigne drank on Tuesday caused him three stools and was all voided before noon. Wednesday morning he took the same amount as the day before. He finds that when he makes himself sweat in the bath, the next day he makes much less urine and does not pass the water he has drunk; which he experienced also at Plombières. For the water that he takes the next day comes out colored and very scanty, whereby he judges that it promptly changes into nourishment, whether this happens by the evacuation of the preceding sweat or by the fasting; for when he bathed he took only one meal; this was the reason why he bathed only once.

On Wednesday his landlord bought a lot of fish; the said lord asked him why that was. He was told in reply that most people of the said place of Baden ate fish on Wednesdays for religious reasons; which confirmed what he had heard, that those here who hold to the Catholic religion are much more strict and devout because they are surrounded by the contrary faith. He argued thus, that when confusion and mixture occurs in the same town and spreads in one and the same government, this relaxes the affections of men, for the mingling reaches down to individuals, as happens at Augsburg and in the Imperial towns; but when a town has only one system of government (for the towns of Switzerland have each their separate laws and government, apart from one another, and do not depend on one another in the matter of their administration; they are united as a league only in certain general respects), the towns that each form a separate state and a separate civil body with all its members have the wherewithal to fortify and maintain themselves; they are undoubtedly strengthened and further joined and united by the impact of the neighboring contagion.

We quickly adapted ourselves to the warmth of their stoves, and not one of us felt any discomfort from it. For once you have swallowed a certain smell in the air that strikes you as you come in, all that remains is a gentle and even warmth. Monsieur de Montaigne, who slept in a room with a stove in it, was very pleased with it and with feeling all night a pleasant and moderate warmth of air. At least you do not burn either your face or your boots, and you are free from the smoke you get in France. Also, whereas we put on our warm furred dressing gowns when we enter the house, they on the contrary stay in their doublets and go bareheaded in the heated room, and get dressed warmly to go back into the open air.

On Thursday he drank the same amount; the water operated both in front and behind, and he voided gravel, not in any great quantity; and he found the waters even more active than others he had tried, whether by the strength of the water or because his body was so disposed; and yet he drank less of them than he had of any others, and passed them not as undigested as the others.

On this Thursday he spoke to a minister of Zurich, a native of this place, who arrived here, and found that the Zurichers' first religion had been Zwinglian; from which this minister told him they had come closer to the Calvinist, which was a little milder. And questioned about predestination, the minister replied that they held a mean between Geneva and Augsburg, but that they did not bother their people with this dispute. Of his own private judgment he inclined more to the extreme of Zwingli, and praised it highly as the creed that came closest to primitive Christianity.

On Friday, the 7th of October, after breakfast, at seven o'clock in the morning, we left Baden; and before leaving, Monsieur de Montaigne again drank his measure of the said waters; thus he drank here five times. On the doubtful question of their operation, in which he sees as much occasion for good hope as in any others, both for the drinking and for the bathing, he would recommend these baths as gladly as any others he had seen until then; inasmuch as the lodgings are so conveniently located, so clean, so well distributed (each person having the share he wants, without dependence or difficulty of access from one room to another), that there are quarters for private persons of low condition and others for the great; separate baths, galleries, kitchens, cabinets, chapels, for separate parties. And in the inn next to ours, which is called the Town Court, ours being the Rear Court (they are public houses belonging to the co-ruling cantons, and are kept by tenants)—in the said inn next to ours they also have some fireplaces, French style. The master bedrooms all have stoves.

The payment exacted of foreigners is a bit tyrannical, as in all countries and especially our own. Four rooms furnished with nine beds, two of which had stoves and a bath, cost us a crown a day for each of the masters; and for the servants, four batzen each, that is to say nine sous and a little over; the horses six batzen, which is about fourteen sous a day; but besides that they added several thievish charges, contrary to their custom.

The Swiss keep guard in their towns and even in the borough where the baths are, which is only a village. Every night there are two sentinels who do the rounds of the houses, not so much to guard against enemies as for fear of fire or other disturbance. When the hours strike, one of them is obliged to shout out aloud at the top of his voice to the other and ask him what time it is; to which the other in the same voice answers with news of the time, and adds that he should keep good watch.

The women here do their washing in the open and in the public laundry, setting up near the waters a little wood fire over which they heat their water; and they do it better, and also scour their pots and pans much better, than in our hostelries in France. In the hostelries each chambermaid has her own particular job, also each manservant.

It is a misfortune for a stranger that, however diligently you try, it is impossible to get information about the notable sights of each place from the people of the country, unless you come across some who are abler than the ordinary; and they do not know what you are asking them. I say this apropos of the fact that, after staying here for five days and showing all possible curiosity, we had not heard about what we found on the way out of town: a stone of the height of a man, which seemed to be a part of some pillar, without ornament or carving on it, planted at the corner of a house to be visible to those passing on the highroad, on which there is a Latin inscription that I had no means of transcribing; but it is simply a dedication to the emperors Nerva and Trajan.

We came and crossed the Rhine at the town of Kaiserstuhl, which is one of the allies of the Swiss, and Catholic; and beyond it we followed the said river through a very beautiful flat country until we came upon some waterfalls where it breaks against the rocks, and which they call the cataracts, like those of the Nile. The reason is that below Schaffhausen the Rhine encounters a bed full of big rocks, where it is broken up; and below, in these same rocks, it comes to a fall about two pikes high where it makes a great drop, foaming and making an amazing noise. This stops the course of boats and interrupts navigation on the said river. We came on without a stop and had supper at

SCHAFFHAUSEN, four leagues, the capital town of one of the cantons of the Swiss, of the religion I have mentioned above, that of the people of Zurich. On leaving Baden we left Zurich on the right, where Monsieur de Montaigne had planned to go, being only two leagues away; but it was reported to him that the plague was there.

At Schaffhausen we saw nothing rare. They are building a citadel that will be rather handsome. There is a butt for crossbow shooting and a place for this practice, as beautiful, large, and well provided with shade, seats, galleries, and rooms, as can be; and there is a similar place for harquebus shooting. There are water mills for sawing wood, of which we had seen several elsewhere, and for pounding flax and shelling millet.

There is also a tree, fashioned like others we had seen, especially at Baden, but not of comparable size. The first and lowest branches they use to form the floor of a round gallery twenty paces in diameter; these branches they then bend upward and make them embrace this gallery all around and rise up as high as they can. Afterward they clip the tree, and keep it from throwing out branches up to the height that they want to give this gallery, which is about ten feet. There they take the other branches that come from the tree, which they lay over certain wicker mats to form the roof of the chamber, and then bend them down to make them join those that are climbing up, and they fill all the gaps with verdure. After this they again clip the tree up to the top, where they let the branches spread freely. This makes a very beautiful appearance and a very handsome tree. Besides this, at the foot of the tree they have made a fountain spring up, which spouts up above the floor of this gallery.

Monsieur de Montaigne paid a visit to the burgomasters of the town, who, to do him honor, came with other public officers to sup at our inn, and there presented some wine to Monsieur d'Estissac and him. This was not without several ceremonious speeches on both sides. The principal burgomaster was a gentleman, brought up as a page with the late duke of Orléans, but he had already forgotten all his French.

The canton professes to be strongly on our side, and has given recent evidence of it by refusing, in our favor, the confederation that the late duke of Savoy sought with the cantons, of which I have made mention above.

On Saturday, the 8th of October, at eight o'clock in the morning, after breakfast, we left Schaffhausen, where the Crown offers very good lodgings. A learned man of the country had a talk with Monsieur de Montaigne and told him among other things that the inhabitants of this town are not in reality very well disposed toward our court; so that in all the deliberations he had attended concerning the alliance with the king, most of the people were always in favor of breaking it off; but owing to the intrigues of certain rich men this turned out differently.

As we were leaving we saw an iron machine, such as we had also seen elsewhere, by which they raise large stones to load the wagons without using manpower.

We passed along the Rhine, which we had on our right hand, as far as Stein, a little town allied to the cantons, of the same religion as Schaff-hausen (and yet along the road there were lots of stone crosses), where we recrossed the Rhine over another wooden bridge; and skirting the river bank, having it on our left hand, we passed by another little town, also one of the allies of the Catholic cantons. There the Rhine expands to a marvelous width, as does our Garonne at Blaye, and then it narrows again as far as Constance.

Germany, Austria, and the Alps (October 8-27, 1580)

CONSTANCE, four leagues, where we arrived around four o'clock. This is a town of the size of Châlons, belonging to the archduke of Austria, and Catholic. Because it was once, and in the last thirty years, held by the Lutherans, whom the Emperor Charles V forcibly dislodged from it, the churches still show this in the absence of images. The bishop, who is a nobleman of this country and a cardinal, living at Rome, draws a good forty thousand crowns of revenue from it. There are canonries in the Church of Our Lady which are worth fifteen hundred florins a year and are held by noblemen. We saw one of these on horse-back, coming from outside, licentiously dressed as a warrior; and indeed they say there are many Lutherans in the town.

We climbed the bell tower, which is very high, and found there a man posted as a sentinel, who never leaves there, whatever the occasion, and is confined there.

They are erecting on the bank of the Rhine a big covered building fifty paces long and forty wide, or thereabouts; they will put in it twelve or fifteen great wheels, by means of which they will continually raise a great quantity of water to a floor which will be one story higher, and other, iron wheels in like number (for the lower ones are of wood); and they will raise the water in the same way from this floor to another above. This water, having been raised to this height, which is about fifty feet, will flow out through a big wide artificial canal and be led into their town to set several mills grinding. The artisan who was super-vising this construction had five thousand seven hundred florins for his labor alone, and was furnished with wine besides. At the very bottom of the water they are making a platform, closed all around, to break the course of the water, they say, and so that it may come to rest in this box and thus be drawn up more easily. They are also erecting some machines by means of which they can raise or lower all this wheelwork according as the river happens to be high or low.

The Rhine does not have that name here; for at the head of the town it spreads out into the form of a lake, which is fully four German leagues wide and five or six long. They have a beautiful terrace overlooking the pointed end of this big lake, where they unload the merchandise; and fifty paces from the lake a handsome little house where they keep a sentinel continually; and they have attached to it a chain by which they close the entrance to the port, having driven many piles which enclose on two sides the part of the lake in which boats are docked and loaded. At the Church of Our Lady there is a conduit which proceeds above the Rhine into the suburbs of the town.

We recognized that we were leaving the country of Switzerland by the fact that a little before we arrived in the town we saw several noblemen's manors; for you hardly see any in Switzerland. But as for private houses, both in the towns and in the country along the route we followed, they are incomparably more handsome than in France, and lack nothing but slate roofs; and especially in the hostelries, where the treatment is better, for what they lack for our service is due not to indigence—this is readily recognizable from the rest of their equipment; and there is not an inn but where everyone drinks out of large silver vessels, most of them gilded and chased—but to custom. It is a very fertile country, notably in wines.

To come back to Constance: we were badly lodged at the Eagle, and received from the landlord a sample of the barbaric German unruliness and pride, over the quarrel of one of our footmen with our guide from Basel. And because the thing even came before the judges, to whom Monsieur de Montaigne went to complain, the provost of the place—an Italian gentleman who has settled and married here and has long had the right of citizenship—answered Monsieur de Montaigne, when he asked whether his servants would be believed in their testimony on our behalf, that yes, they would be believed, provided Monsieur de Montaigne discharged them; but that immediately afterward he could take them back into his service. This was a remarkable piece of subtlety.

The next day, which was Sunday, we remained until after dinner because of this disturbance, and changed our lodging to the Pike, where we were very well off. The son of the commandant of the town, who was brought up as a page with Monsieur de Méru,[1] always attended the gentlemen of our party at their meals and elsewhere; yet he knew not a word of French.

The courses at their tables are changed frequently. Here, and often since, after the cloth was removed, they were given other new courses with the wine: the first, *canaules*,[2] as the Gascons call them; then gingerbread; and for the third a soft white bread cut into slices but still holding together; between the slices they toss a lot of spices and salt, and also on top of the crust of the loaf.

[1] Charles de Montmorency, seigneur de Méru, third son of the Constable Anne de Montmorency.

[2] A cake shaped like a crown.

This country is extremely full of leper hospitals, and the roads are all full of lepers.

The village people serve their laborers for breakfast very flat *fouaces*[3] in which there is fennel, and on top of the *fouaces* little bits of bacon cut up very small, and cloves of garlic.

Among the Germans, to pay honor to a man, they always go to his left side, in whatever position he may be, and consider it an offense to place themselves on his right, saying that in order to show deference to a man you must leave him free on his right side to put his hand to his weapons.

Sunday after dinner we left Constance, and after crossing the lake one league away from the town, we came to sleep at

MARKDORF, two leagues, which is a little Catholic town, and we stayed at the Cologne, the posthouse which is situated here for the Emperor for the trip from Italy into Germany. Here, as in several other places, they fill the mattresses with leaves from a certain tree, which serve the purpose better than straw and last longer. It is a town surrounded by a vast region of vineyards, where very good wines are produced.

On Monday, October 10th, we left after breakfast; for Monsieur de Montaigne was lured by the fine day to change his plan of going to Ravensburg that day, and turned aside a day's journey to go to Lindau. Monsieur de Montaigne never ate breakfast; but they would bring him a piece of dry bread that he ate on the way, and this was sometimes helped down by the grapes he found; for the vintage was still under way in that region and the country was full of vines, especially around Lindau. They raise them from the ground on trellises and thus leave a quantity of fine roads surrounded by verdure, which are very beautiful. We passed a town named Buchhorn,[4] which is Imperial and Catholic, on the shore of the Lake of Constance, into which town all the merchandise from Ulm, Nuremberg, and elsewhere is brought in wagons, and beyond there they take the Rhine route across the lake. We arrived about three o'clock in the afternoon at

LINDAU, three leagues, a small town situated a hundred paces into the lake, which hundred paces you pass over a stone bridge; there is only this entrance, all the rest of the town being surrounded by this lake. The lake is a good league wide, and beyond it rise the mountains of the Grisons. This lake and all the rivers hereabouts are low in winter and swollen in summer, because of the melted snows.

In all this country the women cover their head with a fur hat or bonnet like our calotte; the outside is of some better sort of fur such as squirrel, and the inside of lambskin; and such a bonnet costs only three testons. The window that is in the front of our calottes they wear behind, and through it appears all their braided hair. They are usually shod with boots, either red or white, which are not unbecoming to them.

---

[3] A thick cake cooked fast in coals, the occasion for the war in Rabelais' *Gargantua*.

[4] Now Friedrichshafen.

Both religions are practiced. We went to see the Catholic church, built in the year 866 and preserved in its entirety; and we also saw the church used by the [Protestant] ministers. All the Imperial towns are free to choose their religion, Catholic or Lutheran, according to the wish of the inhabitants. They attach themselves more or less to the one they favor. At Lindau there are only two or three Catholics, from what the priest told Monsieur de Montaigne. The priests do not fail for all that to receive their revenues freely and to perform their service, as do also some nuns who are here. The said sieur de Montaigne also spoke to the minister, from whom he did not learn much of anything except that they feel the usual hatred of Zwingli and Calvin. They say that in truth there are few towns that do not have something particular in their belief; and under the authority of Martin, whom they accept as their chief, they get up many disputes over the interpretation of the meaning of Martin's writings.[5]

We lodged at the Crown, which is a handsome inn. On the paneled wall of the dining room there was a sort of cage, of the same length as the wall, to lodge a great number of birds; it had alleyways hung and fitted with brass wire, which gave the birds room to move about from one end of the room to the other.

Their furniture and woodwork is all of pine only, which is the most common tree in their forests; but they paint, varnish, and scour it with care, and even have brushes of hair with which they dust their benches and tables.

They have a great abundance of cabbage, which they chop up small with a special instrument, and they put a great quantity of it thus chopped up into vats with salt and make soups out of it all winter.

Here Monsieur de Montaigne tried covering himself in bed with a feather quilt, as is their custom; and he was greatly pleased with this practice, finding that it was a covering both warm and light. In his opinion there is nothing to complain of, except, for delicate souls, the bedding; but if anyone brought a mattress, which is unknown here, and a curtain, in his baggage, he would find nothing lacking. For as to table fare, they are so abundant in provisions, and diversify their courses with so many sorts of soups, sauces, salads—for example, besides the dishes that we are accustomed to, some of them offered us soups made of quinces; others, baked apples cut into slices on the soup, and cabbage salads; they also make broths without bread, of various sorts, as with rice, into which everyone fishes together, for there is no individual serving—and all this of such good flavor in the good inns, that the cuisines of the French nobility hardly seemed comparable; and there are few French noblemen that have dining rooms so well adorned.

They have a great abundance of good fish, which they serve in with the meat course; they disdain trout, and eat only the roe; they have lots

[5] In his chapter "Of Experience" (*Essays* III:13, p. 818) Montaigne wrote later: "I have observed in Germany that Luther has left as many divisions and altercations over the uncertainty of his opinions, and more, as he raised about the Holy Scriptures."

of game, woodcocks, young hares, which they dress in a manner very different from ours, but at least as good. We never saw victuals so tender as they ordinarily serve them. They mix stewed plums and pear and apple tarts with the meat course, and sometimes serve the roast first and the soup at the end, sometimes the other way around. Their fruit for dessert is only pears and apples, which are very good, nuts, and cheese. Together with the meat they bring out a tray of silver or pewter with four compartments, in which they put various sorts of powdered spices; and they mix caraway, or some similar seed, which is tangy and hot, with their bread; and their bread is mostly made with fennel. After the meal they put full glasses back on the table and serve two or three courses of various things that provoke thirst.

Monsieur de Montaigne found three things lacking in his travels: one, that he had not brought along a cook to instruct in their ways so that some day the cook could try them at home; another, that he had not brought along a German valet or sought the company of some gentleman of the country—for to live at the mercy of some poor block-head of a guide he found to be a great inconvenience; the third, that before making the trip he had not looked into the books that might have informed him about the rare and remarkable things in each place, or that he did not have a Münster[6] or some other such book in his coffers.

In truth there entered into his judgment a bit of passion, a certain scorn for his country, which he regarded with hatred and indignation for other considerations; but at all events, he preferred the conveniences of this country to the French, beyond comparison, and conformed to them even to drinking wine without water. As for drinking bouts, he was never invited to any except out of courtesy, and never attempted any.

The cost of living in Southern Germany is higher than in France; for by our reckoning a man and horse cost at least a sun-crown a day. The landlords reckon, in the first place, the meal at four, five, or six batzen each for table d'hôte. They make another item of all you drink before and after these two meals, and even the smallest collations; so that Germans commonly set out in the morning from their inn without drinking. The courses that are served after the meal and the wine that is drunk with these, which constitutes the principal expense of them, are put on the account with the collations. In truth, to see the profusion of their services, and notably of wine, especially where it is extremely dear and brought from distant parts, I find their dearness excusable.

They themselves invite the servants to drink with them and keep them at table for two or three hours. Their wine is served in vessels like big pitchers, and it is a crime to see an empty goblet and not fill it immediately; and never any water, not even for those who ask for some, unless they are held in great respect.

Afterward they reckon the oats for the horses, and then the stable,

---

[6] Sebastian Münster. Montaigne owned a copy of his *Cosmographie universelle*.

which also includes the hay. There is this good thing about them, that they tell you almost with their first words what they charge; and you do not gain much by haggling. They are vainglorious, choleric, and heavy drinkers; but, said Monsieur de Montaigne, they are neither traitors nor thieves.

We left Lindau after breakfast, and around two o'clock in the afternoon came to

WANGEN, two leagues, where an accident to our baggage mule, which was injured, forced us to stop, and we were constrained to hire a wagon for the next day at three crowns a day; the wagoner, who had four horses, paid his own expenses out of that. This is a little Imperial town that has never been willing to harbor a congregation of any other religion than the Catholic; in which scythes are made, so famous that they send them to be sold even as far as Lorraine.

Monsieur de Montaigne left the next day, which was Wednesday, October 12th, in the morning, and turned off short toward Trent by the most direct and usual route, and we came to dine at

ISNY, two leagues, a little Imperial town, very pleasantly laid out.

Monsieur de Montaigne, as was his custom, promptly went and found a doctor of theology of this town, to pick up information, and this doctor dined with our party. He found that all the people were Lutherans, and saw the Lutheran church, which, like the others that they hold in the Imperial towns, has been usurped from the Catholic churches. Amid other talk that they had together about the sacrament, Monsieur de Montaigne noted that some Calvinists had informed him along the way that the Lutherans mingled in with the original opinions of Martin several strange errors, such as Ubiquitism, maintaining that the body of Jesus Christ is everywhere, as in the host; whereby they fall into the same difficulty as Zwingli, though by a different path, the one by being too sparing of the presence of the body, the other by being too prodigal of it (for by this reckoning the sacrament has no privilege over the body of the Church or the assembly of three good men). And that their principal arguments were that the divinity was inseparable from the body, wherefore, the divinity being everywhere, the body was everywhere also; and second, that since Jesus Christ had always to be at the right hand of the Father, he was everywhere, inasmuch as the right hand of God, which is the power, is everywhere. This good doctor loudly denied this imputation, and defended himself against it as against a calumny; but in fact it seems to Monsieur de Montaigne that he did not defend himself very well.

He kept Monsieur de Montaigne company in going to visit a very beautiful and sumptuous monastery, where Mass was being said; and he entered and watched without taking off his bonnet until Messieurs d'Estissac and de Montaigne had finished their prayers. In a cellar of the abbey they went to see a long, cylindrical stone, without any other workmanship, taken, so it seems, from a column, on which is this inscription in very legible Latin letters: "that the emperors Pertinax and Antonius Verus have repaired the roads and bridges at a distance of eleven

thousand paces from Campidonum," which is Kempten, where we went
for the night. This stone might have been there because the road was
under repair; for the said town of Isny is not thought to be very ancient.
However, having reconnoitered the approaches to the said Kempten in
both directions, not only did we find that there is no bridge, but we could
not recognize any repair work worthy of such workmen. There are indeed some mountains cut through, but no handiwork on a grand scale.

KEMPTEN, three leagues, a town of the size of Sainte-Foy, very beautiful and populous and abounding in good lodgings. We were at the
Bear, which is a very handsome inn. They served us silver cups of more
different kinds (which are used only for ornament, very elaborately
worked and covered with the coats of arms of various lords) than you
will find in any but a few noblemen's houses. Here there was evidence
of what Monsieur de Montaigne was saying elsewhere, that they omit
what they do of our usage because they despise it; for though they had
a great abundance of pewter plate, scoured just as at Montaigne, they
served only on wooden plates, well polished indeed and very handsome.

The seats in all this country are supplied with cushions to sit on, and
most of their wainscoted ceilings are vaulted in a half-moon shape,
which gives them a lovely grace. As for the linen, of which we were
complaining at the beginning, we have never since had any lack of it;
and for my master I have never failed to get some to make him curtains
for his bed. And if one napkin was not enough for him, they changed
it for him several times.

In this town there is a certain merchant who does a business of a
hundred thousand florins a year in linen. Monsieur de Montaigne, on
leaving Constance, would have gone to that canton in Switzerland[7] from
which linens come for all Christendom, except that to return to Lindau,
he would have had a four or five hour crossing of the lake.

This town is Lutheran; and what is strange is that here too, as at Isny,
the Catholic church holds very solemn services; for the next day, which
was Thursday morning, a working day, Mass was said in the abbey outside the town as it is at Notre Dame de Paris on Easter Day, with music
and organ, and there were only monks present. The people outside these
Imperial towns have not had this freedom to change their religion.
Those here go to this service on holidays. It is a very beautiful abbey.
The abbot holds it by right of principality, and it is worth fifty thousand
florins of income to him. He is of the house of Stein. All the monks are of
necessity gentlemen. Hildegarde, wife of Charlemagne, founded it in
the year 783, and is buried here and held to be a saint; her bones have
been disinterred from a vault where they used to be and placed in a
shrine.

The same Thursday morning Monsieur de Montaigne went to the
church of the Lutherans, which was like the others of their sect and of
the Huguenots, except that at the place of the altar, which is at the head
of the nave, there are some wooden benches that have elbow rests on

---

[7] Appenzell.

them, so that those who take their Lord's Supper may kneel as they normally do. Here he met two old ministers, one of whom was preaching in German to a not very large congregation. When he had finished, they sang a psalm in German in a chant somewhat remote from ours. After each verse the very fine organ, recently installed, gave a musical response. As often as the preacher named Jesus Christ, both he and the people took off their bonnets. After the sermon the other minister went over and stood by the altar with his face turned toward the people and a book in his hand; and a young woman came before him, head bare and hair loose, and there made a slight curtsy in the mode of the country, and remained standing there alone. Shortly afterward a young man, who was an artisan, with a sword at his side, also came forward and took his place by the side of this woman. The minister said a few words to both in their ear, then ordered each to say the paternoster, and afterward began to read out of a book. He read certain rules for people who marry; and he had them touch each other's hands, without kissing. This done, he went away, and Monsieur de Montaigne caught up with him. They had a long talk together; he took the said lord to his house and study, which was handsome and well fitted out. His name is Johannes Tilianus, of Augsburg. The said lord asked about a new confession which the Lutherans have drawn up and which all the doctors and princes who support it have signed; but it is not in Latin.

As they were leaving the church, the violins and drums attending the newlyweds were leaving by the other side. Asked whether they permitted dancing, the minister answered, "Why not?" Asked why they had Jesus Christ and many images painted on the windows and on the new organ, he replied that they did not prohibit images intended to instruct people, provided people did not worship them. Then why had they removed the old images from the churches? It was not they that had done this, he replied; it was their good disciples the Zwinglians, incited by the evil spirit, who had passed there before them and committed these ravages, as well as many others. This is the same reply that others of the Lutheran confession had made to the said lord, particularly the doctor at Isny, who, when asked whether he hated the figure and effigy of the cross, immediately exclaimed, "How could I be such an atheist as to hate this figure, so blessed and glorious for Christians?" and that those were diabolical opinions. That same man said quite brazenly at dinner that he would rather hear a hundred Masses than participate in the Calvinist communion.

At this place they served us the meat of white hares. The town is situated on the river Iller. We dined here on the said Thursday, and came away by a hilly and sterile road to sleep at

PFRONTEN, four leagues, a little village, Catholic like all the rest of this country, which belongs to the archduke of Austria.

I had forgotten to say on the subject of Lindau that at the entrance to the town there is a large wall which gives evidence of great antiquity, on which I did not perceive anything written. I understand that its name in German means Old Wall, which they told me comes from that wall.

On Friday morning, although our inn was very wretched, we found no lack of victuals.

It is their custom never to warm either their sheets for sleeping or their clothes for when they get up; and they are offended if you light a fire in their kitchen for this purpose or use the one that is there; and this is one of the biggest quarrels we had in all the inns. Even here, in the midst of mountains and forests where ten thousand feet of pine do not cost fifty sous, they would not allow us to make a fire, any more than elsewhere.

Friday morning we left here and again took the easier road to the left, leaving the mountain path which goes straight to Trent; for Monsieur de Montaigne was minded to make a few days' detour to see certain beautiful towns of Germany, and repented that at Wangen he had abandoned his original plan of going there and had taken this other route. On the way, as we had done elsewhere in several places, we came across some water mills which receive water only through a wooden flume that takes the water at the foot of some rise, and then, raising and supporting it high above the ground, sends it down a very steep slope at the end of this flume. We came to dine at

Füssen, one league. This is a little Catholic town belonging to the bishop of Augsburg. Here we found a lot of people of the retinue of the archduke of Austria, who was at a castle near by with the duke of Bavaria.

Here we placed our baggage on a float, as they call it—some pieces of wood joined together, which are taken apart when you are in port—to be taken to Augsburg on the river Lech, and I[8] and several others went along with it.

There is an abbey here where they showed our gentlemen a chalice and a stole, kept in a reliquary, which had belonged to a saint whom they call Magnus, who they say was a son of a king of Scotland and a disciple of Columbanus. Pepin founded this monastery for the said Magnus and made him its first abbot; and at the top of the nave these words are inscribed, and above these words some notes of music for a tune: *Having heard by fame of the virtue of the blessed Magnus, King Pepin has endowed, with royal liberality, the place where the saint lived.* Charlemagne afterward enriched it, as is also written in the said monastery. After dinner, both parties of us came to sleep at

Schongau, four leagues, a little town of the duke of Bavaria, and consequently strictly Catholic; for this prince, more than any other in Germany, has kept his jurisdiction pure of contagion, and is very stubborn about it.

There are good lodgings at the Star, and with a new ceremonial form: they ranged the saltcellars on a square table from corner to corner, and the candlesticks at the other corners, and made a Saint Andrew's cross of them. They never serve eggs, at least up to now, except hardboiled, cut into quarters in salads, which are very good and made with

[8] The secretary.

fresh herbs; they serve new wine, ordinarily right after it is made; they thresh the wheat in the barns as they need it, and thresh it with the big end of the flail. On Saturday we went on to dine at

LANDSBERG, four leagues, a little town of the said duke of Bavaria, situated on the said river Lech, very handsome for its size: walled inner town, outer town, and castle. We arrived here on a market day, when there was a great number of people. In the middle of a very big square is a fountain which spouts water out of a hundred pipes to the height of a pike and scatters it in a very artful way, the pipes being pointed in whatever direction is wanted. There is a very beautiful church in the town and another in the outer town, which are both on the rise of a steep hill, as is the castle also.

Monsieur de Montaigne here went to see a college of Jesuits, who are very comfortably settled there in a brand new building and are engaged in building a beautiful church. Monsieur de Montaigne had as long a talk with them as his time allowed. Count von Helffenstein is in command at the castle. If anyone even dreams of any other religion than the Roman, he must keep quiet about it.

On the gate that separates the inner from the outer town there is a great Latin inscription of the year 1552, where they say in these words that "the *Senate and the People* of this town have built this monument to the memory of William and Louis, brothers, dukes *of both Bavarias.*"[9] There are lots of other mottoes in this same place, like this one, *It befits a soldier to be rough, not adorned with gold but relying on his courage and his sword,* and at the head, *The world is a cage of fools.* And in another very conspicuous place are certain words extracted from some Latin historian about the battle that the consul Marcellus lost against a king of this nation: *The battle in which Carloman, king of the Bavarians, fought with Marcellus the consul and defeated him,* etc. There are many other good Latin mottoes at the doors of private houses. They often repaint their towns and their churches, which gives them a very flourishing appearance. And, as if precisely in honor of our passage, during the last three or four years these had almost all been renovated where we were; for they put down the dates of their work.

The clock of this town, like many others of this country, strikes all the quarter-hours; and they say that the one in Nuremberg strikes the minutes.

We left here after dinner, through a long plain of very level pasture land, like the plain of Beauce, and came to

AUGSBURG, four leagues, which is considered the most beautiful town in Germany, as Strasbourg is considered the strongest.

The first thing we noticed on our arrival was a strange arrangement, and one that shows their cleanliness: the steps of the staircase of our inn all covered with linen, on which we had to walk, so as not to dirty the steps, which they had just washed and scoured, as they do every Saturday. We have never noticed any cobwebs or mud in their inns. In some

---

[9] Here and below the italicized passages are quoted in Latin.

there are curtains for those who want to draw them over the windows.

There are hardly any tables in the bedrooms, except those that they attach to the foot of each bed, which hang there by hinges and may be raised or lowered as you wish. The footboards of the beds rise two or three feet above the frames, and often to the level of the headboard; the wood in them is very handsome and elaborately carved; but our walnut much surpasses their pine. Also they served here very shiny pewter plates underneath the wooden ones, out of disdain. They often hang against the wall, beside the beds, linen and curtains, so that people may not dirty their wall by spitting.

The Germans are much in love with coats of arms; for in all the inns there are thousands that the gentlemen of the country passing through leave on the walls, and all their windows are furnished with them.

The order of the courses is often changed. Here crayfish were served up first—which everywhere else are served just before the end—and of unusual size. In many hostelries, big ones, they serve everything covered. What makes their panes shine so much is that they have no windows fixed in our style, and that their frames can be taken out when they want, and they furbish their glasswork very often.

The next morning, which was Sunday, Monsieur de Montaigne went to see several churches; and in the Catholic ones, which are in great number, he found the service everywhere very well done. There are six Lutheran churches and sixteen ministers; two of the six are usurped from the Catholic churches, the other four they have built. He saw one this morning which resembles a great college hall: neither images, nor organs, nor crosses. The wall loaded with lots of writings in German, passages from the Bible; two pulpits, one for the minister—and there was one preaching then—and another below where the man is who leads the singing of the psalms. At each verse they wait for him to give the pitch for the following one; they sing pell-mell, whoever wishes, and whoever wishes remains covered. After that a minister who was in the crowd went up to the altar, where he read a lot of prayers out of a book; and at certain prayers the people rose and clasped their hands, and at the name of Jesus Christ made a low bow. After he had finished reading, uncovered, he turned to the altar, on which there was a napkin, a ewer, and a saucer with water in it; a woman, followed by ten or twelve other women, presented to him a child in swaddling clothes, its face uncovered. Three times the minister took water from this saucer with his fingers and sprinkled it over the child's face, saying certain words. This done, two men approached, and each of them put two fingers of his right hand on this child; the minister spoke to them, and it was done. Monsieur de Montaigne spoke to this minister on his way out. They receive no revenue from the churches; the Senate pays them publicly. There was much more of a crowd in this church alone than in two or three of the Catholic churches together.

We did not see one beautiful woman. Their clothes are very different from one another's. Among the men it is hard to distinguish the nobles, for their velvet bonnets are worn by all kinds of people, and everyone wears a sword at his side.

We were lodged at the sign of a tree called *Linden* in this country, next to the palace of the Fuggers.[10] One of this family, dying a few years ago, left two solid millions of French crowns to his heirs; and these heirs, to pray for his soul, gave the Jesuits here thirty thousand florins in ready money, with which they have set themselves up very well. The said house of the Fuggers is roofed with copper. In general the houses are much more beautiful, big, and tall than in any city of France, the streets much wider. Monsieur de Montaigne estimates the city to be of the size of Orléans.

After dinner we went to see some fencing in a public hall where there was a big crowd. You pay on entrance, as you do to see the mountebanks, and extra for seats on the benches. They fought with the poniard, the two-handed sword, the double-ended staff, and the cutlass; afterward we saw some prize contests with the crossbow and the longbow, in a place even more magnificent than at Schaffhausen.

We saw a big channel of water flowing from there to the town gate by which we had entered; this water is conveyed from outside the town by a wooden aqueduct, which runs under the footbridge over which we had passed and above the river that flows through the town moat. This channel of water sets in motion certain very numerous wheels which work several pumps, and by two lead channels these raise the water of a spring, which at this spot is very low, to the top of a tower at least fifty feet high. Here the water pours into a big stone vessel, and from this vessel it comes down through many conduits, and from these is distributed throughout the town, which by this means alone is all crowded with fountains. Individuals who want a rivulet for themselves are allowed it on payment to the town of ten florins of rent a year, or two hundred florins paid up for good. It is now forty years since the town has been adorned with this rich work.

Marriages between Catholics and Lutherans are common, and the more eager party submits to the laws of the other. There are a thousand such marriages; our landlord was Catholic, his wife Lutheran.

They dust their glassware with a hair-duster attached to the end of a stick.

They say that there are very fine horses for forty or fifty crowns.

The corporation of the town did Messieurs d'Estissac and de Montaigne the honor of sending them as a present at their supper fourteen big vessels full of their wine, which were offered them by seven sergeants dressed in livery and an eminent officer of the town, whom they invited to supper; for that is the custom, and you have something given to the porters: they gave them a crown. The officer who supped with them told Monsieur de Montaigne that there were three such officers in the town who were responsible for thus honoring strangers of some quality, and that for this reason they took pains to learn their visitors' rank, in order to observe accordingly the ceremonies that were their due: they give more wines to some than to others. To a duke, one of the

---

[10] The fabulously wealthy banking family, probably the richest in Europe, established in Augsburg since 1368.

burgomasters comes to make the present; they took us for barons and knights. Monsieur de Montaigne, for some reason, wanted our party to dissemble and not tell their ranks; and he walked unattended all day long through the town; he thinks that this served to have them even more highly honored. This was an honor that was paid them in all the towns in Germany.

When he passed through the Church of Our Lady, being extremely cold (for the cold began to prick them on leaving Kempten, and until then they had had the most fortunate weather possible), he had, without thinking about it, his handkerchief to his nose, supposing that since he was thus alone and very plainly dressed, no one would pay attention to him. When they were better acquainted with him, they told him that the church people had found this bearing strange. At last he had fallen into the fault that he most avoided, that of making himself noticeable by some mannerism at variance with the taste of those who saw him; for as far as in him lies, he conforms and falls into line with the ways of the place where he happens to be, and in Augsburg he wore a fur cap around the town.

They say in Augsburg that they are free, not from mice, but from the big rats with which the rest of Germany is infested; and on that subject they relate many miracles, attributing this privilege to one of their bishops who is buried here; and with the earth from his grave, which they sell in little lumps the size of hazelnuts, they say you can drive away this vermin in whatever country you take it to.

On Monday we went to see, in the Church of Our Lady, the marriage ceremony of a rich and ugly girl of the town with an agent of the Fuggers, a Venetian; we saw not one beautiful woman there. The Fuggers, who are many and all very rich, hold the principal positions in the town. We also saw two rooms in their house, the one high, large, paved with marble, the other low, rich in medals ancient and modern, with a little chamber at the end. They are among the most sumptuous rooms I have ever seen. We also saw the dancing of this company; it was nothing but *allemandes*.[11] They break them off at the end of each number, and return the ladies to their seats, which are benches ranged along the sides of the room in two rows, covered with red cloth; the men do not mingle with the women. After a short pause, they go and get them again; the man kisses his hand to the lady; the lady receives him without kissing hers, and then, putting his hand under her armpit, she embraces him cheek to cheek and puts his right hand on her shoulder. The men dance and converse with them uncovered and not very richly dressed.

We saw other houses of these Fuggers in other parts of the town, which is beholden to them for all the expense that they employ in embellishing it; these are pleasure houses for the summer. In one we saw a clock that is worked by the motion of water, which serves as a counterpoise. In the same place were two big covered fish ponds,

[11] A dance somewhat like the waltz.

twenty paces square, full of fish. On all four sides of each pond there are many little pipes, some straight, the others bent upward; through all these pipes the water pours very charmingly into these ponds, some sending the water in straight, the others spurting it upward to the height of a pike. Between these two ponds there is a space ten paces wide floored with planks; through these planks go lots of little brass jets which cannot be seen. While the ladies are busy watching the fish play, you have only to release some spring: immediately all these jets spurt out thin, hard streams of water to the height of a man's head, and fill the petticoats and thighs of the ladies with this coolness. In another place where there is an amusing fountain-pipe, while you are looking at it anyone who wants to can open the passage to little imperceptible tubes, which from a hundred places cast water into your face in tiny spurts; and in that place is this Latin sentence: *You were looking for trifling amusements; here they are; enjoy them.*

There is also an aviary twenty paces square, twelve or fifteen feet high, enclosed on all sides with well-knotted and interlaced brass wire; inside, ten or twelve pine trees and a fountain; this is all full of birds. Here we saw some Polish pigeons, which they call Indian, and which I have seen elsewhere; they are large, and have a beak like a partridge.

We also saw the handiwork of a gardener, who, foreseeing the storms and cold, had transported into a little covered shed lots of artichokes, cabbages, lettuce, spinach, endive, and other plants that he had picked, as if to eat them on the spot; and by putting their roots into a certain sort of earth, he hoped to keep them good and fresh for two or three months; and indeed he then had a hundred artichokes, not at all withered, and yet he had picked them more than six weeks before.

We also saw a bent instrument of lead, open on both sides, and hollow. Having once filled it with water, holding both holes up, you suddenly and dexterously turn it upside down, so that one end drinks out of a vessel full of water, and the other discharges it outside; when you have started this flow, the result is that, to avoid the vacuum, the water always keeps filling the tube and running out without stopping.[12]

The arms of the Fuggers are a shield divided in the middle: on the left, a fleur-de-lys azure on a field or; on the right, a fleur-de-lys or on a field azure; which the Emperor Charles V gave them when he ennobled them.

We went to see some people who were taking two ostriches from Venice to the duke of Saxony. The male was blacker and had a red neck; the female was more grayish, and laid lots of eggs. They were leading them on foot, and they say that the beasts got less tired than they, and were all the time escaping from them; but they keep them attached by a collar that girds them around the loins over the thighs, and another over the shoulders; these go around their whole body; and they have long leashes by which they stop them or turn them as they please.

[12] The instrument described is a siphon.

On Tuesday, by a singular courtesy of the lords of the town, we went to see a postern which is in the said town, by which they admit at all hours of the night anyone who wants to enter, whether on foot or on horseback, provided he tells his name and the person with whom he will stay in town or the name of the hostelry he is seeking. Two trusty men, paid by the town, preside over this entrance. People on horseback pay two batzen to enter, people on foot one. The corresponding outside door is sheathed with iron; at the side, there is a piece of iron attached to a chain, which piece of iron you pull. This chain, by a very long route with many turns, leads to the bedroom of one of the porters, which is very high up, and rings a bell. The porter, from his bed and in his shirt, by a certain machine that he moves back and forth, opens this first door, more than a hundred paces from his room. The man who has entered finds himself on a bridge forty paces long or thereabouts, all covered over, which crosses the town moat; along the bridge is a wooden channel, and along this the machinery moves which opens this first door, which is immediately closed again on those who have entered. When this bridge is passed, you find yourself in a little place where you speak to this first porter and tell him your name and address. Having heard it, he rings a bell to notify his mate, who is lodged one story below in this gateway, where there is a big lodging; he, by working a spring in a gallery adjoining his room, in the first place opens a little iron barrier, and then, by turning a big wheel, raises the drawbridge, without the visitor's being able to perceive any of these movements, which are concealed by the thickness of the walls and doors; and everything is promptly closed again with a great racket. Beyond the bridge a big door opens, very thick, which is of wood and reinforced with many big sheets of iron. The stranger finds himself in a room, and all the way along sees no one to speak to. After he is shut up there, they open another, similar door to him; he enters a second room in which there is a light; there he finds a brass vessel hanging down by a chain; there he puts the money he owes for his passage. This money is pulled up by the porter; if he is not satisfied, he lets the man stew there till morning; if he is satisfied, as he customarily is, he opens for him in the same way still another big door like the others, which closes as soon as he has passed, and there he is in the town.

It is one of the most ingenious things that can be seen. The queen of England sent an ambassador expressly to ask the city government to reveal the working of these machines; it is said that they refused. Under this gateway is a great vault that will lodge five hundred horse under cover, either to be used for help, or to be sent to war without the knowledge of the townspeople.

On leaving there we went to see the Church of the Holy Cross, which is very beautiful. They make a great celebration there about a miracle that occurred nearly a hundred years ago. A woman would not swallow the body of Our Lord. Having taken it out of her mouth and put it, wrapped in wax, into a box, she confessed; and they found the whole thing changed into flesh. For this they cite plenty of attestations, and this miracle is written down in many places in Latin and in German. They show under crystal that wax, and then a little morsel having the redness of flesh. This church is roofed with copper, like the house of the Fuggers, and that is not very rare here.

The church of the Lutherans is right next to this one; here, as elsewhere, the construction and lodgings are like the cloisters of the Catholic churches. At the door of this church they have placed the image of Our Lady holding Jesus Christ, with other saints and some children, and these words: *Suffer the little children to come unto me*, etc.

In our inn there was a machine consisting of two iron pistons which plunged to the bottom of a very deep well. With a boy at the top working a certain mechanism and making these iron pistons go up and down two or three feet, the pistons, one after the other, beat and pressed the water at the bottom of this well and, pushing it with their plungers, forced it to gush through a leaden pipe which delivers it to the kitchens and wherever it is needed.

They have a whitewasher on their payroll who immediately goes over any part of their walls that has been blackened.

They served us pasties, both large and small, in earthenware vessels of the color and exact shape of a pie crust. Few meals pass at which they do not offer you sugar candies and boxes of sweetmeats. The bread is the most excellent possible; the wines are good, and in this region these are more often white; none is grown around Augsburg, and they bring them from five or six days' journey away. For every hundred florins that the landlords spend on wine, the republic demands sixty, and half that amount from other private persons who buy it only for their own use.

They also have in many places the custom of putting perfumes in the bedrooms and dining rooms.

The town was originally entirely Zwinglian. Later, when the Catholics were recalled, the Lutherans took the place of the Zwinglians; at present there are more Catholics in positions of authority, although they are greatly outnumbered. Monsieur de Montaigne also visited the Jesuits here and found some very learned ones.

Wednesday morning, October 19th, we breakfasted here. Monsieur de Montaigne was very sorry, being only a day's journey from the Danube, to leave without seeing it or the town of Ulm, which lies on its course, and a bath half a day's journey beyond which is called Sauerbrunnen. It is a bath in flat country, of cold water, which they heat up to use it for drinking or bathing. It has something stinging in its taste that makes it pleasant to drink, and it is good for maladies of the head and stomach; a famous bath, where you are very magnificently lodged in very well-appointed inns, as at Baden, from what we were told; but wintertime was advancing fast, and then this road was quite in the opposite direction from ours, and we would have had to retrace our steps back to Augsburg; and Monsieur de Montaigne strenuously avoided passing over the same road twice.

I left an escutcheon of the arms of Monsieur de Montaigne in front of the door of the dining room at his lodging; it was very well painted, and cost me two crowns to the painter and twenty sous to the carpenter.

The town is bathed by the river Lech, Lycus. We passed through a very beautiful countryside, fertile in wheat, and came to sleep at

BRUCK, five leagues, a big village in a very handsome setting in the duchy of Bavaria, Catholic. We left there the next day, which was Thursday, October 20th, and after continuing through a great plain of wheat (for this region has no wines) and then a prairie as far as the eye could reach, we came to dine at

MUNICH, four leagues, a city about as big as Bordeaux, chief city of the duchy of Bavaria, where they[13] have their principal residence on the river Isar, Ister. It has a handsome castle and finer stables than I have ever seen in France or Italy, vaulted, to lodge two hundred horses. It is a town strongly Catholic, populous, handsome, and mercantile.

From a day's journey above Augsburg you can plan on spending four livres a day for man and horse, and forty sous per footman, at the least.

Here we found curtains in our bedrooms and no testers, and moreover everything very clean; they clean their floors with sawdust, which they boil.

Everywhere in this country they cut up two varieties of turnip, applying the same care and diligence as in threshing wheat. Seven or eight men, with large knives in each hand, slash them, with a rhythmic beat, in vessels resembling our wine presses; this makes it possible for them to put them up and salt them for the winter, like their cabbages. With those two vegetables they fill, not their gardens, but their lands in the country, and they have harvests of them.

The duke, who is here now, married the sister of the duke of Lorraine, and has by her two rather big boys and a girl. The duke and his brother are both in town; they had gone hunting, ladies and all, the day we were there.

On Friday morning we left here, and, through the forests of the said duke, saw countless numbers of reddish animals[14] in flocks, like sheep; and we came without stopping to

ICKING, six leagues, a wretched little village in the same duchy. The Jesuits, who govern in this region, have caused a great commotion, which makes them hated by the people, by forcing the priests to get rid of their concubines, under great penalties; and to see the priests complain of it, it seems that formerly this was so tolerated that they practiced it as if it were something legitimate; and they are still busy making remonstrances about it to the duke.

Here we had the first eggs that we had been served in Germany on a fish day, or otherwise than cut up into quarters in salads. Also they served us in wooden goblets with staves and hoops like barrels, among many of silver. The lady of a noble house who was in this village sent some of her wine to Monsieur de Montaigne.

[13] The dukes of Bavaria.
[14] Fallow deer.

Early on Saturday morning we left here; and after coming upon the river Isar on our right and a large lake at the foot of the Bavarian mountains, and climbing for an hour's ride a little mountain on top of which there is an inscription saying that a duke of Bavaria had had the rock cut through a hundred years ago or thereabouts, we plunged right into the heart of the Alps by an easy, comfortable, and delightfully well-kept road, the beautiful, serene weather favoring us. On descending this little mountain we came upon a very beautiful lake, a Gascon league in length and as much in breadth, wholly surrounded by very high and inaccessible mountains; and still following this route at the foot of the mountains, from time to time we came upon level patches of very pleasant meadowland, on which there are houses; and without stopping we came on to sleep at

MITTENWALD, a little village belonging to the duke of Bavaria, rather well situated along the river Isar. Here they served us the first chestnuts we had been served in Germany, and quite raw. There is a steam bath in the hostelry where travelers are accustomed to be sweated, for a batz and a half. I went there while the gentlemen were having supper. There were lots of Germans who were being cupped and bled.

The next morning, Sunday, October 23rd, we continued along this path between the mountains, and on it came upon a gate and a house that shuts off the passage. This is the entrance to the district of Tyrol, which belongs to the archduke of Austria. We came to dine at

SEEFELD, a little village and abbey, three leagues, pleasant site. The church is rather fine, famous for the following miracle. In 1384 a certain man, whose name is given in the particulars, not willing to be content on Easter Day with the common host, asked for the great one. When he had it in his mouth, the earth opened under him and swallowed him up to his neck, and he held on to the corner of the altar. The priest took the host out of his mouth. They still show the hole, covered with an iron grill, and the altar that received the imprint of this man's fingers, and the host, which is all reddish, as with drops of blood. We also found here a recent writing, in Latin, about a Tyrolean who, having a few days before tried to swallow a piece of meat which stuck in his throat, and being unable either to swallow it or throw it up for three days, made a vow and came to this church, where he was instantly cured.

On leaving here we found, in the highlands we were crossing, some beautiful villages; and then, having come down a half hour's descent, at the foot of it we came upon a beautiful town, well located; above, on a precipitous hill which seems inaccessible, a handsome castle[15] commands the road of this descent, which is narrow and cut out of the rock. It is not quite wide enough for an ordinary wagon, as indeed is the case in many places in these mountains; so that the carters who venture up here are accustomed to cut down the ordinary wagons by at least a foot.

Beyond we found a valley of great length, through which passes the river Inn, which flows into the Danube at Vienna. In Latin it is called *Aenus*. It is five or six days by water from Innsbruck to Vienna. This

[15] Fragenstein.

valley seemed to Monsieur de Montaigne to present the most agreeable landscape he had ever seen: now contracting as the mountains pressed close, then widening, now on the side we were on, which was the left side of the river, and creating new land for plowing and cultivating on the very slopes of the less steep mountains; now on the other side; and then revealing plains on two or three levels, one above the other; and all full of beautiful noblemen's houses and of churches; and all this closed and walled in on all sides by mountains of measureless height.

On a rocky hill on our side we discovered a crucifix in a place where it is impossible for any man to have gone without the artificial aid of ropes, by which a man could let himself down from above. They say that the Emperor Maximilian, grandfather of Charles V, while hunting, lost his way on this mountain, and in testimony to the danger he had escaped had this image erected. This story is also painted in the town of Augsburg in the hall that serves the crossbowmen. In the evening we went to

INNSBRUCK, three leagues, chief town of the county of Tyrol, *Aenopontum* in Latin. Here dwells Ferdinand, archduke of Austria. A very beautiful little town and very well built in the depth of this valley, full of fountains and streams, which are a very ordinary attraction in the towns we have seen in Germany and Switzerland. The houses are almost all built in terraces along the hillside.

We lodged at the Rose, a very good inn; they served us in pewter plates. As for napkins in the French fashion, we had already had some a few days before. Around some of the beds there were curtains; and to show the character of the nation, they were beautiful and rich, of a certain kind of linen, cut and open-worked, for the rest short and narrow, in short of no use for what we use them for; and a little tester three fingers wide with lots of tassels. They gave me some sheets for Monsieur de Montaigne which had four fingers' width of rich white lacework all around.

As in most of the other towns of Germany, there are men here all night in the streets who call out the hours that have struck.

Everywhere we have been they have this custom of serving fish in with the meat; but on fish days, however, they do not serve meat with the fish, at least not to us.

On the Monday we left here, skirting the said river Inn on our left hand, along that beautiful plain; we went to dine at

HALL, two leagues; and we made this trip just to see it. It is a little town like Innsbruck, the size of Libourne or thereabouts, on the said river, which we crossed again over a bridge. It is from here that they extract the salt that supplies all Germany, and every week nine hundred loaves are made, at a crown apiece. These loaves are of the thickness of a half a hogshead and of about that shape; for the vessel that serves them as a mold is of that kind. This belongs to the archduke; but the expense is very great. For the preparation of the salt I saw more wood here in one place than I ever saw anywhere else; for in several great caldrons made of iron plates, thirty good paces around, they boil this salt water from which they make their salt, which comes from more than two long leagues away, from one of the neighboring mountains.

There are several fine churches, notably that of the Jesuits, which Monsieur de Montaigne visited; and at Innsbruck he visited others, which are magnificently situated and accommodated.

After dinner we again saw that side of the river, for there is a beautiful house in that place where Archduke Ferdinand of Austria is staying, whose hands Monsieur de Montaigne wanted to kiss; and he had stopped by there in the morning, but had found that the archduke was busy in his council, from what a certain count had told him. After dinner we stopped by again and found him in a garden, or least we thought we had caught a glimpse of him. However, those who went to tell him that our gentlemen were there and why, reported that he begged them to excuse him, but that on the next day he would be more at leisure; that at all events if they had any need of his favor they should make this known to a certain Milanese count. This coolness, added to the fact that they were not even allowed to see the castle, offended Monsieur de Montaigne a little; and as he was complaining about it that same day to an officer of the house, he was answered that the said prince had replied that he did not like to see Frenchmen and that the house of France was hostile to his. We returned to

INNSBRUCK, two leagues. Here we saw in a church eighteen very handsome bronze effigies of the princes and princesses of the house of Austria.

We also went to attend a supper party given by the Cardinal of Austria and the margrave of Burgau, sons of the said archduke by a concubine from the town of Augsburg, a merchant's daughter,[16] whom, having had these two sons by her and no others, he married to legitimize them; and in that same year the said woman passed away. The whole court still wears mourning for her.

Their service was about like that of our princes. The hall was hung with black cloth, also the dais and chairs. The cardinal is the elder, and I think he is not yet twenty. The margrave drinks only bottled wine, and the cardinal very diluted wine. They have no special container for their place settings, but these are uncovered; and the service of the courses is in our style. When they come to sit down, it is a bit away from the table, and this is moved close to them, all loaded with food, the cardinal at the head; for the head with them is always the right side.

We saw in this palace some tennis courts and a rather handsome garden. The archduke is a great builder and deviser of such luxuries. We saw at his place ten or twelve field pieces, carrying a ball the size of a large goose egg, mounted on wheels as gilded and enriched as possible, and even the pieces are all gilded. They are only of wood, but the muzzle is sheathed with an iron plate, and the bore is entirely lined with the same kind of plate. One single man can carry one on his back, and

---

[16] Philippine Welser (1527–80), member of one of the big business families of Augsburg.

fire it not as often, but with almost as big a charge, as those cast in metal.

At his castle in the fields we saw two oxen of unusual size, all gray, with white heads, which the duke of Ferrara had given him; for the said duke had married one of his sisters, the duke of Florence another, the duke of Mantua a third. He had three of his sisters at Hall, whom they called the three queens; for the daughters of the Emperor are given these titles, as others are called countesses or duchesses because of their lands; and they give them the surname of the kingdoms possessed by the Emperor. Of the three, two are dead; the third is still there, but Monsieur de Montaigne could not see her; she is shut up like a nun, and has welcomed and established the Jesuits there.

Here they hold that the said archduke cannot leave his estates to his children and that they revert to the successors to the Empire; but they were unable to give us an intelligible reason for this, and what they say about his wife—that she was not of suitable lineage—does not appear plausible, since he married her, and everyone holds that she was legitimate, and also the children. At all events, he is amassing a big pile of money in order to have enough to give them.

On Tuesday we left in the morning and resumed our road, crossing that plain and following the mountain path. At one league from the inn we climbed a little mountain an hour's ride high, by an easy road. On our left hand we had a view of several other mountains, which, having a more extended and gentler incline, are covered with villages and churches, and for the most part cultivated right to the top, very pleasant to see for the diversity and variety of the sites. The mountains on our right hand were a little wilder, and there were only rare spots where there was any habitation. We crossed several streams or torrents with various courses; and on our way, both on the heights and at the foot of our mountains, we found many little towns and big villages and many handsome hostelries, and among other things two castles and gentlemen's houses on our left hand.

About four leagues from Innsbruck, on our right hand, on a very narrow road, we came upon a richly worked bronze tablet, attached to a rock, with this Latin inscription: "The Emperor Charles V, returning from Spain and Italy from receiving the imperial crown, and Ferdinand, king of Hungary and Bohemia, his brother, coming from Pannonia, seeking each other after being eight years without seeing each other, met on this spot in the year 1530, and Ferdinand here ordered this memorial to be made." They are represented embracing each other.[17] A little later, passing through a gateway set up across the road, we found on it some Latin verses making mention of the passage of the said Emperor, and of his lodging in this place, after he had captured the king of France, and Rome.[18]

Monsieur de Montaigne said that he liked this mountain pass very much because of the diversity of the objects to be seen, and we found

[17] This memorial still exists, on the Lueg Pass.
[18] In 1525 (at Pavia) and 1527 respectively.

no discomfort except from the thickest and most unendurable dust that we had ever felt, which accompanied us across this whole pass between the mountains.[19] Ten hours later (Monsieur de Montaigne said that this stretch represented one stage, or post, for him; it is true that his custom, whether or not he is to stop on the road, is to feed his horses oats before leaving the inn in the morning) we arrived, with him still fasting, late at night at

STERZING, seven leagues, a little town of the said county of Tyrol, rather pretty, above which, a quarter of a league away, there is a beautiful new castle.

On the table here they served us rolls, quite round, joined together. In all Germany the mustard is served liquid and is of the taste of French white mustard. The vinegar everywhere is white. Wine is not grown on these mountains, but wheat grows in almost sufficient abundance for the inhabitants. They drink very good white wines.

There is the greatest security in all these passes, and they are heavily traveled by merchants, carriers, and carters. Instead of the cold for which this pass is decried, we had an almost unendurable heat.

The women in this region wear cloth bonnets just like our toques, and their hair hanging in braids, as elsewhere. Monsieur de Montaigne, coming across a pretty young girl in a church, asked her if she could speak Latin, taking her for a schoolboy.

There were curtains for the beds here, of coarse linen dyed red, divided into alternating strips of four fingers' width, one part being of a close weave, the other of a loose weave. We have found no bedroom or public room in all our travel in Germany that was not wainscoted, the ceilings being very low.

Monsieur de Montaigne had the colic this night for two or three hours and was very hard pressed, from what he said in the morning; and in the morning on rising he passed a stone of medium size, which broke easily. It was yellowish on the outside, and, when broken, more whitish on the inside. He had caught a cold the day before and felt bad. He had not had an attack of the colic since the one at Plombières. This one partly removed the suspicion he had that he had taken into his bladder at the said Plombières more sand that he had got rid of, and he feared that some matter had stopped there and become caught and stuck; but seeing that he had got rid of this one, he finds it reasonable to believe that it would have attached itself to the others if there had been any. As soon as he was on the road he complained of pain in his loins, which was the reason, he said, why he lengthened this day's journey, thinking he was more relieved on horseback than he would have been elsewhere.

In this town he sent for the schoolmaster, to talk with him about his Latin; but the man was a fool from whom he was unable to derive any information about the things of this country.

The next day, which was Wednesday, October 26th, after breakfast,

[19] The Brenner Pass.

we left here through a plain half a quarter-league wide, having the river Isarco [Eisack] on our right side. This plain lasted us for about two leagues; and on the neighboring mountains were many cultivated and inhabited spots, often in locations whose approaches we could not even guess at. There are four or five castles on this road. Afterward we crossed the river over a wooden bridge and followed it on the other side. We found many workers repairing the roads merely because they were stony, about as much so as those in Périgord. Afterward, through a stone gateway, we climbed to a height where we found a plain a league wide or thereabouts, and from it discovered on the other side of the river another at an equal height, but both of them barren and stony. The rest of the country, along the river below us, consisted of very handsome meadows. We came, without stopping, to sup at

BRESSANONE, four leagues, a very beautiful little town through which the river passes under a wooden bridge; it is a bishopric. We saw here two very beautiful churches, and were lodged at the Eagle, a handsome inn. The surrounding plain is not very wide; but the mountains round about, especially on our left hand, stretch out so gently that they allow themselves to be combed and primped right up to the ears. Everything seems to be filled with steeples and villages well up into the mountainside, and near the town are many beautiful houses very pleasantly built and situated.

Monsieur de Montaigne said that all his life he had distrusted other people's judgment on the matter of the conveniences of foreign countries, since every man's taste is governed by the ordering of his habit and the usage of his village; and he had taken very little account of the information that travelers gave him; but in this spot he wondered even more at their stupidity, for he had heard, and especially on this trip, that the passes of the Alps in this region were full of difficulties, the manners of the people uncouth, roads inaccessible, lodgings primitive, the air insufferable. As for the air, he thanked God that he had found it so mild, for it inclined rather toward too much heat than too much cold; and in all this trip up to that time we had had only three days of cold and about an hour of rain. But that for the rest, if he had to take his daughter, who is only eight, for a walk, he would as soon do so on this road as on any path in his garden. And as for the inns, he had never seen a country where they were so plentifully distributed and so handsome, for he had always lodged in handsome towns well furnished with victuals and wine, and more reasonably than elsewhere.

There was a way of turning a spit here which was by a machine with several wheels, by which a cord was tightly wound around a big iron vessel. When this began to unwind, they slowed down its unwinding, so that this movement lasted about an hour, and then it had to be wound up again. As for smokejacks, we had seen several already.

They have so great an abundance of iron that besides all the windows being grated, and in various ways, their doors, even the shutters, are covered with iron plates.

Here we found vineyards again, which we had lost sight of since before Augsburg.

Hereabouts most of the houses are vaulted on every floor; and what they do not know how to do in France, to use pantiles to cover very narrow slopes, they do in Germany, even on the steeples. Their tile is smaller and hollower, and in some places plastered over the joints.

We left Bressanone the next morning and came upon that same very open valley, and the hillsides along most of the road were adorned with many beautiful houses. Having the river Isarco on our left hand, we passed through a little town where there are many artisans of all sorts, called Klausen; from there we came to dine at

KOLMANN, three leagues, a little village where the archduke has a pleasure house. Here they served us goblets of painted earthenware among those of silver, and they washed the glasses with white sand; and the first course was served in a very neat little frying pan, which they put on the table with a little iron instrument to support it and raise its handle. In this frying pan were eggs poached in butter.

As we left there the road narrowed on us a bit and some rocks pressed in on us, so that, since the defile was narrow for both us and the river together, we would have been in danger of colliding, if they had not placed between it and the travelers a wall as a barrier, which in various places extends for more than a German league. Although most of the mountains close to us here are wild rocks, some massive, others split and broken up by the flow of the torrents, and others scaly and sending down pieces of astounding size (I believe it must be dangerous here in very stormy weather), we have also seen, just as elsewhere, whole forests of pines torn up from their footing and carrying down in their fall little mountains of earth clinging to their roots; yet the fact remains that the country is so populous that above these first mountains we saw others higher up, cultivated and inhabited, and we learned that on top of them there are big, beautiful fields which furnish wheat to the towns below, and very rich farmers and beautiful houses.

We crossed the river over a wooden bridge, of which there were several, and put it on our left. We discovered, among other things, a castle on the most eminent and inaccessible mountain height that presented itself to our sight, which they say belongs to a baron of the district, who lives in it and has a fine estate and fine hunting grounds up there. Above all these mountains there is still a top fringe of the Alps; these the people leave alone, for they block the outlet from this valley, so that you continually have to return to our channel and come out again by one of the two ends.

The archduke draws from this county of Tyrol, whose whole revenue derives from these mountains, three hundred thousand florins a year; and he has more from here than from all the rest of his domain. We crossed the river once more over a stone bridge and came early to

BOLZANO, four leagues, a town of the size of Libourne, on the said river, rather unattractive compared with the others in Germany, so that Monsieur de Montaigne exclaimed that he clearly recognized that he was beginning to leave Germany: the streets narrower, and no handsome public square. There still remained fountains, streams, painted houses, and glass windows.

There is so great an abundance of wines here that they supply all Germany with them. The best bread in the world is eaten all along these mountains. Here we saw the church, which is one of the most beautiful. Among other things there is a wooden organ; it is high up, near the crucifix, before the high altar; and yet the person who plays it sits more than twelve feet below, at the foot of the pillar to which it is attached; and the bellows are outside the wall of the church, more than fifteen paces behind the organist, supplying him with their wind from underground.

The open space in which this town lies is scarcely bigger than is needed to contain it; but the mountains, especially on our right hand, stretch out their flanks a little and enlarge it.

From this place Monsieur de Montaigne wrote to François Hotman, whom he had seen at Basel, that he had taken such great pleasure in visiting Germany that he left it with great regret, although it was Italy he was going to; that foreigners had to suffer here as elsewhere from the exactions of innkeepers; but that he thought this might be corrected if a man was not at the mercy of guides and interpreters, who sell accommodations and participate in this profit. All the rest seemed to him full of comfort and courtesy, and especially of justice and security.

We left Bolzano on the Friday morning early and came, to give a measure of oats to the horses and have breakfast ourselves, to

BRONZOLO, two leagues, a little village above which the river Isarco, which had led us thus far, comes to mingle with the river Adige, which runs on to the Adriatic Sea, and runs on wide and peaceful, no longer in the manner of those we had come upon among these mountains above, noisy and furious. So this plain, as far as Trent, begins to widen a bit, and the mountains to lower their horns a bit in some places; however, they are less fertile on their flanks than the preceding ones. There are some marshes in this valley which hug the road; the rest is very easy and level and almost always in the bottom of the valley.

Two leagues beyond Bronzolo we came to a big town in which there was a great gathering of people because of a fair. Beyond this, another village, well built, named Salorno, where the archduke has a small castle, on our left hand, in a strange location, on the top of a crag.

Italy: The Road to Rome
(October 28-November 29, 1580)

From there we came to sleep at

TRENT, five leagues, a town a little larger than Agen, not very pleasant, and having completely lost the graces of the German towns; the streets mostly narrow and tortuous.

About two leagues above Trent, the Italian language begins. This town is divided in half between these two languages, and there is a quarter in the town and a church which they call that of the Germans, and a preacher of their language. As for the new religions, there has been no talk of them since Augsburg. It is situated on this river Adige. We saw the cathedral, which seems to be a very ancient building, and right near it is a square tower which gives evidence of great antiquity. We saw the new church, of Our Lady, where our Council[1] was held. In this church there is an organ, given by a private person, of surpassing beauty, raised up within a marble structure, elaborately carved with many excellent statues, notably those of certain little singing boys. This church was built, as it tells us, in 1520, by *"Bernardus Clesius, cardinal,"* who was bishop of this town and a native of this same place.

This used to be a free town and under the charge and rule of the bishop. Later, when pressed by war against the Venetians, they called the count of Tyrol to their aid, in return for which he has retained a certain authority and right over their city. The bishop and he are in dispute, but the bishop, who is at present Cardinal Madruccio, has possession.

Monsieur de Montaigne said he had taken note along the way of the citizens who have benefited the towns of their birth: the Fuggers at Augsburg, to whom is due most of the embellishment of that city, for they have filled all the street corners with their palaces, and the churches with many works; and this Cardinal Clesius, for besides this church and several streets that he restored at his own expense, he had some very fine building done in the castle of the town. It is not much on the outside, but inside it is the best furnished and painted and decorated and the most livable to be seen anywhere. All the panels on the ground floor have many rich paintings and mottoes; the raised work is elaborately gilded and carved; the floor, of a certain earth hardened and painted like marble, partly arranged in our style, partly in German style, with stoves. One of these is of earthenware, burnished like brass, and made in the form of several large human figures, which receive the fire into their limbs; and one or two others, near a wall, give out water that comes from the fountain in the court very far below: it is a fine piece of work. Here we also saw, among the other paintings on the ceiling, a nocturnal triumph by torchlight,[2] which Monsieur de Montaigne greatly admired. There are two or three round chambers; in one there is an inscription saying that this Clesius, in the year 1530, had been sent to the coronation of the Emperor Charles V, which was performed by Pope Clement VII on Saint Matthew's Day, as ambassador from Ferdinand, king of Hungary and Bohemia, count of Tyrol, and brother of the said Emperor; and that there, from being bishop of Trent, he was made a cardinal. And around the chamber he has had placed and hung on the wall

---

[1] The Council of Trent, held in the Church of Santa Maria Maggiore from 1545 to 1563.

[2] The Triumph of Caesar.

the arms and names of the gentlemen who accompanied him on this trip, about fifty, all vassals of this bishopric and counts or barons. There is also a trap door in one of the said chambers by which he could slip into town without using his doors. There are also two rich fireplaces.

He was a good cardinal. The Fuggers built, but for the service of their descendants; this man built for the public; for he has left this castle furnished with better than a hundred thousand crowns' worth of furniture, which is still there, for the bishops his successors; and in the public purse of the succeeding bishops a hundred and fifty thousand thalers in ready money, which they enjoy without damage to the capital; and yet they have left his Church of Our Lady unfinished, and him rather meanly buried. Among other things there are several paintings from the life and a lot of maps. The bishops that succeeded him have added no furniture to this castle—and there is some for both seasons, winter and summer—and it cannot be alienated.

We are now going by the Italian miles, five of which come to one German mile; and they count up to twenty-four hours a day without dividing them in the middle.[3] We lodged at the Rose, a good inn.

We left Trent Saturday after dinner and followed a similar road in that valley, now widened and flanked by high uninhabited mountains, having the said river Adige on our right hand. Here we passed a castle of the archduke which commands the road, as elsewhere we have found many similar obstacles that close off the roads and hold them subject; and when it was already very late (and until then we had not yet had any taste of evening damps, so regularly did we schedule our travel), we arrived at

ROVERETO, fifteen miles, a town belonging to the said archduke. Here we found our own style of lodging again, and found lacking not only the cleanliness of the bedrooms and furniture of Germany, and their windowpanes, but also their stoves, in which Monsieur de Montaigne found much more comfort than in fireplaces.

As for food, the crayfish here failed us; in which connection Monsieur de Montaigne remarked as a great wonder that they had been served us at every meal since Plombières, and for nearly two hundred leagues of country. Here, and along these mountains, they very commonly eat snails, much larger and fatter than in France, and not so good in taste. They also eat truffles, which they peel and put, in very fine slices, into oil and vinegar; these are not bad. At Trent they served some that had been kept a year. Here again, and to Monsieur de Montaigne's taste, we found lots of oranges, lemons, and olives.

On the beds are slit curtains of linen or a kind of rough serge, in broad bands, and fastened at intervals. Monsieur de Montaigne also regretted those featherbeds that are used as a covering in Germany. They are not beds such as ours, but of very fine down, enclosed in very

---

[3] Most subsequent references to the time of day in the *Journal* follow this pattern. Since they also reckon by starting the day at sunset, this translation simply gives the equivalents in our system of counting the time.

white fustian at the good inns. The underbedding even in Germany is not of this sort, and you cannot use it as a cover without discomfort.

I truly believe that if Monsieur de Montaigne had been alone with his own attendants he would rather have gone to Cracow or toward Greece by land than make the turn toward Italy; but the pleasure he took in visiting unknown countries, which he found so sweet as to make him forget the weakness of his age and of his health, he could not impress on any of his party, and everyone asked only to return home. Whereas he was accustomed to say that after spending a restless night, he would get up with desire and alacrity in the morning when he remembered that he had a new town or region to see. I never saw him less tired or complaining less of his pains; for his mind was so intent on what he encountered, both on the road and at his lodgings, and he was so eager on all occasions to talk to strangers, that I think this took his mind off his ailment.

If someone complained to him that he often led his party, by various roads and regions, back very close to where he had started (which he was likely to do, either because he had been told about something worth seeing, or because he had changed his mind according to the occasions), he would answer that as for him, he was not going anywhere except where he happened to be, and that he could not miss or go off his path, since he had no plan but to travel in unknown places; and that provided he did not fall back upon the same route or see the same place twice, he was not failing to carry out his plan. And as for Rome, which was the goal of the others, he desired less to see it than the other places, since it was known to every man, and there was not a lackey who could not tell them news of Florence and Ferrara. He also said that he seemed to be rather like people who are reading some very pleasing story and therefore begin to be afraid that soon it will come to an end, or any fine book; so he took such pleasure in traveling that he hated to be nearing each place where he was to rest, and toyed with several plans for traveling as he pleased, if he could get away alone.

On Sunday morning, wishing to reconnoiter Lake Garda, which is famous in that country, and from which comes very excellent fish, he hired three horses for himself and the seigneurs de Cazalis and de Mattecoulon, at twenty batzen each; and Monsieur d'Estissac hired two others for himself and the sieur du Hautoy, and without any servant, leaving their own horses at this inn (at Rovereto) for that day, they went to dine at

TORBOLE, eight miles, a little village within the jurisdiction of Tyrol. It is situated at the head of this great lake. At the other side of this head there is a little town and a castle, called La Riva, to which they were taken on the lake, which is five miles going and as much coming back; and they made the trip with five rowers in three hours or thereabouts. They saw nothing at the said La Riva but a tower which seems to be very old, and, by chance, the lord of the place, who is Signor Fortunato Madruccio, brother of the cardinal who is at present bishop of Trent. The view down the lake is boundless, for it is thirty-five miles long. The width, all they could discover of it, was only the said five miles. This head of the lake belongs to the county of Tyrol, but all the lower part, on both sides, is under Venetian rule; here there are lots of beautiful churches, and plenty of beautiful parks of olive and orange trees, and other such fruit trees. This lake becomes furiously agitated when there is a storm. The surroundings of the lake are mountains more forbidding and arid than any others that we had seen on our road, from what the said lords reported; adding that on leaving Rovereto they had crossed the river Adige and left the road to Verona on their left hand, and had entered a low valley where they had found a very long village and a little town; that it was the roughest road they had seen, and the wildest view, because of these mountains which obstructed their way. Leaving Torbole, they returned for supper to

ROVERETO, eight miles. Here they put their baggage on some of those rafts which they call floats in Germany, to be taken to Verona on the said river Adige for a florin, and the next day I had charge of taking it there. At supper they served us poached eggs for the first course, and a pike, amid great plenty of every kind of flesh.

The next day, which was Monday, they left here early in the morning; and following this valley, rather populous but hardly fertile, and flanked by high scaly and arid mountains, they came to dine at

BORGHETTO, fifteen miles, which is still in the county of Tyrol; this county is very large. In this connection, Monsieur de Montaigne, asking whether it consisted of anything but this valley through which we had passed and the mountaintops that had been offered to our sight, was given this answer: that there were many such mountain valleys, just as big and fertile, and other handsome towns, and that it was like a dress which we see only pleated, but that if it were spread out the Tyrol would be a very big country.

We[4] still had the river on our right hand. Leaving here after dinner, we followed the same sort of road as far as Chiusa, which is a little fort that the Venetians have won, in the hollow of a rock on this river Adige; we descended along this river by a steep slope of massive rock, where horses have a hard time getting secure footing, and went through the said fort, where the state of Venice, whose jurisdiction we had entered one or two miles after leaving Borghetto, maintains twenty-five soldiers. They came to sleep at

VOLARGNE, twelve miles, a little village and a miserable inn, as are all those on this road as far as Verona. Here, from the castle of the place, a maiden lady, sister of the absent lord, sent some wine to Monsieur de Montaigne.

The next morning they completely lost the mountains on their right hand, and left far on one side on their left hand a chain of hills. For a long time they followed a barren plain, which then, approaching the said river, became a little better, and fertile in vines trained on trees,

---

[4] The "we" does not include the secretary, who usually refers to the rest of the party as "they." The same discrepancy occurs occasionally later.

as they are in this country; and on All Saints' Day, before Mass, they arrived at

VERONA, twelve miles, a city of the size of Poitiers, and like it having a vast quay, on the said river Adige, which goes through it and over which there are three bridges. I also arrived here with my baggage. Without the health certificates that they had gotten at Trent and had confirmed at Rovereto, they could not have entered the city; and yet there was no rumor of danger from the plague; but it is out of custom, or in order to filch some quattrino or so that they cost.

We went to see the cathedral, where Monsieur de Montaigne found the behavior of the men strange on such a day, at High Mass: they were talking right in the choir of the church, covered, standing, their backs turned toward the altar, and looking as if they were not thinking of the service except at the elevation. There was an organ, and some violins which accompanied it during Mass. We also saw some other churches, in which there was nothing singular—nothing in the adornment or beauty of the women, among other things.

They went to the Church of Saint George, among other places; the Germans have left plenty of evidence of having been there, and many escutcheons. There is one inscription, among others, stating that certain German noblemen, having accompanied the Emperor Maximilian in taking Verona from the Venetians, placed some work or other on an altar here. He thought it remarkable that the Signory preserves in its city the evidence of its losses, as also it preserves in their entirety the proud tombs of the poor lords of La Scala.[5] It is true that our host of the Little Horse, which is a very good inn where we were treated to a superfluity of food at a cost of one-fourth more than in France, enjoys possession of one of these tombs for his family. We saw the castle here, and the party was shown through by the lieutenant of the governor of the castle. The Signory maintains sixty soldiers there: rather, from what they told Monsieur de Montaigne at the castle itself, against the townspeople than against foreigners.

We also saw a convent of monks who are called the Jesuates of Saint Jerome. They are not priests, and neither say Mass nor preach, and are mostly ignorant; and they pride themselves on being excellent distillers of orange-flower liqueurs and similar waters, both here and elsewhere. They are dressed in white, and wear dark brown robes and little white birettas; many are handsome young men. Their church is very well accommodated, as is their refectory, where their table was already laid for supper. Our gentlemen saw here certain old ruins, very ancient, of the time of the Romans, which these men say were an amphitheater, and they patch them up with other fragments that are discovered underneath. On our return from there we found that they had perfumed their cloisters for us, and they had us enter a cabinet full of phials and earthenware vessels, and there they perfumed us.

The finest thing we saw here, and what Monsieur de Montaigne said

[5] More commonly known as the Scaligers.

was the handsomest building he had seen in his life, was a place they call the Arena. This is an oval amphitheater, which seems almost entire—all the seats, all the arches and outer structure—except the extreme end of the outer part: in short, there is enough left to reveal the shape and use of these buildings as they were. The Signory is employing some criminals' fines on it, and has repaired some bit; but what they are doing is very far from what would be needed to restore it entirely; and he strongly doubts whether the whole city is up to this restoration. It is oval in shape; there are forty-three tiers of steps, each a foot or more high, and it is about six hundred paces around at the top. The noblemen of the country still use it for jousting and other public pleasures.

We also saw the Jews, and Monsieur de Montaigne was in their synagogue and had quite a talk with them about their ceremonies.

There are some very beautiful squares and beautiful market places. From the castle, which is up high, we could make out Mantua in the plain, twenty miles away on the right of our road. They have no lack of inscriptions; for they never even repair some little gutter, either in town or on the roads, without inscribing on it the name of the podestà and that of the workman. They have this in common with the Germans, that they all have coats of arms, the merchants as well as others; and in Germany not only the big towns but most of the small ones have some sort of coat of arms of their own.

We left Verona and saw on our way out the Church of Our Lady of the Miracles, which is famous for several strange incidents, in consideration of which they are rebuilding it anew, of a very handsome round shape. The steeples here are covered in many places with bricks laid crosswise. We passed over a long plain of varied nature, now fertile, now otherwise, having the mountains very far off on our left hand and some on our right, and, without stopping, came to sup at

VICENZA, thirty miles. This is a big city, a little smaller than Verona, where there are plenty of noblemen's palaces.

The next day we saw several churches, and the fair that was being held here: in a big square, many booths that are built of wood on the spot for this purpose.

We also saw some Jesuates, who have a handsome monastery here; and we saw their shop for waters, which they sell to the public; and we got two bottles of perfume for a crown;[6] for they also make medicinal waters for all maladies. Their founder is P. Urb.[7] Saint Giovanni Colombini, a Sienese gentleman, who founded the order in the year 1367. Cardinal di Pelveo is for the present their protector. They have no monasteries except in Italy, and there they have thirty. They have a

---

[6] The Italian crown (scudo) was worth 10 giulii, 100 baiocchi, or in French money 50 sous or .833 crown (écu). It is not always clear, however, in the Italian part of the *Travel Journal*, whether Montaigne is speaking in terms of French or Italian crowns.

[7] In the papacy of Urban V. This is an addition made by Montaigne, according to Querlon.

very handsome habitation. They flagellate themselves every day, they say; each of them has his little chains at his place in their oratory, where they pray God without singing, and are there together at certain hours.

The old wines were then already beginning to fail us, and it troubled me because of his colic that he should drink those muddy wines—which were otherwise good, however. We regretted leaving those of Germany, although they are for the most part spiced and have various scents which the Germans find delicious, especially sage; and they call that sage wine, which is not bad when you get used to it, for otherwise their wine is good and generous.

We left here Thursday after dinner; and by a very level, wide, straight road, with ditches on both sides, and a little raised, having on all sides a very fertile terrain, with the mountains, as usual, visible a long way off, we came to sleep at

PADUA, eighteen miles. The hostelries cannot be compared for any sort of treatment with those of Germany. It is true that they are a third less expensive and very near the same as in France.

The city is indeed very vast, and in my opinion its enclosed area is at least the size of Bordeaux. The streets are narrow and ugly; very sparsely populated, few beautiful houses; the situation very pleasant, with an open plain extending very far all around.

We were here all the next day, and saw the fencing, dancing, and riding schools, where there were more than a hundred French gentlemen; which Monsieur de Montaigne reckoned as a great disadvantage for the young men of our country who go there, inasmuch as this society accustoms them to the ways and language of their own nation and deprives them of the means of acquiring foreign acquaintances.

The Church of Saint Anthony seems to him beautiful; the roof is not in one piece, but in several domelike projections. There are many rare sculptures in marble and bronze. He looked with a kindly eye at the bust of Cardinal Bembo, which shows the sweetness of his character and something indefinable of the elegance of his mind.

There is a hall, the biggest I ever saw without pillars, where their justice is dispensed; and at one end is the head of Livy, thin, showing him as a studious and melancholy man: an ancient work that lacks only speech. His epitaph is there also; when they found it they erected it thus to do themselves honor, and with reason. Paulus, the jurisconsult, is also there, over the door of this place; but Monsieur de Montaigne thinks this is a recent work. The house which is on the site of the ancient Arena is worth seeing, and so is its garden. The students live here very reasonably at seven crowns a month for the master and six for the valet, in the most decent pensions.

We left there Saturday morning early by a very fine causeway along the river, having on either side very fertile plains of wheat, very well shaded with trees sown in orderly rows in the fields where they have their vines, and the road furnished with plenty of beautiful pleasure houses, and among others a house of the Contarini family, at the gate of which an inscription states that the king[8] lodged there on his way back from Poland. We came to

FUSINA, twenty miles, where we dined. This is only a hostelry, from which one embarks for Venice. Here all the boats along this river land, by means of machines and pulleys turned by two horses in the manner of those that turn oil mills. They transport these boats, with wheels that they put underneath, over a wooden flooring, and launch them into the canal which goes on into the sea, in which Venice is situated. We dined here, and having got into a gondola, we came to sup at

VENICE, five miles. Next day, which was Sunday morning, Monsieur de Montaigne saw Monsieur du Ferrier, ambassador of the king, who gave him a very cordial welcome, took him to Mass, and kept him to dinner with him.[9] On the Monday Monsieur d'Estissac and he dined there again. Among other remarks of the said ambassador, this one seemed strange to him: that he had no dealings with any man of the city, and that they were such a suspicious sort of people that if one of their gentlemen spoke to him twice, they would hold him suspect; and also this, that the city of Venice was worth fifteen hundred thousand crowns in revenue to the Signory.

For the rest, the rarities of this town are well enough known. Monsieur de Montaigne said he had found it different from what he had imagined, and a little less wonderful. He reconnoitered it and all its particulars with extreme diligence. The government, the situation, the arsenal, the Square of Saint Mark, and the crowds of foreign people seemed to him the most remarkable things.

On Monday, November 7th, at supper, Signora Veronica Franca,[10] a Venetian gentlewoman, sent a man to present him with a little book of letters that she had composed; he had the said man given two crowns.

On the Tuesday after dinner he had the colic, which lasted him two or three hours—not one of the most extreme, to look at him—and before supper he passed two big stones, one after the other.

He did not find here that famous beauty that they attribute to the ladies of Venice, and yet he saw the noblest of those who make a traffic of it; but it seemed to him as wonderful as anything else to see such a number of them as a hundred and fifty or thereabouts spending like princesses on furniture and clothes, having no other funds to live on except from this traffic; and many of the nobles of the place even keeping courtesans at their expense in the sight and knowledge of all.

For his own service he hired a gondola for day and night at two lire, which is about seventeen sous, without any expense for the boatman.

---

[8] Henry III of France, who was king of Poland for about five months before becoming king of France in 1574.

[9] A note on the manuscript in Montaigne's hand reads (according to Querlon): "This old man, who has passed seventy-five, from what he says, enjoys a healthy and cheerful old age. His manners and his talk have something scholastic about them; little vivacity or incisiveness. His opinions very evidently lean, in the matter of our affairs, toward the Calvinistic innovations."

[10] One of the many distinguished Venetian courtesans.

Food is as expensive as in Paris, but still this is the city where you live at the cheapest rate in the world, inasmuch as a train of valets is of no use to us at all here, for everyone goes around by himself; and the expense for clothes likewise; and then there is no need of a horse.

On Saturday, November 12th, we left here in the morning and came to

FUSINA, five miles, where we took a boat, men and baggage, for two crowns. Monsieur de Montaigne has customarily been afraid of the water; but in the belief that it is the motion alone which upsets his stomach, and wanting to test whether the movement of this river, which is even and uniform, since the boat is drawn by horses, would upset it, he tried it and found that he had no trouble from it. You have to pass two or three locks on this river, which close and open for travelers. We came by water to sleep at

PADUA, twenty miles. Here Monsieur de Cazalis left the party and stayed on here as a boarder for seven crowns a month, well lodged and treated. He could have kept a lackey for five crowns; and yet these are pensions of the highest class, where there was good company, and especially the sieur de Millac, son of Monsieur de Salagnac. They usually have no valets and only a houseboy or some women who wait on them; each one has a very clean bedroom; the fire for their rooms, and candles, they furnish for themselves. They treat you well, as we saw. You live here very reasonably; which is in my opinion the reason why many foreigners, even those who are no longer students, reside here. It is not the custom to go about the town on horseback or with many attendants. In Germany I noticed that everyone wears a sword at his side, even the workmen; in the territories of this Signory, quite to the contrary, no one wears one.

Sunday, November 13th, after dinner we left here to see some baths which were on our right hand. Monsieur de Montaigne headed straight for Abano. This is a little village near the foot of the mountains, three or four hundred paces above which there is a somewhat elevated stony place. This height, which is very spacious, has many springs of boiling hot water spouting from the rock. Around the source it is too hot to bathe in, let alone to drink. It leaves a trace around its course that is quite gray, like burned ash, and a lot of sediment that is in the form of hard sponges. The taste is a bit salty and sulphurous. The whole countryside is full of steam; for the streams that flow here and there in the plain carry this heat and the smell very far.

There are two or three little houses here, rather poorly accommodated for sick people, into which they turn aside canals of these waters to make them into baths for the houses. Not only is there steam where the water is, but the rock itself steams through all its crevices and joints and gives out heat all over, so that they have pierced holes in some places where a man can lie down and get hot and sweaty from this exhalation; which happens instantly. Monsieur de Montaigne put some of this water into his mouth after it had stood a long time and lost its excessive heat; he found its taste more salty than anything else.

Further along, on our right hand, we discovered the abbey of Praglia, which is very famous for its beauty, its wealth, and its courtesy in receiving and entertaining strangers. He would not go there, considering that he was to revisit all this region, notably Venice, at his leisure,[11] and thought nothing of this visit; and what had made him undertake it was his extreme hunger to see that city. He said that he could not have stayed peacefully in Rome or anywhere else in Italy without having had a look at Venice; and for that purpose he had turned out of his way. In this hope he left at Padua, with one Master François Bourges, a Frenchman, the works of Cardinal Cusanus, which he had bought in Venice.

From Abano we passed on to a place called San Pietro Basso, and we still had the mountains on our right very near. It is a countryside of meadows and pastures which is likewise all steaming in various places from these waters, some boiling, others tepid, others cold; the taste a little more dead and insipid than the others'; less smell of sulphur, indeed virtually none at all; a little saltiness.

We found here some traces of ancient buildings. There are two or three wretched little houses round about to lodge the sick; but in truth this is all very primitive, and I would not be minded to send my friends here. They say it is the Signory that takes little care of the place and fears the influx of foreign lords. These last baths, he said, reminded him of those of Préchacq, near Dax. The trace of these waters is all reddish, and left some of the mud on his tongue; he found no taste in it; he thinks the waters contain more iron.

From here we passed by a very beautiful house belonging to a gentleman of Padua, where the Cardinal d'Este, ill with the gout, had been staying for more than two months, to enjoy the comfort of the baths and, even more, the proximity of the ladies of Venice; and right near there we stopped to sleep at

BATTAGLIA, eight miles, a little village on the Frassine canal, which, having no depth, sometimes only two or three feet, nevertheless conveys surprisingly big boats. Here we were served on earthenware dishes and wooden plates for lack of pewter; otherwise passably enough.

Monday morning I went on ahead with the mule. They went to see some baths which are five hundred paces from here, by the levee along this canal. There is, so Monsieur de Montaigne reported, only one house over the bath, with ten or twelve rooms. In April and May they say that plenty of people go there, but most of them lodge in the said village or in this château of the Signor Pic, in which the Cardinal d'Este was dwelling. The water of the baths comes down from a little mountain ridge, and flows through channels into the said house and on below; they do not drink it at all, and rather drink that of San Pietro, which they send for. It comes down from this same ridge by channels right near the good sweet water; according as it takes a shorter or longer course, it is more or less hot. He went to the top of the hill to see the source; they could

---

[11] He never did return. Presumably this is one of the plans interrupted by his recall to France as mayor of Bordeaux.

not show it to him, and put him off by saying that it came from underground. He finds little taste to it in the mouth, like that of San Pietro, little smell of sulphur, little saltiness; he thinks that if anyone drank it he would get the same effect as from that of San Pietro. The trace it leaves in its conduits is red.

In this house there are baths and other places where the water only trickles down, and you place the sick member under it; they told him that it is usually the forehead for head ailments. They have also, in some places in these channels, made little stone cells in which you shut yourself up, and then, when you open the airhole to the channel, the steam and heat immediately make you sweat hard; these are dry vapor-baths, of which they have several kinds.

The principal use made is of the mud bath. They fetch the mud from a big basin that is below the house, in the open, by means of an instrument with which they draw it to take it to the house, which is quite near. There they have several wooden instruments fit for legs, arms, thighs, and other parts, to lay and enclose the said limbs in after filling this wooden vessel full of this mud, which they renew according to the need. This mud is black like that of Barbotan, but not so granulated, and greasier, warm with a moderate warmth, and with virtually no smell. All these baths have no great advantage unless it is the proximity to Venice; everything about them is crude and unattractive.

They left Battaglia after breakfast and followed that canal, which they call the Two-Road Canal, from the causeways on either side. Very near there they came upon the bridge of the canal.[12] In this place they have made highways on the outside of the canal walls, at the height of the said causeways, on which travelers pass; the highways on the inside go down to the level of the bottom of the canal. At that point there is a stone bridge which joins these two highways, over which bridge flows the canal from one arch of a viaduct to the other. Over this canal there is a very high bridge; the boats which follow the canal pass under it and above those which want to cross this canal. There is another big stream right at the bottom of the plain which comes from the mountains and whose course crosses this canal. In order to conduct it without interrupting this canal, this stone bridge has been made across which the canal flows and under which flows this stream, cutting across the canal, over a planking dressed with wood on the sides, so that this stream is capable of carrying boats: there would be enough room both in width and in height. And then with other boats continually passing on the canal and coaches on the arch of the highest bridge, there were three roads, one above the other.

From there, still keeping this canal on our right hand, we skirted a

---

[12] The original of the following passage is even more confusing than this translation of it and may well include many misreadings of the manuscript. Modern editors offer a variety of conjectures, none of them very comprehensible. This much at least should be clear: a mountain stream flows between artificial banks across and beneath the canal. The canal at this point flows over a viaduct. A bridge crosses it above.

little town called Monselice, low-lying, but whose confining wall goes up to the top of a mountain and encloses an old castle which used to belong to the lords of this town; now it is nothing but ruins. And leaving the mountains on our right, we followed the road to the left, raised, handsome, level, and which in the hot season must be well shaded; on either side of us there were very fertile plains that have, according to the custom of the country, amid their wheat fields many trees arranged in rows, from which hang their vines. Very big gray oxen are so common here that I no longer found strange what I had noted about those of the Archduke Ferdinand. We came onto a raised causeway, and on both sides were marshes more than fifteen miles wide stretching as far as the eye could reach. These were formerly great ponds, but the Signory attempted to dry them up to get farmland; they have succeeded in some places, but very few. At present it is a huge extent of muddy land, sterile and full of reeds. They lost more than they gained by trying to change its nature.

We crossed the river Adige on our right, on a ferry: a deck resting on two little boats, with a capacity of fifteen or twenty horses, which slides along a rope attached on the other side of the water, more than five hundred paces away; and to keep the rope in the air there are several little boats in between, which support this long rope with forked sticks.

From there we came to sleep at

Rovigo, twenty-five miles, a very small town still in the territory of the said Signory. We lodged outside the town. They began to serve us salt in blocks, from which you take some like sugar. There is no less abundance of food than in France, whatever people are accustomed to say; and the fact that they do not lard their roast takes away hardly any of its savor. Their bedrooms, for lack of glass and proper closing of the windows, are less clean than in France; the beds better made, smoother, with lots of mattresses; but they have hardly any but badly woven little canopies, and are very parsimonious of white sheets. Anyone who went alone or with a small retinue would get none. The cost as in France, or a little more.

This is the birthplace of the excellent Celius, who took from it the surname Rhodiginus.[13] It is very pretty, and there is a very handsome square; the river Adige passes through the middle.

Tuesday morning, November 15th, we left here, and after doing a long stretch on the causeway, like that at Blois, and crossing the river Adige, which we came upon on our right, and then the Po, which we found on the left, over a ferry like that of the day before (except that on this platform there is a permanent cabin in which you pay the toll while crossing, according to the printed regulations they have posted there; and in the middle of the crossing they stop their boat short to settle accounts and get their pay before landing), and after getting off

---

[13] Author of a popular compilation which Montaigne owned and borrowed from once or twice, the *Lectionum antiquarum libri triginta.*

in a low plain, where it seems as though in very rainy weather the road would be impassable, we came in one stage, in the evening, to
FERRARA, twenty miles. Here for their passports and health certificates they stopped us for a long time at the gate, and everyone else likewise. The city is of the size of Tours, situated in very flat country: many palaces, most of the streets wide and straight, not very populous.

On the Wednesday morning Messieurs d'Estissac and de Montaigne went to kiss the duke's hands. He was informed of their intention; he sent a lord of his court to welcome them and bring them to his cabinet, where he was with two or three others, waiting for them. We passed through several closed chambers where there were several well-dressed gentlemen. They had us all come in. We found him standing at a table waiting for them. He put his hand to his bonnet when they came in, and remained uncovered as long as Monsieur de Montaigne spoke to him, which was rather a long time. He asked him first if he understood the language, and having been answered yes, he told them in very eloquent Italian that he was very glad to see gentlemen of that nation, being at the service of, and under much obligation to, the Most Christian King. They had some other conversation together and then they withdrew, the lord duke never having covered himself.

We saw in a church the effigy of Ariosto, a little fuller in face than he appears in his books; he died at the age of fifty-nine, on the 6th of June, 1533.

They serve fruit here on plates.

The streets are all paved with bricks. The colonnades, which are continuous at Padua and serve as a great convenience for walking about in all weather under cover without getting muddy, are lacking here. At Venice the streets are paved with the same material, and so sloping that there is never any mud.

I had forgotten to say about Venice that the day we left there we found on our path several boats with their holds filled entirely with fresh water; the boatload is worth a crown delivered at Venice and the water is used to drink or to dye cloth. While we were at Fusina we saw how with horses incessantly turning a wheel, water is drawn from a stream and poured into a channel, from which channel the said boats receive it, lining up below.

We were all that day at Ferrara, and there saw many beautiful churches, gardens, private houses, and everything that they told us was remarkable: among other things, at the Jesuates, a rose tree that bears flowers every month of the year; and even then there was one, which was given to Monsieur de Montaigne. We also saw the Bucentaur,[14] which the duke, to emulate the one at Venice, had had made for his new wife, who is beautiful and too young for him, to take her around on the river Po. We also saw the duke's arsenal, in which there is a piece of ordnance thirty-five spans long which carries a shot one foot in diameter.

The cloudy new wines that we were drinking, and the water, just

[14] The state barge.

as muddy as when it comes out of the river, alarmed him about his colic.

On all the bedroom doors in the hostelry is written: Remember your health certificate. As soon as you have arrived you must send your name to the authorities, and the number of your men. Then they send word to give them lodging; otherwise they do not do so.

On Thursday morning we left here[15] and went through a level and very fertile country, difficult for pedestrians in muddy weather, inasmuch as the soil of Lombardy is very rich; and then, the roads being closed in by ditches on either side, they have no space in which to step aside to avoid the mud, so that many people of the country walk with little stilts half a foot high. We went in the evening, without stopping, to

BOLOGNA, thirty miles, a large and beautiful city, much bigger and more populous than Ferrara. At the inn where we lodged, the young seigneur de Monluc[16] had arrived an hour before, coming from France; he had stopped in the said city to attend the schools of fencing and horsemanship.

On Friday we saw the fencing of the Venetian who boasts of having invented new techniques in that art which prevail over all others; and in truth his style of fencing is in many respects different from the usual ones. The best of his students was a young man from Bordeaux named Binet.

Here we saw a square tower,[17] ancient, so constructed that it leans all to one side and seems to threaten its own downfall. We also saw the academy of the sciences, which is the handsomest building I have ever seen for this purpose.

On the Saturday after dinner we saw some comedians, with whom Monsieur de Montaigne was very pleased; and there, or from some other cause, he got a headache, which he had not had for several years; and yet at the same time he said he had a lack of pain in his kidneys more pure than he had been accustomed to for a long time, and enjoyed a comfortable feeling in his stomach such as he had had on returning from Bagnères. His headache passed away during the night.

This is a city all enriched with handsome wide colonnades and a very great number of beautiful palaces. You live as at Padua, or just about, and very reasonably; but the city is a little less peaceable because of the old feuds that exist between factions of certain families in the city, one of which has always had the French on their side, the other the Spaniards, who are here in very great numbers. In the square there is a very handsome fountain.

On Sunday Monsieur de Montaigne had planned to take the road to the left toward Imola, the March of Ancona, and Loreto, to get to Rome;

---

[15] It is curious that the secretary's account says nothing of Montaigne's visit to the poet Tasso, then insane, about which Montaigne speaks bitterly in the *Essays* (II: 12, p. 363).

[16] Blaise de Monluc, grandson of his famous namesake.

[17] Presumably the Torre Garisenda, which has the greater lean of the two leaning towers of Bologna.

but a German told him that he had been robbed by bandits in the duchy of Spoleto. So he turned right, toward Florence. We immediately plunged into a rugged road and mountainous country, and came to sleep at

LOIANO, sixteen miles, a rather uncomfortable little village. There are only two hostelries in this village, which are famous among all those in Italy for the treachery that is practiced on travelers in feeding them with fine promises of every sort of comfort before they set foot to the ground, and laughing at them when they have them at their mercy: about which there are popular proverbs.

We left here early the next morning and until evening followed a road which in truth is the first on our trip that can be called uncomfortable and wild, and in the midst of mountains more difficult than in any other part of this trip; we came to sleep at

SCARPERIA, twenty-four miles, a very small town of Tuscany, where they sell quantities of little cases, scissors, and similar merchandise.

Monsieur de Montaigne took all possible pleasure in the rivalry among the landlords. They have the custom of sending seven or eight leagues to meet strangers and conjuring them to choose their inn. You will often find the landlord himself on horseback, and in various places many well-dressed men in wait for you; and all along the road, Monsieur de Montaigne, who wanted to draw them out, had himself amusingly entertained with the various offers that each one made him; and there is nothing that they will not promise.[18] There was one who offered him a hare purely as a gift if he was willing just to visit his house. Their disputes and competition stop at the gates of the town, and they do not dare say one more word. They have this in common, that they offer you a guide on horseback at their expense to guide you and carry part of your baggage to the inn you are going to; which they always do, and pay their expense. I do not know whether or not they are obliged to by some ordinance because of the danger of the roads.

We had made our bargain as early as Bologna for what we were to pay and get at Loiano. Urged as we were by the people of the inn where we stayed and elsewhere, Monsieur de Montaigne had sent one of us to inspect all the inns, the food, and the wines, and to learn the conditions before we all dismounted; and he chose the best. But it is impossible to make such careful terms that you escape their trickery; for they will make you lack the wood, the candles, the linen, or the hay that you have forgotten to specify.

This route is full of travelers, for it is the ordinary highroad to Rome.

I was here informed[19] of a stupid thing I had done in forgetting to visit a mountaintop ten miles this side of Loiano and two miles off the road, from which, in rainy or stormy weather and by night, you can see flames coming out to a very great height; and my informant told me that

---

[18] A note in the original edition, possibly by Querlon but more probably by Montaigne, here adds: "Anche ragazze et ragazzi"—"Even young girls and young boys."

[19] This paragraph seems to have been written by Montaigne.

in the big upheavals there are sometimes disgorged little pieces of money with some figure or other. We should have seen what all this was.

We left Scarperia the next morning with our landlord as guide and went along a fine road between many populated and cultivated hills. We turned out of our way to the right for about two miles to see a palace that the duke of Florence[20] built here twelve years ago, which he exercises all his five natural senses to embellish. It seems as though he purposely chose an inconvenient, sterile, and mountainous site, yes, and even without springs, so as to have the honor of sending to get water five miles from there, and his sand and lime another five miles. It is a place that has nothing level about it. You have a view of many hills, which is the general shape of the country. The house is called Pratolino. The building is contemptible to see it from far off, but from near it is very beautiful, though not up to the most beautiful in France. They say that there are six score furnished rooms; we saw ten or twelve of the finest. The furniture is pretty, but not magnificent.

There is one miraculous thing, a grotto with several cells and rooms; this part surpasses all that we have ever seen elsewhere. It is encrusted and formed all over of a certain material which they say is brought from certain mountains, and they have joined it invisibly with nails. There is not only music and harmony made by the movement of the water, but also a movement of several statues and doors with various actions, caused by the water; several animals that plunge in to drink; and things like that. At one single movement the whole grotto is full of water, and all the seats squirt water on your buttocks; and if you flee from the grotto and climb the castle stairs and anyone takes pleasure in this sport, there come out of every other step of the stairs, right up to the top of the house, a thousand jets of water that give you a bath.

The beauty and richness of this place cannot be described in detail. Among other things, below the castle there is a walk fifty feet wide and five hundred paces long or thereabouts, which has been made almost level, at great expense. On both sides there are long and very handsome railings of freestone; every five or ten paces along these railings there are springing fountains in the wall, so that there are nothing but fountain jets all along the walk. At the bottom there is a beautiful fountain that pours into a big basin through a conduit set in a marble statue of a woman doing her washing. She is wringing out a tablecloth of white marble, from the dripping of which this water comes out; and underneath there is another vessel where it seems as if there is water boiling for washing. There is also a marble table in a hall of the castle around which there are six seats, at each of which you raise a lid of this marble by a ring, and under the lid there is a vessel attached to the said table. In each of the said six vessels there springs up a fountain of fresh water in which each man may cool his glass, and in the middle is a big one to put the bottle in.

[20] Francis I de' Medici, grand duke of Tuscany.

We also saw some very wide holes in the ground where they keep a large quantity of snow all year round; and it is placed on a litter of broom, and then all this is covered, up to a great height, in the form of a pyramid, with thatch, like a little barn. There are a thousand reservoirs. And they are building the body of a giant, which is three cubits wide at a rough estimate, and the rest in the same proportion; from this will pour a fountain in great abundance. There are a thousand reservoirs and ponds, and all this drawn from two springs by an infinity of earthen pipes. In a very handsome big aviary we saw some little birds like goldfinches, which have two long feathers in their tail like those of a big capon. There is also a singular stove. We stayed here two or three hours and then resumed our journey and went over the top of certain hills to

FLORENCE, seventeen miles, a city smaller in size than Ferrara, situated in a plain, surrounded by a thousand highly cultivated hills. The river Arno passes through and is crossed by bridges. We found no moats around the walls.

That day Monsieur de Montaigne passed two stones and a lot of gravel, without having had any other feeling of it than a slight pain in the lower abdomen.

On the same day we saw the grand duke's stable, very large, vaulted, in which there were not many valuable horses; indeed, he was not there that day. There we saw a sheep of a very strange shape; also a camel, some lions, some bears, and an animal the size of a very big mastiff and the shape of a cat, all marked in black and white, which they call a tiger.

We saw the Church of San Lorenzo, where still hang the flags that we lost under Marshal Strozzi in Tuscany. There are in this church several pieces of flat painting, and very beautiful and excellent statues by Michelangelo. We saw the cathedral, which is a very big church with the bell tower all faced with black and white marble; it is one of the most beautiful and sumptuous things in the world.

Monsieur de Montaigne said that he had never until then seen a nation where there were so few beautiful women as the Italian.

The lodgings he found much less comfortable than in France and Germany; for the food is not half so abundant as in Germany, nor so well prepared. They serve the food without larding in both places; but in Germany it is much better seasoned, and varied with sauces and soups. The lodgings in Italy are much worse: no common rooms; the windows large and wide open, except for a big wooden shutter that keeps out the light if you want to keep out the sun or the wind; which he found much more intolerable and irremediable than the lack of curtains in Germany. Besides, they have only little cots with wretched canopies, one at the most in each bedroom, with a truckle bed underneath; and anyone who hated to lie hard would find himself up against it. An equal or greater lack of linen. The wines generally worse, and for those who hate a sickly sweetness, unbearable in this season. The expense, it is true, is a little less. They say that Florence is the most expensive city in Italy. I had made our bargain, before my master arrived at the hostelry, the Angel, at seven reals a day for man and horse, and four reals for a man on foot.

The same day we saw a palace of the duke, where he himself takes pleasure in working at counterfeiting oriental stones and cutting crystal; for he is a prince somewhat interested in alchemy and the mechanical arts, and above all a great architect.

The next day Monsieur de Montaigne led the way up to the top of the cathedral, where there is a globe of gilt brass which from below seems of the size of a ball, and when you are there proves capable of holding four people.[21] There he saw that the marble with which this church is encrusted, even the black (for this work is all variegated and carved), is already beginning to give way in many places and is cracking from the frost and the sun; which made him fear that this marble was not very genuine.

He wanted to see the houses of the Strozzi and the Gondi, where some of their kin still reside. We also saw the palace of the duke, where Cosimo, the duke's father, has had a painting made of the capture of Siena and the battle we lost. Yet in various places in this city, and especially in the said palace on the old walls, the fleurs-de-lys hold the first rank of honor.

Messieurs d'Estissac and de Montaigne were at a dinner of the grand duke; for so they call him here. His wife was seated in the place of honor; the duke below; below the duke, the duchess's sister-in-law; below her, her husband, the brother of the duchess. This duchess[22] is beautiful by Italian notions, an agreeable and imperious face, big bust, and breasts the way they like them. To Monsieur de Montaigne she seemed certainly clever enough to have bewitched this prince and to keep him devoted to her for a long time. The duke is a stout, dark man of my height, large limbs, face and bearing full of courtesy, passing always uncovered through the throng of his courtiers, who are a handsome group. He has a healthy bearing, that of a man of forty. On the other side of the table were the duke's two brothers, the cardinal and another young man of eighteen.

They bring drink to this duke and his wife in a basin, in which there is an uncovered glass full of wine and a glass bottle full of water; they take the glass of wine, pour as much as they do not want into the basin, fill it with water themselves, and then put the glass back in the basin, which the cupbearer holds for them. The duke put in a good deal of water; she, almost none. The fault of the Germans is to use immoderately big glasses; here it is the opposite, to have them so extraordinarily small.

I do not know why this city should be privileged to be surnamed "the beautiful"; it is so, but without any advantage over Bologna, and little over Ferrara, and it is incomparably inferior to Venice. True, it

[21] The text says "forty," but "four" is probably intended.

[22] Bianca Capello of Venice, who had been the grand duke's mistress during his first marriage.

is fine to discover from this bell tower the infinite multitude of houses that cover the hills all around for a good two or three leagues, and this plain where the city is situated, which seems to extend to a length of two leagues; for the houses seem to touch each other, so thickly are they sown. The city is paved with slabs of flat stone, without method or order.

After dinner the four gentlemen and a guide took post horses to go and see a place of the duke's called Castello. The house has nothing worth while about it; but there are various things about the gardens. The whole estate is situated on the slope of a hill, so that the straight walks are all on a slope, but a soft and easy one; the cross walks are straight and level. One sees there many arbors, very thickly interwoven and covered with all kinds of odoriferous trees such as cedars, cypresses, orange trees, lemon trees, and olive trees, the branches so joined and interlaced that it is easy to see that the sun at its greatest strength could not get in; and copses of cypress and of those other trees disposed in order so close to each other that there is room for only three or four people to pass abreast. There is a big reservoir, among other things, in the middle of which you see a natural-looking artificial rock, and it seems all frozen over, by means of that material with which the duke has covered his grottoes at Pratolino; and above the rock is a large bronze statue of a very old hoary man seated on his rear with his arms crossed, from all over whose beard, forehead, and hair water flows incessantly, drop by drop, representing sweat and tears; and the fountain has no other conduit than that.

Elsewhere they had the very amusing experience of seeing what I have noted above; for as they were walking about the garden and looking at its curiosities, the gardener left their company for this purpose; and as they were in a certain spot contemplating certain marble statues, there spurted up under their feet and between their legs, through an infinite number of tiny holes, jets of water so minute that they were almost invisible, imitating supremely well the trickle of fine rain, with which they were completely sprinkled by the operation of some underground spring which the gardener was working more than two hundred paces from there, with such artifice that from there on the outside he made these spurts of water rise and fall as he pleased, turning and moving them just as he wanted. This same game is found here in several places.

They also saw the master fountain, which issues from a conduit in two very big bronze effigies, of which the lower holds the other in his arms and is squeezing him with all his might;[23] the other half fainting, his head thrown back, seems to spurt this water forcibly out of his mouth; and it shoots out with such power that the stream of water rises thirty-seven fathoms above the height of these figures, which are at least twenty feet high. There is also a chamber among the branches of an evergreen tree, but much richer than any other that they had seen; for it is all filled out with the live green branches of the tree, and on all

---

[23] Hercules squeezing Antaeus, figures by Bartolommeo Ammannati.

sides this chamber is so closed in by this verdure that there is no view
out except through a few apertures that must be opened up by pushing
aside the branches here and there; and in the center, through a concealed pipe, a jet of water rises right in this chamber through the center
of a small marble table. Water music is also made here, but they could
not hear it, for it was late for people who had to get back to town. They
also saw the duke's escutcheon here high over a gateway, very well
formed of some branches of trees fostered and maintained in their natural strength by fibers that one can barely discern. They were here in the
most unpropitious season for gardens, and were all the more amazed.
There is also a handsome grotto, where you see all sorts of animals represented to the life, spouting the water of these fountains, some by the
beak, some by the wing, some by the claw or the ear or the nostril.

I forgot to say that in the palace of this prince, in one of the big
rooms, is seen the figure of a four-footed animal in bronze relief on a
pillar, represented to the life, of a strange shape, the front all scaly, and
on the backbone something that looked like horns. They say that it was
found in a mountain cavern of this country and brought here alive a few
years ago.[24] We also saw the palace where the Queen Mother was
born.[25]

In order to try out all the comforts of this city, as he had of others,
Monsieur de Montaigne wanted to see the rooms to let and the conditions of the boarding houses; he found nothing worth while. You find
rooms to let only in the hostelries, so they told him; and those that he
saw were dirty and much more expensive than in Paris or even in Venice;
and the board wretched, at more than twelve crowns a month for the
master.

Also there is no worth-while practice either of arms, or of horsemanship, or of letters.

Pewter is rare in all this region, and food is served only in vessels of
painted earthenware, rather dirty.

Thursday morning, November 24th, we left here and found a country moderately fertile, very thickly populated and cultivated everywhere, the road bumpy and stony; and in one stretch, which was very
long, we came very late to

Siena, thirty-two miles, four stages; they make them of eight miles,
longer than ours ordinarily are.

On Friday Monsieur de Montaigne examined the town with curiosity, notably in respect to our wars.[26] It is an irregular town, planted on
the ridge of a hill, on which the better part of the streets are situated; its
two slopes are covered with various streets in tiers, and some of these go
climbing to still greater heights. It is numbered among the beautiful
towns of Italy, but not of the first rank, nor of the size of Florence. Its

[24] This seems to be a sculptured Etruscan chimaera, discovered around 1558.
The travelers either misunderstood their informant or were misinformed, perhaps
deliberately.

[25] Catherine de' Medici was born in the Pitti Palace.

[26] Siena was captured by the French under Lansac in 1552; though heroically
defended under Monluc in 1554–55, it was finally lost.

appearance testifies to its great antiquity. It has a great abundance of fountains, from which most of the private persons drain off small streams for their particular service. They have good, cool cellars here.

The cathedral, which scarcely yields to that of Florence, is coated almost all over, inside and out, with this same marble: square pieces of marble, some a foot thick, others less, which they apply like wainscoting to these buildings made of brick, the ordinary building material of this country.

The handsomest part of the town is the round plaza,[27] very beautiful and grand, curving in from all directions toward the palace that forms one of the fronts of this circle and is less curved than the rest. Opposite the palace, at the upper end of the place, there is a very beautiful fountain, which, through several conduits, fills a great basin where everyone can draw very fine water. Several streets converge in this circle by graded stone steps. There are plenty of very ancient streets and dwellings: the principal ones are those of the Piccolomini, the Ciaia, the Tolomei, and the Colombini, and that of the Cerretani. We saw evidences of three or four hundred years of age. The arms of the city, which you see on many pillars, are the she-wolf with Romulus and Remus hanging at her teats.

The duke of Florence treats the noblemen who favored our side courteously, and has near his person Silvio Piccolomini, the most able nobleman of our time in every kind of knowledge and exercise of arms. As one who has to guard himself principally against his own subjects, he lets his towns take care of fortifying themselves, and concentrates on citadels, which are supplied with arms and guarded with all possible expense and diligence, and with such suspicion that very few people are permitted to approach them.

The women mostly wear hats on their heads. We saw some who took them off out of reverence, like the men, at the point of the elevation during Mass.

We were lodged at the Crown, fairly well, but still without window-panes or frames.

Monsieur de Montaigne, asked by the gatekeeper at Pratolino whether he was amazed at the beauty of the place, after praising it, strongly condemned the ugliness of the doors and windows—big pine planks, without shape or workmanship, and clumsy and awkward locks like those in our villages—and then the roofing of hollow tiles; and he said that if there was no means of getting slate or lead or brass, they should at least have hidden these tiles by the shape of the building, which the gatekeeper said he would repeat to his master.

The duke still allows the ancient mottoes and emblems of this town to exist, and everywhere these ring of liberty; yet they have taken from their places and hidden in a certain spot in the town the tombs and epitaphs of the Frenchmen who died,[28] under color of some improvement in the building and shape of their church.

---

[27] The Piazza del Campo.
[28] Those who died in the capture or in the defense of Siena.

On Saturday the 26th after dinner we continued the journey through a countryside of similar aspect and came to sup at

BUONCONVENTO, twelve miles, a *castello* of Tuscany: so they call walled villages which, because of their smallness, do not deserve the name of towns.

Sunday morning very early we left here, and since Monsieur de Montaigne wanted to see Montalcino because of the associations the French have had with it, he turned out of his way to the right, and with Messieurs d'Estissac, de Mattecoulon, and du Hautoy, went to the said Montalcino, which they say is a badly built town of the size of Saint-Emilion, situated on one of the highest mountains in the whole region, but accessible. They happened to arrive there as High Mass was being said, and they heard it. At one end there is a castle where the duke keeps his garrisons; but in Monsieur de Montaigne's opinion, all this is not very strong, for the place is commanded on one side by another higher mountain within a hundred paces of it.

In this duke's territories the memory of the French is maintained in such great affection that you can scarcely remind the people of the French without tears coming to their eyes; for even war seems sweeter to them, if accompanied by some form of liberty, than the peace they enjoy under tyranny. When Monsieur de Montaigne inquired there whether there were not some tombs of the Frenchmen, he was answered that there had been several in the Church of Saint Augustine, but that they had been covered up by the duke's command.

The road of this day's journey was mountainous and stony, and brought us in the evening to

LA PAGLIA, twenty-three miles, a tiny village of five or six houses at the foot of several barren and forbidding mountains.

The next morning early we resumed our trip along a very stony bottom, where we crossed and recrossed a hundred times a torrent which runs all the length of it. We came to a big bridge built by the present Pope Gregory, where the territories of the duke of Florence end, and entered those of the Church. We came upon Acquapendente, which is a little town; and it is so named, I believe, because of a torrent which right next to it hurtles over some rocks into the plain. From there we passed San Lorenzo, which is a walled village, and through Bolseno, which is another, turning about the lake that is named Bolseno, thirty miles long and ten miles wide, in the middle of which are seen two rocks like islands, on which they say there are monasteries. We continued without a halt, by this mountainous and barren road, to

MONTEFIASCONE, twenty-six miles, a little town situated on the top of one of the highest mountains in all the district. It is small, and shows signs of considerable age.

We left here in the morning and crossed a beautiful fertile plain in which we came upon Viterbo, which is in part situated on the crest of a hill. It is a beautiful town, of the size of Senlis. We noticed here many beautiful houses, a great abundance of workmen, beautiful and pleasant streets; in three parts of town, three very beautiful fountains. Monsieur de Montaigne would have stopped here because of the beauty of the place, but his mule, which went ahead of him, had already passed on. Here we began to climb a high mountainside, at the nearer foot of which is a little lake which they call Vico. From there, through a very pleasant valley surrounded by low hills on which there is lots of timber (a somewhat rare commodity in these parts), and by this lake, we came in good time to

RONCIGLIONE, nineteen miles, a little town and castle belonging to the duke of Parma,[29] as there are also on these roads many houses and lands belonging to the house of Farnese.

The inns on this road are of the best, since it is the ordinary post highway. They take five giulii per day to rent a horse, or two giulii per post; and the rate is the same if you want them for two or three posts or for several days, your horse being cared for at no expense to you: for from place to place the landlords take charge of the horses of their fellow landlords; indeed, if your hired one fails you, they stipulate that you can take another instead somewhere else on your road. At Siena, we had the experience of seeing a Fleming who was in our company—unknown, a foreigner, all alone—being trusted with a hired horse which was to take him to Rome. There is this exception, that you pay the hire before starting out; but for the rest, the horse is at your mercy, subject to your word that you will leave him where you promise to.

Monsieur de Montaigne rejoiced in their custom of dining and supping late, in accordance with his humor; for here they do not dine in the good houses before two in the afternoon or sup before nine; so that in places where we found actors, the play begins only at six o'clock, by torchlight, and lasts two or three hours, and then you go to supper. He said that it was a good country for lazy people, for you get up very late.

We left here the next day three hours before daylight, so eager was he to see the pavement of Rome. He found that the night damp gave his stomach as much trouble morning as evening, or very little less, and felt bad because of it until daylight, although the night was clear. At a distance of fifteen miles we caught sight of the city of Rome, and then lost it again for a long time. There are some villages on the road, and hostelries. We came across some districts with roads raised and paved with very big paving stones, which, to look at them, seemed something ancient; and nearer the city some evidently very ancient ruins, and some stones which the popes have reerected in honor of their antiquity. Most of the ruins are of brick, witness the Baths of Diocletian—a small, simple brick like ours, not of the size and thickness that is seen in the antiquities and old ruins in France and elsewhere.

Rome did not make a great show to see it from this road. We had far on our left the Apennines; the country is unpleasant, full of humps and deep clefts, incapable of allowing the passage of troops in battle formation; the land bare, treeless, to a large extent barren; the country very open for more than ten miles around; and almost all of this sort, with very few houses.

[29] Ottavio Farnese.

(November 30, 1580-April 19, 1581)

Through this sort of country we arrived at about eight in the evening on the last day of November, the feast of Saint Andrew, at the Porta del Popolo, in

ROME, thirty miles. Here they made some difficulties for us, as elsewhere, because of the plague at Genoa.

We took lodgings at the Bear, where we also stayed the next day; and on the second day of December we took rented rooms in the house of a Spaniard, opposite Santa Lucia della Tinta. Here we were well accommodated with three handsome bedrooms, dining room, larder, stable, and kitchen, at twenty crowns a month, out of which the host provided a cook and fire for the kitchen.

The inns are generally furnished a little better than in Paris, since they have a great deal of gilt leather, with which the lodgings of a certain class are upholstered. We could have had lodging at the same price as our own at the Gold Vase, rather near there, upholstered with cloth of gold and silk, like that of kings. But besides that the bedrooms were not separate, Monsieur de Montaigne thought that this magnificence was not only useless but also troublesome on account of the care required by this furniture, for each bed was worth four or five hundred crowns. At our inn we had made a bargain to be supplied with linen about the same as in France; the custom of the country is to be a little more sparing.

Monsieur de Montaigne was annoyed to find so great a number of Frenchmen here that he met almost no one in the street who did not greet him in his own language. New to him was the sight of so great a court, so thronged with prelates and churchmen, and it seemed to him more populous in rich men, and coaches, and horses, by far, than any other that he had ever seen. He said that the appearance of the streets in many respects, and especially in the multitude of people, reminded him more of Paris than any other city he had ever been in.

The modern city is built all along the river Tiber, on both sides. The hilly quarter, which was the site of the old city, where he went every day and took a thousand walks, is occupied by a few churches and some remarkable houses and gardens of the cardinals. He judged by very clear appearances and by the height of the ruins that the shape of these mountains and of the slopes was completely changed from the old shape; and he held it as certain that in many places we were walking on the tops of entire houses. It is easy to judge, by the Arch of Severus, that we are more than two pikes' length above the ancient street level; and in truth, almost everywhere, you walk on the top of old walls which the rain and the coach ruts uncover.

He disagreed with those who compared the freedom of Rome to that of Venice, principally on these grounds: that even the houses were so unsafe that those who brought rather ample means were ordinarily advised to give their purse in keeping to the bankers of the city, so as not to find their strongbox broken open, as had happened to many. *Item,* that going about at night was hardly very safe. *Item,* that in this month of December, our first month here, the general of the Franciscans was suddenly dismissed from his office and locked up for having condemned in his sermon, at which the Pope and the cardinals were present, the idleness and pomp of the prelates of the Church, without going into any particulars, and merely using, with some asperity in his voice, some ordinary commonplaces on this subject. *Item,* that his [Montaigne's] baggage had been inspected by the customs on his entry into the city, and examined right down to the smallest articles, whereas in most of the other cities of Italy these officers were content when you merely offered your baggage for inspection; and that besides this, they had taken from him all the books they had found in order to examine them, which took so long that a man who had anything else to do might well consider them lost; besides, the rules were so extraordinary here that the book of hours of Our Lady, because it was of Paris, not of Rome, was suspect to them, and also the books of certain German doctors of theology against the heretics, because in combating them they made mention of their errors. In this connection he was grateful for his good luck because, though he had not been warned at all that this was to happen to him, and though he had passed through Germany and was of an inquiring nature, he had no forbidden book in the lot. However, some lords of the city told him that even if some had been found, he would have got off with the loss of the books.

Twelve or fifteen days after our arrival he felt ill; and because of an unusual defluxion of his kidneys which threatened him with some kind of ulcer, by the prescription of a French doctor of the Cardinal de Rambouillet, aided by the dexterity of his apothecary, he overcame his scruples one day and took some cassia in big doses on the end of a knife first lightly dipped in water, which he swallowed very easily, and had two or three stools from it. The next day he took some Venetian turpentine, which they say comes from the mountains of Tyrol, two large doses done up in a wafer on a silver spoon, sprinkled with one or two drops of some good-tasting syrup; he observed no other effect from it than a smell of March violets in his urine. After that he took three times, but not in quick succession, a certain sort of drink that had precisely the taste and color of almond milk, and indeed his doctor told him it was just that; however, he thinks there were some *quatre-semences-froides*[1] in it. There was nothing difficult or extraordinary in the taking of this last except the hour of the morning: all that, three hours before the meal. Nor did he feel what good that almond milk did him, for the same indisposition still lasted afterward; and later, on the twenty-third of December, he had a very severe colic, for which he took to his bed around

---

[1] A combination of the four "cold" seeds: cucumber, gourd, melon, and pumpkin.

noon and was there until evening, when he ejected a lot of gravel, and after that a big hard stone, long and smooth, which stopped five or six hours in passing through the penis. All this time, since his baths, his bowels had been in good order, and he thought that this protected him against many worse accidents. At this time he skipped several meals, now dinner, now supper.

On Christmas Day we went to hear the Pope's Mass at Saint Peter's, where Monsieur de Montaigne had a convenient place for seeing all the ceremonies at his ease. There are several particular forms: the Gospel and the Epistle are said first in Latin and then in Greek, as is also done on Easter Day and Saint Peter's Day. The Pope gave Communion to several others, and with him at this service there officiated the cardinals Farnese, Medici, Caraffa, and Gonzaga. There is a certain instrument for drinking from the chalice, in order to provide safety from poison. It seemed novel to him, both at this Mass and others, that the Pope and cardinals and other prelates are seated, and, almost all through the Mass, covered, chatting and talking together. These ceremonies seem to be more magnificent than devout.

For the rest, it seemed to him that there was nothing special about the beauty of the women worthy of that preeminence that reputation gives to this city over all the others in the world; and moreover that, as in Paris, the most singular beauty was found among those who put it on sale.

On December 29th Monsieur d'Elbène, who was then ambassador, a studious gentleman and long a good friend of Monsieur de Montaigne, recommended that he kiss the Pope's feet. Monsieur d'Estissac and he got into the said ambassador's coach. When the ambassador was admitted to audience, he had them called by the Pope's chamberlain. They found the Pope and with him the ambassador alone, which is the fashion; he has beside him a little bell that he rings when he wants someone to come to him. The ambassador was seated at his left hand, uncovered; for the Pope never takes off his cap for anyone whatever, nor is any ambassador with him with his head covered. Monsieur d'Estissac entered first, and after him Monsieur de Montaigne, and then Messieurs de Mattecoulon and du Hautoy. After one or two steps into the chamber, in the corner of which the said Pope is seated, those who enter, whoever they may be, put one knee on the ground and wait for the Pope to give them his benediction, which he does; after that they get up again and proceed until about the middle of the room. It is true that most people do not go straight to him, cutting across the room, but sidle along the wall in order, after turning, to make straight for him. At this halfway point they once more get down on one knee and receive the second benediction. This done, they go toward him as far as a velvet carpet spread out at his feet seven or eight feet farther forward. At the edge of this carpet they go down on both knees. There the ambassador, who was presenting them, knelt on one knee and pulled back the Pope's robe from his right foot, on which there is a red slipper with a white cross on it. Those who are on their knees drag themselves in this position up to his foot and lean down to the ground to kiss it. Monsieur de Montaigne said he had raised the end of his foot a bit. They made way for one another to kiss, then withdrew to one side, still in this posture. This done, the ambassador covered the Pope's foot again, and, rising from his seat, told him what seemed proper for the recommendation of Monsieur d'Estissac and Monsieur de Montaigne. The Pope, with a courteous countenance, admonished Monsieur d'Estissac to pursue study and virtue, and Monsieur de Montaigne to continue in the devotion he had always borne to the Church and the service of the Most Christian King, and said that he would gladly be of service to them whenever he could: those are Italian phrases of service. They for their part said not a word to him; but having there received another benediction before the Pope rose, which is the sign of dismissal, went back the same way. This is done according to each person's notion; however, the commonest way is to move away backward, or at least to withdraw to the side, in such a way that one always looks the Pope in the face. At the halfway point, as in coming, they again went down on one knee and had another benediction; and at the door, again on one knee, the final benediction.

The language of the Pope is Italian, smacking of the Bolognese patois, which is the worst idiom in Italy; and then by nature his speech is halting.[2] For the rest, he is a very handsome old man, of middle height, erect, his face full of majesty, a long white beard, more than eighty years old, as healthy and vigorous for his age as anyone can wish, without gout, without colic, without stomach trouble, and not subject to any ailment: of a gentle nature, not very passionate about the affairs of the world; a great builder, and in that respect he will leave in Rome and elsewhere exceptional honor to his memory; a great almoner, I should say beyond all measure. Among other evidences of this, there is not a girl about to marry whom he does not aid in setting up house, if she is of low estate; and in this respect they count his liberality as ready money. Besides that,[3] he has built colleges for the Greeks, and for the English, Scots, French, Germans, and Poles, and has endowed each one with more than ten thousand crowns a year in perpetuity, besides the huge expense of the buildings. He has done this to call to the Church the children of those nations, corrupted by evil opinions against the Church; and there the boys are lodged, fed, dressed, instructed, and provided with everything, without one quattrino of their own going into it for anything whatever. The troublesome public charges he readily casts off on the shoulders of others and avoids giving himself trouble.

He gives as many audiences as one wants. His replies are short and decided, and you waste your time if you combat his reply with new

---

[2] This is Pope Gregory XIII (Ugo Buoncompagno of Bologna, 1502–1585), Pope from 1572 until his death, a strong fighter against Protestantism, who publicly celebrated the Massacre of Saint Bartholomew's Day. Most of the details given here, except for his age, are confirmed by other witnesses.

[3] These few lines, from "there is not" to "Besides that," are an addition to the manuscript in Montaigne's hand.

arguments. In what he judges to be just, he trusts himself; and even for his son, whom he loves with a frenzy, he will not stir a bit against this justice of his. He gives advancement to his relations, but[4] without any prejudice to the rights of the Church, which he preserves inviolable. He is very lavish in public buildings and the improvement of the city's streets; and in truth, his life and his conduct have nothing very extraordinary about them one way or the other, but incline much more to the good.

On the last day of December the two of them [Montaigne and d'Estissac] dined at the house of the cardinal of Sens, who observes more of the Roman ceremonies than any other Frenchman. The very long Benedicites and Graces were said by two chaplains in response to each other in the fashion of the church service. During his dinner a paraphrase of the Gospel of the day was read in Italian. They washed with him both before and after the meal. Everyone is served with a napkin to wipe his mouth and hands with; and in front of those to whom they want to do particular honor, who are seated beside or opposite the master, they place big silver squares on which their saltcellar stands, of the same sort as those they put before the great in France. On top of this there is a napkin folded in four, and on this napkin the bread, knife, fork, and spoon. On top of all this there is another napkin, which you are to use, and leave the rest in the state it is in; for after you are at table, they give you, beside this square, a silver or earthenware plate which you use. Of all that is served at table the carver gives portions on plates to those who are seated, in the order of seating, and they do not put their hand to the dish, least of all to the master's dish.

They also served Monsieur de Montaigne with drink, as they ordinarily did at the ambassador's when he ate there, in this way: they presented to him a silver basin on which there was a glass with wine and a little bottle, of the size of those you put ink in, full of water. He takes this glass with his right hand and this bottle with the left, and pours as much water as he likes into his glass, and then puts this bottle back into the basin. When he drinks, the man who serves him offers the said basin under his chin, and he himself then replaces his glass in the said basin. This ceremony is performed only for one or two persons at most below the master.

The table was removed immediately after grace, and the chairs promptly arranged along one side of the room, on which the cardinal had them sit, after him. Then there appeared two churchmen, well dressed, with I know not what instruments in their hands, who knelt before the cardinal and informed him of I know not what service that was being performed in some church. He said nothing at all to them, but as they rose after speaking and were going away, he raised his cap to them a little.

---

[4] The following passage, from "but without" to "the city's streets," and the shorter one a few lines later, "but incline much more to the good," are additions to the manuscript in Montaigne's hand.

A little later he took them in his coach to the Hall of the Consistory, where the cardinals assembled to go to vespers. The Pope arrived and dressed to go to vespers too. The cardinals did not kneel at his benediction, as the people do, but received it with a deep inclination of the head.

On the third day of January, 1581, the Pope passed in front of our window. In front of him walked about two hundred horses bearing persons of his court of one or the other robe.[5] Beside him was the Cardinal de' Medici, who was conversing with him covered and was taking him to dine with him. The Pope had on a red hat, his white apparel and red velvet hood, as usual, and was mounted on a white hackney harnessed with red velvet with gold fringes and lace. He mounts on horseback without the help of a groom, and yet is in his eighty-first year. Every fifteen steps he gave his benediction. After him came three cardinals, and then about a hundred men-at-arms, lance on thigh, in full armor except for the head. There was also another hackney with the same trappings, a mule, a handsome white charger, and a litter following him, and two robe bearers who carried valises at their saddlebow.

That same day Monsieur de Montaigne took some turpentine, without any reason except that he had a cold, and afterward he passed a lot of gravel.

On January 11th, in the morning, as Monsieur de Montaigne was leaving the house on horseback to go to the bankers', it happened that they were taking out of prison Catena, a famous robber and bandit captain who had kept all Italy in fear and to whom some monstrous murders were ascribed, especially those of two Capuchins whom he had made to deny God, promising on that condition to save their lives, and then massacred without any reason either of advantage or of vengeance. Monsieur de Montaigne stopped to see this spectacle. Besides the formalities used in France, they carry in front of the criminal a big crucifix covered with a black curtain, and on foot go a large number of men dressed and masked in linen, who, they say, are gentlemen and other prominent people of Rome who devote themselves to this service of accompanying criminals led to execution and the bodies of the dead; and there is a brotherhood of them. There are two of these, or monks dressed and masked in the same way, who attend the criminal on the cart and preach to him; and one of them continually holds before his face a picture on which is the portrait of Our Lord, and has him kiss it incessantly; this makes it impossible to see the criminal's face from the street. At the gallows, which is a beam between two supports, they still kept this picture against his face until he was launched. He made an ordinary death, without movement or word; he was a dark man of thirty or thereabouts.

After he was strangled, they cut him into four quarters. They hardly ever kill men except by a simple death, and exercise their severity after death. Monsieur de Montaigne here remarked what he has said else-

---

[5] Churchmen or laymen.

where,[6] how much the people are frightened by the rigors exercised on dead bodies; for these people, who had appeared to feel nothing at seeing him strangled, at every blow that was given to cut him up cried out in a piteous voice. As soon as a criminal is dead, one or several Jesuits or others get up on some high spot and shout to the people, one in this direction, the other in that, and preach to them to make them take in this example.

We remarked in Italy, and especially in Rome, that there are almost no bells at all for the service of the Church, and less in Rome than in the smallest village in France; also that there are no images, unless they have been made very recently. Many old churches have not a one.

On January 14th he again took turpentine without any apparent effect.

On this same day I saw two brothers executed, former servants of the Castellano's secretary, who had killed him a few days before in the city by night, in the very palace of the said Signor Giacomo Buoncompagno, the Pope's son. They tore them with red-hot pincers, then cut off their fist in front of the said palace, and having cut it off they put on the wound capons that they had killed and immediately opened up. They were executed on a scaffold: first they were clubbed with a big wooden mace, and then their throats were cut immediately. This is a punishment they say is sometimes used in Rome, though others maintained that it had been adapted to the misdeed, since they had killed their master in that way.

As for the size of Rome, Monsieur de Montaigne said that the space enclosed by the walls, which is more than two-thirds empty, including ancient and modern Rome, might equal the enclosure you would make around Paris if you walled in all the *faubourgs* that surround it. But if you count the size by the number and crowding of houses and habitations, he thinks that Rome does not come within a third of the size of Paris. In the number and size of public squares, and beauty of streets and houses, Rome wins by far.

He also found the cold of winter very nearly approaching that of Gascony. There were heavy frosts around Christmas, and some unbearably cold winds. It is true that even then there is very often thunder, hail, and lightning.

The palaces are divided into numerous apartments, one leading to another; you thread your way through three or four rooms before you are in the principal one. In certain places where Monsieur de Montaigne dined in ceremony, the buffets are not where you dine but in another room through which you pass first, and they go there to get you a drink when you ask for it; and the silver plate is on display there.

Thursday, January 26th, Monsieur de Montaigne—after going to see Mount Janiculum, beyond the Tiber, and to look at the sights of that place (among others a large piece of old wall that had fallen in ruins two days before), and to contemplate the configuration of all the parts

---

[6] *Essays* II: 11, p. 315.

of Rome, which may not be seen so clearly from any other place; and from there having gone down to the Vatican to see the statues enclosed in the niches of the Belvedere and the beautiful gallery that the Pope is erecting for paintings from all parts of Italy, which is very nearly finished—lost his purse and what was in it; and he thought what had happened was that in giving alms two or three times, the weather being very rainy and unpleasant, instead of putting his purse back into his pocket he had slipped it through the slashings of his breeches.

All these days he spent his time only in studying Rome. At the beginning he had taken a French guide; but when this man quit because of some fancy or other, he made it a point of pride to learn all about Rome by his own study, aided by various maps and books that he had read to him in the evening; and in the daytime he would go on the spot to put his apprenticeship into practice; so that in a few days he could easily have guided his guide.

He said that one saw nothing of Rome but the sky under which it had stood and the plan of its site; that this knowledge that he had of it was an abstract and contemplative knowledge of which there was nothing perceptible to the senses; that those who said that one at least saw the ruins of Rome said too much, for the ruins of so awesome a machine would bring more honor and reverence to its memory: this was nothing but its sepulcher. The world, hostile to its long domination, had first broken and shattered all the parts of this wonderful body; and because, even though quite dead, overthrown, and disfigured, it still terrified the world, the world had buried its very ruin. These little signs of its ruin that still appear above the bier had been preserved by fortune as testimony to that infinite greatness which so many centuries, so many conflagrations, and all the many conspiracies of the world to ruin it had not been able to extinguish completely. But it was likely that these disfigured limbs which remained were the least worthy, and that the fury of the enemies of that immortal glory had impelled them to destroy first of all what was most beautiful and most worthy; and the buildings of this bastard Rome which they were now attaching to these ancient ruins, although fully adequate to carry away the present age with admiration, reminded him precisely of the nests which sparrows and crows in France suspend from the arches and walls of the churches that the Huguenots have recently demolished.

He feared further, seeing the space that this tomb occupies, that we were not aware of all of it, and that the sepulcher itself was for the most part buried; and that judging from the fact that such paltry rubble as pieces of tile and broken pots had built up in ancient times to a pile of such excessive size that it equals in height and breadth several natural mountains (for he compared it in height to the hill of Gurson and estimated it to be twice as broad),[7] this must have been an express ordinance of the Fates, to make the world feel that they had conspired for

---

[7] The short passage in parentheses is an addition to the manuscript in Montaigne's hand.

the glory and preeminence of this city by so novel and extraordinary
a testimonial to its greatness.

He said he could not easily make people agree, seeing the small
space occupied by some of these seven hills, and notably the most famous ones, like the Capitoline and the Palatine, that so great a number
of buildings had been arrayed there. Merely to see what remains of the
Temple of Peace, beside the Forum Romanum, of whose quite recent
fall you still see evidence, as of a great mountain broken up into many
horrible rocks, it does not seem that two such buildings could fit into
the whole space of the Capitoline Hill, where there were fully twenty-
five or thirty temples, besides many private houses.

But in truth, many conjectures that we make from the description of
this ancient city have hardly any verisimilitude, since even its site has
infinitely changed in form, some of the valleys having been filled up,
even in the lowest places that were there; as for example, in the place
of the Velabrum, which because of its lowness received the sewage of
the city and had a lake, hills have arisen of the height of the other, natural hills that are round about, as a result of the piling and heaping up of
the ruins of these great buildings; and Mount Savello is nothing but the
ruin of a part of the Theater of Marcellus. He thought that an ancient
Roman could not recognize the site of his city even if he saw it. It has
often happened that after digging deep down into the ground people
would come merely down to the head of a very high column which was
still standing down below. They do not seek any other foundations for
their houses than old ruined buildings or vaults, such as are seen at the
bottom of all the cellars, nor the support of the ancient foundation or
of a wall which is in its place; but on the very broken pieces of the old
buildings, however fortune has located them, they have planted the feet
of their new palaces, as on great chunks of rocks, firm and assured. It
is easy to see that many streets are more than thirty feet below those of
today.

On January 28th Monsieur de Montaigne had the colic, which did
not keep him from any of his ordinary actions, and passed a rather big-
gish stone and other smaller ones.

On the 30th he went to see the most ancient religious ceremony
there is among men, and watched it very attentively and with great
profit: that is, the circumcision of the Jews.

He had already seen their synagogue at another time, one Saturday
morning, and their prayers, in which they sing without order, as in the
Calvinist churches, certain lessons from the Bible in Hebrew, that are
suited to the occasion. They sing the same songs, but with extreme dis-
cord, because they do not keep time and because of the confusion of
so many voices of every sort of age; for the children, even the very
youngest, take part, and all without exception understand Hebrew.
They pay no more attention to their prayers than we do to ours, talking
of other affairs in the midst of them and not bringing much reverence to
their mysteries. They wash their hands on coming in, and in that place
it is an execrable thing to doff one's hat; but they bow the head and

knees where their devotions ordain it. They wear over their shoulders or on their head a sort of cloth with fringes attached: the whole thing would be too long to describe. After dinner their doctors each in turn give a lesson on the Bible passage for that day, doing it in Italian. After the lesson some other doctor present selects some one of the hearers, and sometimes two or three in succession, to argue with the reader about what he has said. The one we heard seemed to him to argue with great eloquence and wit.

But as for the circumcision, it is done in private houses, in the most convenient and lightest room in the boy's house. Where he was, because the house was inconvenient, the ceremony was performed at the entrance door. They give the boys a godfather and a godmother, as we do; the father names the child. They circumcise them on the eighth day from their birth. The godfather sits down on a table and puts a pillow on his lap; the godmother brings him the infant there and then goes away. The child is wrapped in our style; the godfather unwraps him below, and then those present and the man who is to do the operation all begin to sing, and accompany with songs all this action, which lasts a short quarter of an hour. The minister may be other than a rabbi, and whatever he may be among them, everyone wishes to be called to this office, for they hold that it is a great blessing to be employed at it often: indeed, they pay to be invited to do it, offering, one a garment, another some other commodity for the child; and they hold that he who has circumcised up to a certain number, which they know, when he is dead has this privilege, that the parts of his mouth are never eaten by worms.

On the table where this godfather is seated there is also a great preparation of all the instruments necessary for this operation. Besides that, a man holds in his hands a phial full of wine and a glass. There is also a brazier on the ground, at which brazier this minister first warms his hands, and then, finding this child all stripped, as the godfather holds him on his lap with his head toward him, he takes his member and with one hand pulls back toward himself the skin that is over it, with the other pushing the glans and the member within. To the end of this skin which he holds toward the said glans he applies a silver instrument which stops the said skin there and keeps the cutting edge from injuring the glans and the flesh. After that, with a knife he cuts off this skin, which they immediately bury in some earth which is there in a basin among the other preparations for this mystery. After that the minister with his bare nails plucks up also some other particle of skin which is on this glans and tears it off by force and pushes the skin back beyond the glans.

It seems there is much effort and pain in this; however, they find no danger in it, and the wound is always cured in four or five days. The boy's outcry is like that of ours when they are baptized. As soon as this glans is thus uncovered, they hastily offer some wine to the minister, who puts a little in his mouth and then goes and sucks the glans of this child, all bloody, and spits out the blood he has drawn from it, and immediately takes as much wine again, up to three times. This done, they offer him, in a little paper cup, some red powder which they say is dragon's blood,[8] with which he salts and covers the whole wound; and then he very tidily wraps this boy's member with cloths cut specially for this. That done, they give him a glass full of wine, which wine they say he blesses by some prayers that he says. He takes a swallow of it, and then dipping his finger in it he three times takes a drop of it with his finger to the boy's mouth to be sucked; and afterward they send this glass, in the same state, to the mother and the women, who are in some other part of the house, to drink what wine is left. Besides that, another person takes a silver instrument, round as a tennis ball, held by a long handle (which instrument is pierced with little holes, like our casso- lettes), and carries it to the nose, first of the minister, and then of the child, and then of the godfather: they suppose that these are odors to confirm and enlighten minds for devotion. He meanwhile still has his mouth all bloody.

On the 8th, and then again on the 12th, he had a touch of colic and passed some stones without great pain.

The Shrovetide that took place in Rome that year was more licen- tious, by permission of the Pope, than it had been for several years be- fore: we found, however, that it was not much of a thing. Along the Corso, which is a long street in Rome that gets its name from this very thing, they race, now four or five boys, now some Jews, now some old men stark naked, from one end of the street to the other. You have no pleasure in it except in seeing them pass in front of the place where you are. They do the same with horses, on which are little boys who drive them with whips, and with donkeys and buffaloes driven with goads by men on horseback. For each race there is a prize offered which they call *il palio*: pieces of velvet or cloth. The gentlemen, in a certain part of the street where the ladies have a better view, run at the quintain on fine horses, and have good grace at it; for there is nothing that this no- bility so commonly knows how to do well as exercises on horseback. The stand which Monsieur de Montaigne had made cost them three crowns. It was indeed situated in a very fine place in the street.

On those days all the beautiful gentlewomen of Rome were seen at leisure: for in Italy they do not mask themselves as in France, and show themselves with faces quite uncovered. As for perfect and rare beauty, there is no more of it, he said, than in France, and except in three or four he found no excellence; but commonly they are more attractive, and you do not see so many ugly ones as in France. Their heads are without comparison more advantageously dressed, and the lower part below the girdle. The body is better in France: for here they are too loose around the girdle and carry that part like our pregnant women. Their countenance has more majesty, softness, and sweetness. There is no comparison between the richness of their apparel and of ours: all is full of pearls and precious stones. Wherever they let themselves be

---

[8] A red resin used as an astringent.

seen in public, whether in a coach, at a festival, or in the theater, they are apart from the men; however, at dances they intermingle freely enough, where there are occasions for talking and touching hands.

The men are very simply dressed, for all occasions, in black and Florentine serge; and because they are a little darker than we are, they somehow do not look like dukes, counts, and marquises, which they are, but have a rather mean appearance; for the rest, they are as courteous and gracious as possible, whatever the common run of Frenchmen say, who cannot call people gracious who find it hard to endure their excesses and their ordinary insolence. In every way we do all we can to get a bad reputation here. However, they have an ancient affection or reverence for France which makes those people very respected and welcome who deserve the least bit to be, and who merely control themselves without offending them.

On Thursday before Lent he went to the feast of the Castellano. A good deal of preparation had been made, notably an amphitheater very artfully and richly disposed for combat in the lists, which combat took place at night, before supper, in a square barn with an oval-shaped entrenchment in the middle. Among other singularities, the pavement was painted in an instant with various designs in red: having first coated the pavement with some sort of plaster or lime, they laid over it a piece of parchment or leather cut into a stencil of the devices they wanted; and then they passed a brush dipped in red over this piece and printed through the openings what they wanted on the pavement, and so quickly that in two hours the whole nave of a church would be painted so.

At supper the ladies are served by their husbands, who stand about them and give them drink and what they ask for. They served a great deal of roast fowl dressed in its natural feathers as if alive; capons cooked entire in glass bottles; quantities of hares, rabbits, and live birds in pasties; admirably folded linen. The ladies' table, which was of four dishes, could be taken off in pieces, and underneath there was another all served and' covered with sweetmeats.

The men do not wear masks when they go visiting. They do wear inexpensive masks when they walk about town in public or set up teams for tilting at the ring. There were two fine rich companies got up in this fashion on Shrove Monday to run at the quintain; they surpass us above all in abundance of very handsome horses.

[THE JOURNAL BY MONTAIGNE IN FRENCH]

Having dismissed the one of my men who was doing this fine job, and seeing it so far advanced, whatever trouble it may be to me, I must continue it myself.

On February 16th, returning from the station,[9] I came across a priest in vestments in a little chapel busy curing a possessed man: he was a melancholy man and as if half dead. They were holding him on his knees before the altar, with some kind of cloth around his neck by which

[9] A church where a procession goes for a service.

they held him fast. The priest read in his presence lots of prayers and exorcisms, commanding the devil to leave this body, and he read them from his breviary. After this he turned his remarks to the patient, now speaking to him, now speaking to the devil in his person, and then insulting him, beating him with great blows of his fist, spitting in his face. The patient replied to his questions with a few inept replies: now for himself, saying how he felt the movements of his malady; now for the devil, how much he feared God and how much these exorcisms acted against him. After that, which lasted a long time, the priest, for his last effort, retired to the altar and took the pyx, in which was the *Corpus Domini,* in his left hand, in the other hand holding a lighted taper upside down so that he made it melt and be consumed, meanwhile uttering prayers, and at the end harsh and threatening words against the devil, in the loudest and most magisterial voice he could. As the first candle went out close to his fingers, he took another, and then a second and third additional one. This done, he replaced the pyx, that is to say the transparent vessel containing the *Corpus Domini,* and came and joined the patient again, speaking to him now as to a man, had him untied, and returned him to his people to take him back home.

He told us that this devil was of the worst type, obstinate, and would cost a lot of effort to cast out. And to ten or twelve of us gentlemen who were there he told several stories about this science and his ordinary experience of it, notably that the day before he had rid a woman of a big devil who, in coming out, had pushed nails, pins, and a tuft of his hair out of this woman through her mouth. And because someone answered him that she was not yet completely recovered, he said that this was another sort of spirit, lighter and less harmful, who had returned into her that morning; but that this sort (for he knows their names, their divisions, and their most particular distinctions) was easy to conjure. That is all I saw. My man made no other face than to gnash his teeth and twist his mouth when they presented the *Corpus Domini* to him, and he sometimes mouthed these words, *si fata volent;*[10] for he was a notary, and knew a little Latin.

On the first day of March I went to the station of Saint Sixtus.[11] At the high altar the priest who was saying Mass was beyond the altar, his face turned toward the people; behind him there was no one. The Pope went there that same day; a few days before he had had removed from this church the nuns who were there, because that place was a little too far out of the way, and had accommodated there all the poor who were begging throughout the city—a very fine arrangement. The cardinals gave twenty crowns each to start this movement off, and extremely generous alms were given by other private persons. The Pope endowed this hospital with five hundred crowns a month.

In Rome there are a great many private devotions and brotherhoods

---

[10] "If the Fates will."

[11] The Sistine Chapel. The nuns were removed (and replaced by the poor) not from the chapel itself but from a neighboring convent.

in which many great evidences of piety are seen. The people as a whole seem to me less devout than in the good towns in France, though indeed more ceremonious, for in that respect they are extreme. I am writing here in freedom of conscience. Here are two examples.

While a certain man was in bed with a courtesan, amid the license of that relationship, behold at midnight the Ave Maria rang; she immediately jumped out of bed onto the floor and got on her knees to say her prayer. When a man was with another courtesan, behold the good mother (for the young ones especially have old governesses, whom they treat as mothers or aunts) comes banging at the door, and with anger and fury tears from this young one's neck a ribbon from which hung a little Madonna, so as not to contaminate it with the filth of her sin. The young one felt extreme contrition for having forgotten to take it from her neck as she was accustomed to do.

The ambassador from the tsar of Muscovy also came that day to this station, dressed in a scarlet mantle and a cassock of cloth of gold, with a hat in the form of a nightcap, of cloth of gold, furred, and beneath it a skullcap of cloth of silver. He is the second ambassador who has come from Muscovy to the Pope. The other was in the time of Pope Paul III. There they maintained that his mission was to move the Pope to interpose in the war that the king of Poland was making on his master, alleging that it was up to his master to sustain the first attack of the Turk, and that if his neighbor weakened him he would remain incapable of the other war, which would be a great window opened to the Turk to come at us; offering besides to give ground on certain differences in religion that he had with the Roman Church. He was lodged with the Castellano, as the other one had been in the time of Pope Paul, and was entertained at the Pope's expense. He strongly insisted on not kissing the Pope's feet but only his right hand, and would not give in until it was attested to him that the Emperor himself was subject to that ceremony: for the example of kings was not enough for him. He did not know how to speak any language but his own, and had come without an interpreter. He had only three or four men in his retinue, and said that he had passed through great danger in crossing Poland in disguise. His nation is so ignorant of the affairs of this part of the world that he brought to Venice letters from his master addressed to the Grand Governor of the Signory of Venice. Questioned about the meaning of this inscription, he said that they thought Venice was under the dominion of the Pope and that he sent governors there as he did to Bologna and elsewhere. God knows with what relish these magnificos received this piece of ignorance! He made presents, both there and to the Pope, of sables and black fox, which is a still rarer and richer fur.

On March 6th I went to see the Vatican Library, which is in five or six large rooms all in a row. There are a large number of books attached onto several rows of desks; there are also some in coffers, which were all opened to me; lots of books written by hand, and especially a Seneca and the *Moral Essays* of Plutarch. Among the remarkable things I saw there were the statue of the good Aristides with a handsome bald head, a thick beard, a big forehead, a look full of gentleness and majesty: his name is written on the very ancient pedestal; a book from China, in strange characters, the leaves made of some material much softer and more pellucid than our paper; and because this cannot endure the stain of ink, the writing is on only one side of the sheet, and the sheets are all double and folded at the outside edges, by which they hold together. They think it is the membrane of some tree. I also saw a bit of the ancient papyrus, on which there were unknown characters: it is the bark of a tree. I saw the breviary of Saint Gregory, written by hand; it bears no evidence of the year, but they hold that it has come down from him from hand to hand. It is a missal about like ours, and was brought to the last Council of Trent to serve as a testimony of our ceremonies. I saw a book by Saint Thomas Aquinas in which there are corrections in the hand of the author himself, who wrote badly, a small lettering worse than mine. *Item*, a Bible printed on parchment, one of those that Plantin has just done in four languages, which King Philip sent to the present Pope, as is stated in the inscription on the binding; the original of the book that the king of England[12] composed against Luther, which he sent about fifty years ago to Pope Leo X, inscribed with his own hand, with this most elegant Latin distich, also in his own hand:

To Leo Ten, Henry, king of the English, sends
This work, a pledge of loyalty between two friends.

I read the prefaces, the one to the Pope, the other to the reader: he excuses himself because of his military occupations and lack of ability; for scholastic Latin, it is good.

I saw the library without any difficulty; anyone can see it thus, and can make whatever extracts he wants; and it is open almost every morning. I was guided all through it and invited by a gentleman to use it whenever I wanted. Our ambassador was leaving Rome at that time without having seen it, and complained that they wanted him to pay court to Cardinal Sirleto, master of this library, for this permission: and, he said, he had never been able to see that handwritten Seneca, as he hugely desired to do. Fortune brought me to it, since on this testimony of his I considered the thing hopeless. All things are easy in this way from certain angles, and inaccessible from others. Opportunity and opportuneness have their privileges, and often offer to the common people what they refuse to kings. Curiosity often gets in its own way, as also do greatness and power.

I also saw here a handwritten Virgil in extremely large lettering and those long, narrow characters that we see here in the inscriptions of the time of the emperors, as for example around the age of Constantine, which have a sort of Gothic fashion and have lost that square proportion that is in the old Latin writings. This Virgil confirmed me in what I have always judged, that the first four lines that they put in the

[12] Henry VIII.

Aeneid[13] are borrowed: this book does not have them. There is an Acts of the Apostles written in very beautiful gold Greek lettering, as fresh and recent as if it were of today. This lettering is massive and has a solid body raised on the paper, so that if you pass your hand over it you feel the thickness. I think we have lost the use of this kind of writing.

On March 13th an old patriarch of Antioch, an Arab, very well versed in five or six languages of that part of the world, and having no knowledge of Greek or any other of our tongues, with whom I had become quite intimate, made me a present of a certain mixture to help my stone, and prescribed the use of it for me in writing. He enclosed it for me in a little earthenware pot, and told me that I could keep it ten or twenty years, and hoped for such results from it that from the first taking I should be completely cured of my malady. In order that, if I should lose his writing, I may find it here: "You must take this drug as you are going to bed after a light supper, in a dose the size of two peas, and mix it with lukewarm water after crumbling it with your fingers, and take it five times, leaving out every other day."

Dining one day in Rome with our ambassador, with Muret[14] and other learned men present, I got on the subject of the French translation of Plutarch;[15] and against those who esteemed it much less highly than I do, I maintained at least this: that where the translator missed the real meaning of Plutarch, he has substituted another that is probable and well in keeping with what precedes and what follows. In order to show me that even in this I was granting him too much, two passages were produced. One, the critique of which they attribute to the son of Monsieur Mangot, advocate in the Parlement of Paris, who had just left Rome, is in the "Life of Solon," at about the middle, where he says that Solon boasted of having freed Attica and removed the boundaries that separated inherited plots of land. He was wrong, for the Greek word signifies certain marks which were placed on lands that were mortgaged or alienated, so that purchasers should be warned of this mortgage. What he substituted about "limits" has no recognizable sense, for that would be making the lands not free but common. Estienne's Latin[16] comes closer to the truth. The second passage, right at the end of the treatise "On the Education of Children": "The observation of these rules," he says, "may rather be wished than advised." The Greek, they say, suggests "is more to be desired than hoped for," a sort of proverb that is found elsewhere. Instead of this clear and easy meaning, the one

[13] These lines are not included in the text in modern editions.

[14] Marc-Antoine Muret (1526–85), one of the leading Latinists of his time, a teacher of Montaigne at the Collège de Guyenne in Bordeaux, author of a Latin play *Julius Caesar*, commentator of Ronsard's first *Amours*. He fled from France to Italy in 1554 because of a morals charge, and from 1563 on taught at the University of Rome. Montaigne praises him in the *Essays* (I: 26, p. 129) as the best orator of his time.

[15] The famous Amyot translation of the *Lives* (1559) and *Moral Essays* (1572), which were Montaigne's favorite books. See *Essays* II: 4, p. 262, and *passim*.

[16] The Latin translation by Henri Estienne (Stephanus) in 1572.

the translator has substituted is weak and strange. Wherefore, accepting their assumptions about the proper meaning of the words, I admitted their conclusion in good faith.

The churches in Rome are less beautiful than in most of the good towns of Italy, and likewise in Italy and Germany in general they are ordinarily less beautiful than in France. At Saint Peter's one sees, at the entrance of the new church, banners hanging as trophies: their inscription states that they are banners won by the king [of France] from the Huguenots; it does not specify where and when. Beside the Gregorian chapel, in which you see an infinite number of votive tablets attached to the wall, there is among others a little square picture, rather wretched and badly painted, of the battle of Montcontour. In the room next to the Sistine Chapel (where, on the wall, there are several paintings of memorable incidents concerning the Holy See, such as the naval battle of John of Austria),[17] there is a picture representing that Pope treading underfoot the head of that Emperor[18] who came to ask his pardon and kiss his feet; but not the words spoken by both men according to history. There are also two places where the wounding and the death of Admiral de Châtillon[19] are painted very authentically.

On March 15th Monsieur de Monluc[20] came to get me at daybreak to carry out the plan we had made the day before of going to see Ostia. We crossed the Tiber by the Bridge of Our Lady and went out by the Porta del Porto, which in ancient times they called Portuensis; from there we followed an uneven road, through country moderately fertile in wines and wheat; and after about eight miles, returning to the Tiber, we descended into a large plain covered with meadows and pasture land, at the end of which was once situated a large town, many great and handsome ruins of which may be seen on the shores of the Lake of Trajan, which is an overflow of the Tyrrhenian Sea and into which ships used to come; but now the sea comes into it only very little, and still less into another lake a little above this place, which they call the Port of Claudius. We might have dined here with the cardinal of Perugia, who was there; and in truth there is nothing so courteous as these lords and their servants. And the said lord cardinal sent me word by one of my men who promptly went to convey my respects that he had reason to complain of me; and this same valet was taken for a drink to the wine cellar of the said cardinal, who had no friendship or acquaintance with me, and in this was practicing only an ordinary hospitality toward all

17 The great victory of the Spaniards and Venetians over the Turks at Lepanto in 1571.

18 Pope Alexander III and Frederick Barbarossa, in Venice, in 1177. The Emperor acknowledged Saint Peter's right to tread enemies underfoot, and the Pope then claimed it equally for himself.

19 Châtillon, better known as Coligny, the Protestant leader, was killed in the Massacre of Saint Bartholomew's Day in 1572. Pope Gregory XIII hailed the news of the massacre with great joy.

20 Blaise de Monluc, grandson of the marshal, whom Montaigne had already seen in Bologna. See Travel Journal, p. 926.

strangers who have some breeding. However, I was afraid that the day-light might fail us for making the tour I wanted to make, since I had greatly lengthened my trip in order to see these two banks of the Tiber.

Here we crossed by boat a little branch of the Tiber and entered the Sacred Isle, about the length of a good Gascon league, covered with pasture land. There are some ruins and marble columns, as there are many in this place Porto, where the old city of Trajan used to be; and the Pope has some of them dug up every day and taken to Rome. When we had crossed this island we came upon the Tiber, and since we had no suitable means of getting the horses across, we were about to retrace our steps; but by chance, behold there arrived on the other bank several gentlemen—the sieur du Bellai, the baron de Chasai, the sieur de Mari-vau, and others. Whereupon I crossed the river and made a deal with these gentlemen that they should take our horses and we theirs. Thus they returned to Rome by the road on which we had come, and we by theirs, which was the one straight to Ostia.

OSTIA, fifteen miles, is situated along the old bed of the Tiber; for the river has changed its course a little and moves farther from the old course every day. We had a snack for breakfast at a little tavern. Be-yond we saw La Rocca, a small, rather strongly fortified castle; no guard is mounted there. The popes, especially the present one, have erected on this seacoast big towers or lookouts, about every mile, to provide against the raids that the Turks often used to make, especially at vin-tage time, taking cattle and men. From these towers, by means of a cannon shot, they warn one another with such great speed that imme-diately the alarm is flying to Rome. Around Ostia are the salt marshes, which supply all the territories of the Church: there is a large marshy plain into which the sea flows.

All along this road from Ostia to Rome, which is the Via Ostensis, there are great marks of its ancient beauty: a great many causeways, many ruins of aqueducts, and almost the entire length of it sown with great ruins, and more than two-thirds of the said road still paved with those big square black slabs with which they used to pave their high-ways. Seeing this bank of the Tiber, you easily accept as true the opin-ion that on both sides this road was lined with residences all the way from Rome to Ostia. Among other ruins, about halfway to Rome we came across on our left hand a very beautiful sepulcher of a Roman praetor, the inscription of which is still seen entire. The ruins of Rome are discernible for the most part only by the solidity and thickness of the construction. They used to make stout brick walls and then encrust them with slabs either of marble or of some other white stone, or a certain cement, or big tiles coated on the outside. This crust, on which the inscriptions were, has almost everywhere been ruined by the years; whereby we have lost most of our knowledge of such things. Inscrip-tions are seen wherever the building has walls of thick and massive stone.

The approaches to Rome, almost everywhere, look uncultivated and barren, either for want of soil, or, what I consider more likely, because this city has hardly any laborers and men who live by the work of their hands. When I came here I found on the way many groups of villagers who came from the Grisons and Savoy to earn something in the season by laboring in the vineyards and the gardens; and they told me that every year this was their source of income.

The city is all court and all nobility: every man shares in the ecclesiastical idleness. There are no shop-lined streets, or fewer than in a small town: it is nothing but palaces and gardens. You see no Rue de la Harpe or Rue de Saint-Denis; it seems to me that I am always on the Rue de Seine or on the Quai des Augustins in Paris. The city hardly changes its appearance from a working day to a holiday. All through Lent they do the rounds of the stations; there is no less of a crowd on a working day than on any other. At this time there are nothing but coaches, prelates, and ladies. We returned to sleep at

ROME, fifteen miles. On March 16th I wanted to go and try the Roman steam baths, and went to those of Saint Mark, which are considered among the noblest. Though I was unattended, I was treated there moderately well and with all possible respect. The custom is to bring lady friends if you want, who are rubbed down with you by the attendants. There I learned that quicklime and orpiment mixed with lye, two parts of lime and the third of orpiment, go to make that drug and unguent with which they make the body hair fall out, after applying it for a short half of a quarter hour.

On the 17th I had my colic for five or six hours, endurable, and some time after passed a stone as big as a big pine nut, and of that shape.

At this time we had roses in Rome, and artichokes; but as for me, I found the heat nothing extraordinary, keeping dressed and covered as at home.

Fish are less abundant than in France; their pike especially is no good at all, and they leave it for the people. They rarely have soles and trout; very good barbel, much bigger than in Bordeaux, but expensive. Dorados are highly prized, and the mullets bigger than ours and a little firmer. The oil here is so excellent that the pricking which remains in my throat in France when I have eaten much of it, I do not have at all here. They eat fresh grapes here all year long, and even as late as this time of year there are very good ones hanging from the trellises. Their mutton is no good and is held in scant esteem.

On the 18th the ambassador of Portugal made obeisance to the Pope for the kingdom of Portugal on behalf of King Philip—the same ambassador who was here to represent the deceased king and the Cortes opposed to King Philip.

On my return from Saint Peter's I met a man who informed me humorously of two things: that the Portuguese made their obeisance in Passion week;[21] and then, that on this same day the station was at San Giovanni Porta Latina, in which church a few years before certain Portuguese had entered into a strange brotherhood. They married one

---

[21] The point being that they suffered in making it.

another, male to male, at Mass, with the same ceremonies with which we perform our marriages, read the same marriage gospel service, and then went to bed and lived together. The Roman wits said that because in the other conjunction, of male and female, this circumstance of marriage alone makes it legitimate, it had seemed to these sharp folk that this other action would become equally legitimate if they authorized it with ceremonies and mysteries of the Church. Eight or nine Portuguese of this fine sect were burned.

I saw the Spanish ceremony. They fired a salvo of cannon from the Castle of Sant' Angelo, and the ambassador was conducted to the palace by the Pope's trumpeters and drummers and archers. I did not go in to watch the harangue and the ceremony. The ambassador from the tsar of Muscovy, who was at a decorated window to see this ceremony, said that he had been invited to see a great assemblage, but that in his country, when they speak of troops of horse, it is always twenty-five or thirty thousand; and he laughed at all this ado, from what I was told by the very man who was commissioned to talk to him through an interpreter.

On Palm Sunday I found in a church at vespers a boy sitting beside the altar on a chair, dressed in a great new robe of blue taffeta, head bare, with a crown of olive branches, holding in his hand a lighted torch of white wax. He was a boy of fifteen or thereabouts, who, by order of the Pope, had been delivered from prison that day; he had killed another boy.

At Saint John Lateran some transparent marble is to be seen.

The next day the Pope did the seven churches. He had on boots with the hairy side in, and on each foot a cross of whiter leather. He always takes a Spanish horse, a hackney and a mule, and a litter, all decked out in the same way; that day the horse was missing. His groom had two or three pairs of gilt spurs in his hand and was waiting for him at the foot of Saint Peter's stairs; he refused them and asked for his litter, in which there were two red hats of almost the same fashion hanging on nails.

On this day in the evening my *Essays* were returned to me, corrected according to the opinion of the learned monks. The Master of the Sacred Palace[22] had been able to judge them only by the report of some French friar, since he did not understand our language at all; and he was so content with the excuses I offered on each objection that this Frenchman had left him that he referred it to my conscience to redress what I should see was in bad taste. I begged him on the contrary to follow the opinion of the man who had made the judgment, admitting in certain things—such as having used the word "fortune," having named heretic poets, having excused Julian, and the objection to the idea that anyone who was praying should be free from evil impulses at the time; *item*, esteeming as cruelty whatever goes beyond plain death; *item*, that

[22] The Master of the Sacred Palace at this time was Sisto Fabri (1541–94), professor of theology at the University of Rome, soon (1583) to be made general of the Dominican Order.

a child should be brought up to do anything;[23] and other things of that sort—that this was my opinion, and that they were things I had put in, not thinking they were errors; in other matters denying that the corrector had understood my thought. The said Master, who is an able man, was full of excuses for me, and wanted me to realize that he was not very sympathetic to these revisions; and he pleaded very ingeniously for me, in my presence, against another man, also an Italian, who was opposing me.

They did not return to me the book on the histories of the Swiss, translated into French, solely because the translator—whose name, however, is not given—is a heretic; but it is a marvel how well they know the men of our countries. And the best part was that they told me that the preface was condemned.

That same day, in the Church of Saint John Lateran, in place of the ordinary penitents who are seen performing this office in most of the churches, Monsignor the Cardinal San Sisto was seated in a corner, tapping on the head, with a long wand that he had in his hand, the passersby, including the ladies, but with a smiling face, and with greater courtesy according to their rank and beauty.

On the Wednesday of Holy Week I did the seven churches with Monsieur de Foix[24] before dinner, and we put in about five hours at it. I do not know why some people are scandalized to see the vice of some particular prelate freely accused, when it is known and public; for that day, both at Saint John Lateran and at the Church of the Holy-Cross-in-Jerusalem, I saw the history, written at full length in a very conspicuous place, of Pope Sylvester II, which is the most damaging that can be imagined.

The tour around the city, which I have made several times on the city side from the Porta del Popolo to the Porta San Paolo, can be made in a good three hours or four, traveling light and at a walk; the tour of the part on the other side of the river is made in an hour and a half at the most.

Among other pleasures that Rome furnished me in Lent were the sermons. There were excellent preachers, such as that renegade rabbi who preaches to the Jews on Saturday after dinner in the Church of the Trinity. There are always sixty Jews there; this number is compelled to attend. He was a very famous doctor among them, and by their very

---

[23] The passages criticized in the *Essays*, in order of mention, are these, or others like them: Fortune: II:4, p. 263, and *passim*. Heretic poets (Beza and Buchanan): II: 17, p. 502. Julian: II: 19, *passim*. Praying: I: 56, *passim*. Torture: I: 31, p. 155; II: 11, p. 314. Training a child: I: 26, p. 123.

Montaigne made no changes because of the criticisms, probably in part at least in order not to alter his self-portrait. In the *Essays* later he once alludes to his use of the word "fortune" (I: 56, p. 234), and once defends himself for praising heretics as poets (III: 10, p. 775).

[24] Paul de Foix (1528–84), to whom Montaigne dedicated La Boétie's French verses. After the death of Foix, Montaigne praised him highly in the *Essays* (III: 9, p. 731).

arguments, by their rabbis, and by the text of the Bible, he combats their belief. In that science and in the languages used in it he is admirable.

There was another preacher who preached to the Pope and the cardinals, named Padre Toledo (in depth of learning, in pertinence, and in readiness, he is a very rare man); another, very eloquent and popular, who was preaching to the Jesuits, with much ability, besides his excellent language; the last two are Jesuits. It is a marvel how much of a place this College holds in Christendom; and I believe there never was a brotherhood and body among us that held such a rank, or, to sum up, that produced such results as these men will, if their plans continue. They will soon possess all Christendom: it is a nursery of great men in every sort of greatness. It is the one limb of our Church that most threatens the heretics of our time.

One preacher's joke was that we turned our coaches into astrolabes. The commonest exercise of the Romans is to promenade through the streets; and ordinarily the enterprise of leaving the house is undertaken solely to go from street to street, without having any place in mind to stop at; and some streets are particularly affected to that use. To tell the truth, the greatest profit that is derived from this is to see the ladies at the windows, and notably the courtesans, who show themselves at their Venetian blinds with such treacherous artfulness that I have often marveled how they tantalize our eyes as they do; and often, having got off my horse immediately and obtained admission, I wondered at how much more beautiful they appeared to be than they really were. They know how to present themselves by their most agreeable feature; they will show you only the upper part of the face, or the lower, or the side, and cover themselves or show themselves in such a way that not one single ugly one is seen at the window. All the men are there taking off their hats and making deep bows, and receiving an ogling glance or two as they pass. The gain from having spent the night there for a crown, or for four, is to pay court to them the next day in public. Some ladies of quality are also seen at the windows, but of a different style, and with a bearing very easy to discern. On horseback you see better; but that is a matter either for unimportant folk like me or for the young men mounted on hired horses, which they show off. The people of rank go only in coaches; and the more licentious, in order to have more of a view upward, have the top of the coach open with skylights. That is what the preacher meant about astrolabes.

On Maundy Thursday in the morning, the Pope, in full pontificals, takes his stand on the first portico of Saint Peter's, on the second story, attended by the cardinals, himself holding a torch in his hand. There, on one side, a canon of Saint Peter's reads aloud a Latin bull by which are excommunicated an infinite variety of people, among others the Huguenots, under that very name, and all the princes who have appropriated some part of the territories of the Church; at which articles the cardinals de' Medici and Caraffa, who were next to the Pope, laughed very hard. This reading lasts a good hour and a half; for at each article that this canon reads in Latin, Cardinal Gonzaga on the other side, also uncovered, reads as much in Italian. After that the Pope threw this lighted torch down to the people, and, for sport or otherwise, Cardinal Gonzaga threw another; for there were three of them lighted. This falls on the people; down below the greatest scramble in the world ensues to see who will get a bit of this torch, and they fight very roughly with fists and sticks. While this condemnation is being read, there is also a big piece of black taffeta which hangs over the parapet of the said balcony in front of the Pope. The excommunication done, they turn up this black drape, disclosing another of a different color; the Pope then gives public blessings.

On these days they show the Veronica, which is a disfigured face, of a dark and somber color, in a square frame like a big mirror.[25] It is shown with great ceremony from the height of a pulpit five or six paces wide. The hands of the priest who holds it are clad in red gloves, and there are two or three other priests who support him. There is nothing viewed with such great reverence as this, the people prostrate on the ground, most of them with tears in their eyes, with cries of commiseration. A woman who they said was possessed of a spirit became frantic on seeing this face, screamed, stretched out and twisted her arms. These priests, walking around this pulpit, display the image to the people, now this way, now that; and at every movement the people to whom it is presented cry out.

They also show at the same time and with the same ceremony the lance-head in a crystal bottle. Several times on this day this exhibition takes place, with an assemblage of people so huge that even very far outside the church, as far as this pulpit can be seen, there is a tremendous crush of men and women.

It is a true papal court: the pomp of Rome, and its principal grandeur, lies in displays of devotion. It is fine to see the ardor for religion of so innumerable a people on these days.

They have a hundred brotherhoods and more, and there is hardly a man of quality who is not attached to some one of these; there are some for foreigners. Our kings belong to that of the Gonfalon. These private societies perform many acts of religious fellowship, which are principally practiced in Lent; but on this day they walk in companies, dressed in linen; each company has its fashion, white, red, blue, green, or black; most of them have their faces covered.

The noblest and most magnificent thing I have seen here or elsewhere is the incredible number of people scattered throughout the city on this day at their devotions, and especially in these companies. For besides a large number of others that we had seen by day and who had come to Saint Peter's, as night began this city seemed to be all on fire: these companies marching in order toward Saint Peter's, each man carrying a torch, and almost all these of white wax. I think there passed before me twelve thousand torches at the least; for from eight in the

---

[25] This is the cloth with which it is said Saint Veronica wiped the face of Jesus on the cross, and which retained his image in his blood.

evening until midnight the street was always full of this procession, conducted in such good and measured order that although there were various companies and parties, starting from various places, there was never a breach or interruption to be seen; each body having a large choir of music, always singing as they went, and in the center of the ranks a file of Penitents, who scourge themselves with ropes; there were five hundred of them at least, their backs all flayed and bleeding in a piteous fashion.

This is an enigma that I do not yet well understand. They are all torn and cruelly wounded, and torment and beat themselves without stopping. Yet to see their bearing, the steadiness of their steps, the firmness of their speech (for I heard several speak), and their faces (for many were uncovered in the street), it did not appear that they were even in the midst of a painful or indeed a serious action, and yet there were some as young as twelve or thirteen. Right in front of me there was a very young one who had a pleasant face; a young woman lamented to see him wound himself so. He turned toward us and said to her, laughing: "That's enough. Tell her that I'm doing this for her sins, not for mine." Not only do they show no distress or constraint in this action, but they do it cheerfully, or at least with such nonchalance that you see them talk with one another about other matters, laugh, yell in the street, run, and jump, as people do in a crowd so great that the ranks are broken.

There are men among them who carry wine, which they offer the Penitents to drink; some of them take a swallow. They also give them sugar candy; and very often those who carry this wine put some in their mouth and then blow it out and with it wet the end of the scourges, which are made of cord and become so clotted and glued together with blood that they have to be wet to separate the thongs; for some they blow this same wine on their wounds.

To see their shoes and hose, it is quite apparent that they are people of very little means who sell themselves for this service, at least most of them. I was told indeed that they greased their shoulders with something; but I have seen their wounds so raw and the beating so lengthy that there is no medicament that could take away the feeling of it; and then what do those who hire them do it for, if it is only a counterfeit?[26]

This ceremony has many other particularities. When they arrived at Saint Peter's they did nothing, except that they were shown the *Holy Face*, and then they went out again and made room for others.

On that day the ladies have great freedom; for all night the streets are full of them, and they almost all go on foot. However, in truth, the city seems to be very well-behaved, especially in this sort of debauchery. All oglings and amorous manifestations cease.

The handsomest sepulcher is that of the Santa Rotonda, because of the illuminations. Among other things, there are a great number of lights, from top to bottom, incessantly rolling and turning.

On the eve of Easter I saw at Saint John Lateran the heads of Saint

[26] Montaigne speaks of this scene also in the *Essays* (I: 14, p. 41).

Paul and Saint Peter that are shown there, which still have their flesh, color, and beard, as if they were alive: Saint Peter, a white and slightly longish face, his color ruddy and inclined to the sanguine, a forked gray beard, his head covered with a papal miter; Saint Paul, dark, his face broad and stouter, the head bigger, the beard gray, thick. They are up high in a special place. The way of showing them is that they call the people by the sound of bells, and by fits and starts lower a curtain behind which are these heads, side by side. They let them be seen for the time it takes to say an Ave Maria, and immediately raise the curtain again; after that they lower it again in the same way, and this up to three times. They repeat this exhibition four or five times during the day. The place is about as high as a pike, and then there is a heavy iron grill through which you look. They light several tapers around it on the outside; but it is hard to discern very clearly all the details. I saw them two or three times. The polish of these faces had some resemblance to our masks.

On the Wednesday after Easter, when Monsieur Maldonado, who was then in Rome, asked me what opinion I had of the mores of this city, and especially in the matter of religion, he found his judgment entirely in conformity with mine: that the common people were incomparably more devout in France than here; but the rich, and especially the courtiers, a little less. He told me further that to those who alleged that France was totally lost in heresy, and especially to Spaniards, of whom there are a great number in his College, he maintained that there were more men who were truly religious in the city of Paris alone than in all Spain put together.

They have their boats towed upstream on the river Tiber with ropes by three or four pairs of buffaloes.

I do not know how others feel about the air of Rome; for myself, I found it very pleasant and healthy. The sieur de Vialard said that he had lost his subjection to migraines here; which went to support the opinion of the people, that it is very bad for the feet and good for the head. There is nothing so hostile to my health as boredom and idleness; here I had always some occupation, if not as pleasant as I could have desired, at least sufficient to overcome boredom: like visiting the antiquities and the vineyards, which are gardens and pleasure spots of singular beauty, and where I learned how aptly art can make use of a rugged, hilly, and uneven spot; for here they derive from them charms that cannot be duplicated in our level places, and very artfully take advantage of this diversity. Among the most beautiful vineyards are those of the cardinals d'Este at Monte Cavallo, Farnese on the Palatine, Orsini, Sforza, Medici; that of Pope Julius, that of Madama;[27] the gardens of Farnese and of Cardinal Riario at Trastevere, and of Cesio outside the Porta del Popolo. These are beauties open to anyone who wants to enjoy them, and for whatever purpose, even to sleep there, even in company if the masters are not there, and they do not like to go there much.

[27] The duchess of Parma, daughter of Charles V.

Or I could go to hear sermons, which they have at all times, or theological disputations; or else sometimes visit some woman of the public sort, in which I found this disadvantage: that they sell their mere conversation as dear (which was what I was looking for, to hear them talk and be in on their subtleties), and are as sparing of it, as the whole business.

All these amusements kept me busy enough; for melancholy, which is the death of me, and irritability, I had no occasion, either inside or outside my house. Thus Rome is a pleasant place to live in; and I can argue from that how much I would have enjoyed it if I could have tasted it more privately; for in truth, despite my craft and the trouble I have taken, I have known it only by its public visage, which it offers to the meanest stranger.

On the last of March I had an attack of colic which lasted me all night but was bearable enough; it disturbed my belly with gripings and gave a sting to my urine beyond the usual. I passed some large gravel and two stones.

On Low Sunday I saw the ceremony of alms for maidens. The Pope has, besides his ordinary equipage, twenty-five horses that are led ahead of him with caparisons and saddlecloths of cloth of gold, very richly decked out, and ten or twelve mules with saddlecloths of crimson velvet, all this led by his armed lackeys on foot; his litter covered with crimson velvet. In front of him four men on horseback carried, on the end of certain staffs covered with red velvet and gilded at the handle and the ends, four red hats. He himself was on his mule. The cardinals who followed him were also on their mules, decked in their pontifical vestments; the tails of their gowns were attached with a cord to their mules' headstalls. The maidens were a hundred and seven in number, each accompanied by an old female relative. After Mass they came out of the church and formed a long procession. On their return from there, one after the other, passing through the choir of the Church of Santa Maria sopra Minerva, where this ceremony is performed, they kissed the Pope's feet; and he, after giving them the benediction, gave each one with his own hand a white damask purse containing a promissory note. It is understood that when they have found a husband they collect their alms, which is thirty-five crowns a head, besides a white dress which they each get for the wedding and which is worth five crowns. Their faces are covered with a linen veil, with only a place open for seeing.

I used to say about the advantages of Rome, among other things, that it is the most universal city in the world, a place where strangeness and differences of nationality are considered least; for by its nature it is a city pieced together out of foreigners; everyone is as if at home. Its ruler embraces all Christendom with his authority; his princely jurisdiction is binding on foreigners in their own homes just as here. At his own election and that of all the princes and grandees of his court the consideration of their origin has no weight. The freedom of the government of Venice, and the advantages of its trade, people it with foreigners; but they are nevertheless as if at someone else's house. Here they

hold their own offices, property, and responsibilities; for it is the seat of
ecclesiastics. You see as many or more foreigners in Venice (for the influx of foreigners you see in France, in Germany, or elsewhere, does not
come into comparison with the number here), but of resident, domiciled
foreigners, far fewer. The common people are no more dismayed at our
fashion in dress, or the Spanish or German fashion, than at their own;
and you hardly see a beggar who does not ask alms of us in our own
language.

I therefore sought, and employed all my five natural senses, to ob-
tain the title of Roman citizen, were it only for the ancient honor and
the religious memory of its authority. I found some difficulty in this;
however, I surmounted it without any Frenchman's favor or even knowledge. The authority of the Pope was employed in it through the medium
of Filippo Musotti,[28] his majordomo, who had taken a singular liking to
me and went to great pains for this. And letters-patent were dispatched
to me on "the 3rd day before the Ides of March, 1581," which were delivered to me on the 5th of April, very authentic, in the same form and
favorable terms as were used for the lord Giacomo Buoncompagno,
duke of Sora, son of the Pope. It is a vain title; but at all events I received much pleasure in having obtained it.[29]

On April 3rd I left Rome early in the morning by the Porta San
Lorenzo Tiburtina. I went along a rather level road, through a country for the most part fertile in wheat, and, like all the approaches to
Rome, little inhabited. I crossed the river Teverone, which is the ancient
Anio, first by the bridge of Mammolo, and second by the Lucano bridge,
which still retains its ancient name. On this bridge there are some ancient inscriptions, and the principal one is very legible. There are also
two or three Roman tombs along this road; there are no other traces of
antiquity and very little of that big ancient paving, and yet this is the
Via Tiburtina. I came to dine at

TIVOLI, fifteen miles. This is the ancient Tiburtum, lying at the roots
of the mountains, the town extending along the first rather steep slope,
which makes its situation and view very rich, for it commands an im-
mense plain in all directions, and great Rome itself. Its view is toward
the sea, and it has the mountains behind it. This river Teverone bathes
it, and near there takes a marvelous leap, coming down from the mountains and disappearing through a hole in the rock five or six hundred
paces below, and then coming into the plain, where it meanders along
playfully and joins the Tiber a little above the city.

Here are to be seen that famous palace and garden of the cardinal
of Ferrara:[30] it is a very beautiful thing, but incomplete in many parts,
and the work is not being continued by the present cardinal. Here I
examined everything most particularly. I would try to describe it here,

---

[28] Alessandro (not Filippo) Musotti, prefect of the apostolic palace, later to be
papal nuncio at Venice.

[29] Near the end of the chapter "Of Vanity" (Essays III: 9, p. 765), Montaigne
quotes this document in full.

[30] Cardinal d'Este. The palace is the Villa d'Este.

but there are published books and pictures on the subject. The gushing of an infinity of jets of water checked and launched by a single spring that can be worked from far off, I had seen elsewhere on my trip, both at Florence and at Augsburg, as has been stated above. The music of the organ, which is real music and a natural organ, though always playing the same thing, is effected by means of the water, which falls with great violence into a round arched cave and agitates the air that is in there and forces it, in order to get out, to go through the pipes of the organ and supply it with wind. Another stream of water, driving a wheel with certain teeth on it, causes the organ keyboard to be struck in a certain order; so you hear an imitation of the sound of trumpets. In another place you hear the song of birds, which are little bronze flutes that you see at regals; they give a sound like those little earthenware pots full of water that little children blow into by the spout, this by an artifice like that of the organ; and then by other springs they set in motion an owl, which, appearing at the top of the rock, makes this harmony cease instantly, for the birds are frightened by his presence; and then he leaves the place to them again. This goes on alternately as long as you want.

Elsewhere there issues a noise as of cannon shots; elsewhere a more frequent smaller noise, as of harquebus shots. This is done by a sudden fall of water into channels; and the air, laboring at the same time to get out, engenders this noise. All these inventions, or similar ones, produced by these same natural causes, I have seen elsewhere.

There are ponds or reservoirs, with a stone margin all around and many tall freestone pillars above this parapet, about four paces apart from each other. From the head of these pillars water comes out with great force, not upward, but toward the pond. The mouths, being thus turned inward and facing one another, cast and scatter the water into this pond with such force that these shafts of water come to meet and clash in the air, and produce a thick and continual rain falling into the pond. The sun, falling upon it, engenders, both at the bottom of this pond and in the air and all around this place, a rainbow so natural and vivid that it lacks nothing of the one we see in the sky. This I had not seen elsewhere.

Under the palace there are great hollows, artificially made, and air holes which give out a cold vapor and cool off all the lower part of this house enormously; this part, however, is not completed.

I also saw many excellent statues there, and notably one sleeping nymph, one dead one, a celestial Pallas, the Adonis[31] in the home of the bishop of Aquino; the bronze she-wolf and the boy taking out a thorn, in the Capitol; the Laocoön and the Antinous of the Belvedere; the Comedy in the Capitol, the Satyr in the vineyard of Cardinal Sforza; and of modern workmanship, the Moses[32] in the sepulcher of San Pietro in

---

[31] The passage that follows, from "the Adonis" to "in Rome," at the end of the paragraph, seems to be a later addition referring to original statues in Rome, not, as one might suppose, to copies at Tivoli.

[32] By Michelangelo.

Vinculis, the beautiful woman at the feet of Pope Paul III in the new Church of Saint Peter—these are the statues I have liked best in Rome.

It was to rival this place that Pratolino was built. As to the richness and beauty of the grottoes, Florence is infinitely superior; as to abundance of water, Ferrara;[33] in variety of sports and amusing mechanisms derived from water, they are equal, unless the Florentine has a little more elegance in the arrangement and order of the whole body of the place; Ferrara excels in ancient statues, and in the palace, Florence.[34] In situation and beauty of prospect Ferrara is infinitely superior; and I should say the same in all nature's favors, if it did not have this extreme misfortune, that all its waters, except the fountain that is in the little garden all the way at the top, and which is seen in one of the palace rooms, is only water from the Teverone, a branch of which the cardinal has taken over and diverted to a separate channel for his service. If this water were as clear and good to drink as on the contrary it is muddy and ugly, this place would be incomparable, especially its great fountain, which is of the finest workmanship, and more beautiful to see with its adjuncts than anything else either in this garden or elsewhere. At Pratolino, on the contrary, what water there is is spring water and drawn from far away. Because the Teverone comes down from much higher mountains, the inhabitants of this place use it as they will, and the example of several private individuals makes this work of the cardinal's less marvelous.

I left here the next day after dinner, and passed by a great ruin on the right-hand side of the road as we came back, which they say comprises six miles and is a villa. They say it is the *Praedium* of the Emperor Hadrian.

On this road from Tivoli to Rome there is a stream of sulphurous water that cuts across the road. The edges of the channel are all whitened with sulphur, and it gives off a smell for more than half a league away. They do not use it for medicine. In this stream there are small bodies formed of the scum of the water, so closely resembling our sugar-coated candies that there are few people that would not be fooled; and the inhabitants of Tivoli make all sorts of things of this same material, of which I bought two boxes for 7 sous 6 deniers.

There are some antiquities in the town of Tivoli, such as two baths of a very ancient shape, and the remains of a temple in which there are still several pillars entire; which temple they say was that of their ancient Sibyl. However, on the cornices of this church you still see five or six large letters which were not continued; for the following part of the

[33] Throughout this paragraph Montaigne uses "Ferrara" to refer to the Villa d'Este at Tivoli, "Florence" to refer to Pratolino (see pp. 928–29).

[34] The punctuation of the text of this passage is confusing and contradictory. Some editors take it to mean this: "Ferrara excels in ancient statues and in the palace. Florence infinitely surpasses Ferrara in situation of place and beauty of prospect; and I should say in all nature's favors . . ." The part about the Teverone that follows, however, seems to me compatible only with the reading given in our text above, and thus decisive.

wall is still entire. I do not know if there were any letters before these, for that part is broken; but in what can be seen, there is only CE . . . ELLIUS L. F.[35] I do not know what that can be. We returned in the evening to

ROME, fifteen miles; and I made all this trip back by coach without any discomfort, contrary to my wont. They have an observance here much more careful than elsewhere, for they make a distinction between the streets, the quarters of the town, even the apartments of their houses, in respect to health, and set so much store by this that they change their habitation with the seasons; and even of those who rent them, some keep two or three rented palaces at very great expense, so as to move with the seasons in accordance with their doctors' orders.

On April 15th I went to say good-by to the Master of the Sacred Palace[36] and his colleague, who urged me not to make use of the censorship of my book, in which censorship some other Frenchmen had informed them there were many stupid things; saying that they honored both my intention and affection for the Church and my ability, and thought so well of my frankness and conscience that they left it to myself to cut out of my book, when I wanted to republish it, whatever I found too licentious in it, and among other things the uses of the word "fortune." It seemed to me that I left them well pleased with me; and to excuse themselves for having scrutinized my book so attentively and condemned it in certain details, they cited me many books of our time by cardinals and churchmen of very good reputation, censured for a few such imperfections which did not affect in the least the reputation of the author or of the work as a whole. They urged me to help the Church by my eloquence (those are their courteous formulas) and to make my abode in this city, at peace and without interference from them. These are persons of great authority and potential cardinals.

We were eating artichokes, beans, and peas around mid-March. In April it is daylight at their ten o'clock, and I think on the longest days at nine.[37]

At this time I made the acquaintance, among others, of a Pole, the most intimate friend of the late Cardinal Hosyusz, who presented me with two copies of the booklet he had written on the cardinal's death and corrected with his own hand.

The pleasures of residence in this city increased by more than half with acquaintance. I never tasted air more temperate for me or more suited to my constitution.

On April 18th I went to see the inside of the palace of Signor Giovanni Giorgio Cesarini, where there are numberless rare antiquities, and

---

[35] The inscription may have read CURANTE L. CELLIO. L. F., "Supervised by L. Cellius, son of Lucius." This Cellius was at one time in charge of many public works in Rome.

[36] See above, pp. 955–56.

[37] Around 5 A.M. and 4 A.M. respectively, counting from sundown the day before.

notably the authentic busts of Zeno, Posidonius, Euripides, and Car-
neades, as their very ancient Greek inscriptions tell. He has also the
portraits of the most beautiful living Roman ladies and of the Signora
Clelia-Fascia Farnese, his wife, who is, if not the most comely, beyond
comparison the most lovable woman then in Rome, or, as far as I know,
anywhere else. This man says he is of the race of the Caesars, and as
such bears by his own right the banner of the Roman nobility; he is rich,
and has on his coat of arms the column with the bear fastened to it, and
above the column an eagle with wings spread.

A great beauty of Rome is the vineyards and gardens, and the season
for them is well on in the summer.

Italy: From Rome to Loreto and La Villa (April 19-May 7, 1581)

On Wednesday, the 19th of April, I left Rome after dinner, and we
were escorted as far as the Ponte Molle by Messieurs de Noirmoutier,
de la Trémouille, and du Bellai, and other gentlemen. Having crossed
this bridge, we turned to the right, leaving on our left hand the main
road to Viterbo, by which we had come to Rome, and on our right hand
the Tiber and the hills. We followed an open and uneven road, through
country not very fertile and uninhabited, and passed the place they call
Prima Porta, which is the first gate, seven miles from Rome; and some
say that the ancient walls of Rome went as far as this, which I do not
consider at all likely. Along this road, which is the ancient Via Flaminia,
there are some unknown and rare antiquities. We came to sleep at

CASTELNUOVO, sixteen miles, a little walled village belonging to the
house of Colonna, buried among hills in a site that strongly reminded
me of the fertile approaches to our Pyrenees on the Aigues-Caudes road.
The next day, April 20th, we continued through the same country, hilly
but very pleasant, fertile and thickly inhabited, and arrived, in a low
valley along the Tiber, at

BORGHETTO, a little walled village belonging to Duke Ottavio Farnese. We left here after dinner, and after following a very pleasant
valley between these hills, we crossed the Tiber at Orte, where big piles
of stone are still to be seen, relics of the bridge that Augustus had built
there to connect the country of the Sabines, the one toward which we
were heading, with that of the Falisci, which is on the other side. Afterward we came upon Otricoli, a tiny little town belonging to the cardinal
of Perugia. In front of this town you see, in a beautiful site, some great
and important ruins; the hilly and extremely pleasant country offers a
very humpy aspect, but very fertile all over and thickly populated.

On this road one comes across an inscription in which the Pope says that he made and leveled this road, which he calls Via Buoncompagna, after his name. This custom of thus putting in writing and leaving a testimony of such works, which is seen in Italy and Germany, is a very good spur; and a man who does not care about the public will be motivated to do something good by this hope of reputation. In truth, most of this road used to be difficult going, but it has now been made passable even for coaches for as far as Loreto. We came to sleep at

NARNI, ten miles, Narnia in Latin, a little town belonging to the Church, situated on the top of a rock, at the foot of which rolls the river Nera, Nar in Latin. On one side the said town looks out over a very pleasant plain in which the said river plays and winds around itself curiously. In the square there is a very beautiful fountain. I saw the cathedral and noticed this, that the tapestry in it has French inscriptions and rhymes in our ancient language. I was unable to learn how that came about; but I did learn from the people that from time immemorial they have had a great inclination in our favor. The said tapestry bears a picture of the Passion and occupies one whole side of the nave.

Because Pliny says that in this place is found a certain kind of earth that is softened by heat and dried by rains, I asked the inhabitants about it; they knew nothing about it. A mile from there they have some cold springs which have the same effect as our hot ones; sick people use them, but they are not well known. The inn, according to Italian standards, is one of the good ones; yet we had no candle, but oil light everywhere.

On the 21st, early in the morning, we descended into a very pleasant valley in which the said river Nera runs, which river we crossed over a bridge at the gates of Terni, which we passed through; and in the square we saw a very ancient column that is still standing. I perceived no inscription on it, but it has beside it the statue of a lion in relief, beneath which in old letters there is a dedication to Neptune, and also the said Neptunus carved in relief in marble with his train. In this same square there is an inscription that they have set up in a prominent place: to one "A. Pompeius A. F., the inhabitants of this town, which is called Interamna, because of the river Nera that hems it in on one side, and another stream on the other, have erected a statue for the services he has rendered to this people." The statue is not there, but I could judge the age of this inscription by the form of writing with a diphthong *periculeis*[1] and similar words.

This is a beautiful town in a singularly pleasant site. To the rear, from where we came, it has the very fertile plain of this valley, and beyond, the most highly cultivated inhabited hillsides; and among other things, so many olive trees that there is nothing more beautiful to see, since among these hillsides there are sometimes very high mountains which are seen to be cultivated and bearing all sorts of fruits even to the summit. I had my colic very badly, and it had gripped me for twenty-four hours and was then in its last effort; however, I did not fail for all that to enjoy the beauty of that place.

---

[1] Instead of the classical form *periculis*.

Beyond there we penetrated a little further into the Apennines, and found that this new road that the Pope has constructed there is in truth a beautiful, great, and noble work of improvement, great in expense and convenience. The people of the neighborhood were constrained to build it; but they do not complain so much about this as that without any compensation, even where there happened to be tillable fields, orchards, and the like, nothing was spared for this highway. We saw on our right hand a pleasant hilltop occupied by a tiny little town. The people call it Colle Scipoli: they say that in ancient times it was Castrum Scipionis. The other mountains are higher, arid, and stony. Between these and the bed of a winter torrent, we came to

SPOLETO, eighteen miles, a famous and commodious town, situated among these mountains and at their foot. Here we were compelled to show our health certificate, not because of the plague, which was not then in any part of Italy, but for the fear they are in of one Petrino, their fellow townsman, who is the most notorious robber outlaw in Italy and the most famous for his exploits, by whom they and the towns round about are afraid of being surprised.

This region is dotted with many taverns; and where there are no buildings, they have arbors, where there are tables spread with boiled eggs and cheese and wine. They have no butter here, and serve everything fricasseed in oil.

On leaving there, this same day after dinner, we found ourselves in the valley of Spoleto, which is the most beautiful plain between the mountains that it is possible to see, two big Gascon leagues wide. We descried many houses on the nearby crests. The road in this plain is a continuation of that road of the Pope's that I have just spoken of, in a deliberate straight line like a racecourse. We left many towns on either side, among others, on the right hand, the town of Trevi. Servius says, speaking of Virgil, that this is the "olive-bearing Mutusca" that he speaks of in Book Seven.[2] Others deny it and argue to the contrary. At all events, it is a town perched on a high mountain, and in one place extending halfway down all along its slope. This mountain, covered all over with olive trees, is a very pleasant location. By this new road, restored three years ago, which is the finest that can be seen, we came in the evening to

FOLIGNO, twelve miles, a handsome town situated on this plain, which on arrival reminded me of the plan of Sainte-Foy-la-Grande, although it is much richer, and the town beyond comparison much more beautiful and populous. There is a little river or stream that is called Topino. In ancient times this town was called Fulignium, others say Fulcinia; it was built on the site of the Forum Flaminium.

The hostelries on this route, or most of them, are comparable to the French, except that the horses get hardly anything but hay to eat. They serve fish marinated, and have little of it fresh. Throughout Italy they serve beans raw, and also peas and green almonds, and they seldom

[2] *Aeneid* VII. 711: "oliviferaeque Mutuscae."

cook the artichokes. Their floors are paved with tiles. They attach their oxen by the muzzle with a piece of iron that pierces the part between the nostrils, like buffaloes. The baggage mules, of which they have plenty, and very handsome ones, have their forefeet shod not in our way but with a round shoe going all around the hoof and bigger than the hoof. In various places here you come upon monks who give holy water to passers-by and expect alms from them, and many children asking for alms, promising to say their full ten paternosters, which they show in their hands, for whoever gives them money. The wines here are not much good.

The next morning, after leaving this beautiful plain, we again headed along the mountain road, where we again came across many beautiful level spots, sometimes high up, sometimes at the foot of the mountains. But toward the beginning of this morning we had for some time a very handsome view of a thousand varied hills, clad on all sides with all kinds of beautifully shady fruit trees and the finest wheat fields possible, often in a place so steep and precipitous that it was a miracle that even horses could get to them; the most beautiful valleys, an infinite number of streams, so many houses and villages here and there, that I was reminded of the approaches to Florence, except that there is no palace or house of any distinction here; and there the terrain is dry and barren for the most part, whereas in these hills there is not an inch of useless ground. It is true that the spring season brought out the best in them. Often, very far above our heads, we would see a beautiful village, and below our feet, as if at the Antipodes, another, each one having many and various attractions. This fact itself gives them no mean luster, that among such fertile mountains as these the Apennines show their frowning and inaccessible peaks, from which you see many torrents rolling down, which, having lost their first fury, soon after, in these valleys, turn into very pleasant and very gentle streams. Among these summits you discover, both on the heights and down below, many fertile plateaus, sometimes so large as to extend out of sight when looked at from a certain angle. It does not seem to me that any painting can represent so rich a landscape.

From here on the appearance of our road varied, now one way, now another; but the going was always very easy; and we came for dinner to

La Muccia, twenty miles, a tiny little town situated on the river Chienti.

From here we followed a low and easy road through these mountains, and because I had given a box on the ear to our driver, which is a great outrage according to the usage of the country—witness the driver who killed the prince of Tresignano—seeing myself no longer followed by the said driver, and being privately a little concerned that he might lodge a complaint against me or cause some other trouble, I stopped, contrary to my plan (which was to go to Tolentino), for supper at

Valchimara, eight miles, a little village and relay station, on the said river Chienti.

The next day, Sunday, we still followed this valley between cultivated and fertile mountains as far as Tolentino, a tiny little town through
which we passed, and afterward found the country getting flatter, and
we now had on our flanks only very accessible low hills; this country
reminding me very much of the Agenais where it is prettiest, along the
Garonne, except that here, as in Switzerland, you see no castles or gentlemen's houses, but there are many villages or towns on the hillsides.
This was all a very pretty road, following the Chienti, and paved with
bricks toward the end, by which we came to dine at

MACERATA, eighteen miles, a beautiful town of the size of Libourne,
situated on a height approximately round in shape, and rising equally
on all sides toward its center. There are not many handsome buildings.
I noticed here a freestone palace, all cut on the outside into square dia-
mond points, like the palace of the Cardinal d'Este in Ferrara; this form
of structure is pleasing to the sight. The entry to this town is a new gate,
on which is inscribed "Porta Buoncompagna," in letters of gold; it is
part of the series of roads that this Pope has rebuilt. Here is the seat of
the legate for the country of the Marches.

On these roads they give you the boilings of the local wine, when it is
their own wines that they offer: for they boil and cook it until half of it
is gone, to make it better.

We could tell indeed that we were on the highway to Loreto, so full
were the roads of people going and coming: many not only private individuals but companies of rich people making the journey on foot, dressed
as pilgrims; and some with a banner and then a crucifix going on ahead—
and these dressed in livery.

After dinner we went through ordinary country, now cutting across
plains and a few rivers, and then a few easy hills; but the whole very
fertile, and the road for the most part paved with bricks laid edgewise.
We passed the town of Recanati, a long town situated on a height and
stretched out following the folds and contours of its hill, and came in the
evening to

LORETO, fifteen miles. This is a little village enclosed in walls and
fortified against the incursion of the Turks, standing on a slightly raised
site, looking over a very beautiful plain and, from very near, the Adriatic
Sea or Gulf of Venice; so that they say that when the weather is good,
they can make out beyond the gulf the mountains of Sclavonia. In short,
it is a very beautiful site.

There are hardly any other inhabitants than those in the service of
this cult, such as many landlords—and yet the inns are rather dirty—and
many tradesmen, to wit, sellers of wax, of images, beads, Agnus Dei,
Salvators,[3] and such wares, for which there are a large number of handsome and richly furnished shops. I left nearly fifty good crowns there,
for my part.

The priests, churchmen, and College of Jesuits are all gathered in
one big palace which is not old, where there also resides a governor—a

[3] Medals or images of the Lamb of God and of the Savior.

churchman, to whom one applies for all things—under the authority of the legate and the Pope.

The place of devotion is a very small house, very old and mean-looking, built of brick, longer than it is wide. Across the head they have built a partition, which has an iron door on each side; in between the two doors an iron grating; all this crude, old, and without any show of richness. This grill occupies the width between one door and the other; through it you can see right to the end of this little building; and this end, which is about the fifth part of the size of the building, is the location of the principal shrine. Here you see high up on the wall the image of Our Lady, made, they say, of wood; all the rest is so heavily adorned with rich votive tablets from so many places and princes, that all the way to the ground there is not an inch of space empty and not covered with some plate of silver or gold.

I was able to find room there only with the greatest difficulty, and as a great favor, to place a tablet on which there are four silver figures attached: that of Our Lady, my own, that of my wife, that of my daughter. At the foot of mine there is engraved on the silver: "Michel de Montaigne, Gascon Frenchman, Knight of the Order of the King, 1581"; at that of my wife's, "Françoise de La Chassaigne, his wife"; at that of my daughter's, "Léonor de Montaigne, his only daughter."[4] All are in a row on their knees on the tablet, and Our Lady above them in the foreground.

There is an entry into this chapel other than by the two doors I have spoken of, which entry leads to the outside. So as you enter the chapel by that door, my tablet is located on the left hand, opposite the door that is in this corner; and I left it very carefully fixed and nailed there. I had had a little silver chain and ring made with which to hang it on some nail; but they preferred to attach it completely. In this little place is the fireplace of the building, which you see by turning up some old curtains that cover it. Few are permitted to enter; indeed, by the sign on the front of the door, which is of very richly worked metal (and furthermore, there is an iron grill in front of this door), the restriction is that without the governor's permission no one shall enter.

Among other things, for its rarity, they had left with the other, rich presents the candle that a Turk had recently sent here after making a vow to Our Lady of Loreto when he was in some extreme necessity and wanting to catch hold of any sort of rope to help himself.

The other and larger part of this little hut serves as a chapel. It has no daylight, and its altar is beneath the grill against this partition that I have spoken of. In this chapel there is not an ornament, no bench, no railing, no painting or tapestry on the wall: for of itself it serves as a reliquary. One may not wear any sword or weapon here, and there is neither precedence nor regard to high rank.

We received our Easter Sacrament in this chapel, which not all are permitted to do, since there is another place reserved for this purpose

---

[4] These inscriptions are all in Latin.

because of the great crowd of people who ordinarily come to receive Communion. There are so many people who come to this chapel at all hours that you have to see to it early to get a place there. A German Jesuit said Mass for me and administered the Communion to me.

People are forbidden to scratch anything from this wall; and if it were permitted to take anything away, there would not be enough to last three days. This place is full of innumerable miracles, for which I refer to the books; but there are several, and very recent ones, involving mishaps that have befallen those who out of devotion have carried away something from this building, even with the Pope's permission; and a small fragment of brick which had been removed at the time of the Council of Trent has been brought back.

The four walls of this hut are covered and reinforced on the outside by an extremely rich and elaborately carved screen, made of the finest marble that can be had anywhere; few pieces of workmanship are to be seen more exquisite and excellent than this. All around and above this square structure is a beautiful big church; many handsome chapels all around; tombs, and among others that of Cardinal d'Amboise, which Cardinal d'Armagnac has had erected there. This little square structure is like the choir of other churches; there is a choir, but it is in a corner. All this great church is covered with tablets, paintings, and stories. We saw there many rich ornaments, and I was astonished that there were not even more to be seen, in view of the renown of this church, which has been famous for so long. I believe they melt down the old things and use them for other purposes. They estimate the alms in coined money at ten thousand crowns.

There is more show of religion here than in any place I have seen.

What is lost—I mean of money or anything else not merely worth picking up, but worth stealing for people of that profession—the person who finds it puts into a certain public place set aside for this purpose; and whoever wants to get it back gets it back there with no questions asked. When I was there, there were many such things—beads, handkerchiefs, unclaimed purses—that were there for the first comer to take.

In what you buy for the service of the church and to leave there, no artisan wants anything for his labor, in order, they say, to have a share in the grace. You pay only for the silver or the wood. Alms or liberality are permitted, but in fact they refuse it. The church people are as obliging as possible in everything: for confession, for Communion, or for anything else, they take nothing. It is usual to give money to some priest of your choice to distribute to the poor in your name when you have left.

As I was in that sanctuary, along comes a man who offers the first priest he meets a silver cup, saying that he had made a vow to do so; and because he had vowed to spend twelve crowns, which the cup did not amount to, he promptly paid the surplus to the said priest, who argued for the payment of the money as for a thing very exactly due, in order to help in the complete and conscientious execution of his promise; that done, he had this man enter this sanctuary, offer this chalice himself to Our Lady, and say a short prayer there; and the money he threw into the common alms box. These examples they see every day, and they are pretty nonchalant about them. Not everyone who wants to is readily allowed to give; at least it is a favor to be accepted.

I stayed here Monday, Tuesday, and Wednesday morning; after Mass we left. But, to say a word about my experience of this place, which I liked very much: there at the same time was Michel Marteau, seigneur de la Chapelle, a Parisian, a very rich young man with a big retinue. I had him and some of his attendants give me a very particular and careful account of the facts of the cure, which he said he had derived from this place, of one leg of his; it is not possible to represent better or more exactly the effect of a miracle. All the surgeons of Paris and Italy had failed at it. He had spent more than three thousand crowns on it: his knee, swollen, useless, and very painful for more than three years, by this time worse, more red and inflamed, and swollen to the point of giving him a fever; at that point, after abandoning all other medicaments and aids for several days, while sleeping, suddenly he dreams that he is cured and he seems to see a flash of lightning; he wakes up, cries out that he is cured, calls his men, gets up, walks around, which he had never done since his malady; the swelling in his knee goes down, the withered and virtually dead skin all around his knee continues to mend ever since, without any other sort of aid. Now completely cured, he has returned to Loreto; for it was on another trip a month or two before that he had been cured, and he had meanwhile been in Rome with us. From his own mouth and from all his men that is all you can get for certain.

The miracle of the transporting of that little house, which they hold to be the very one in which Jesus Christ was born in Nazareth—its removal first to Sclavonia, and then near here, and finally here—is represented on large marble tablets in the church, attached all along the pillars, in Italian, Sclavonian, French, German, and Spanish. In the choir there hangs an ensign of our kings, and no arms of any other king.

They say that they often see the Sclavonians come to this devotion in large groups, with shouts as soon as they discover the church from the sea, and then on the spot so many protestations and promises to Our Lady to have her return to them, and so many regrets for having given her occasion to abandon them, that it is a wonder.

I found out that from Loreto it is possible to go along the seashore to Naples in eight days, by easy stages, a trip I would like to make. You have to pass by way of Pescara and the city of Chieti, where there is a mail carrier that leaves every Sunday for Naples.

I offered money to a number of priests; most of them were obstinate in refusing it, and those that did accept some did so with all the difficulties in the world.

They store and keep their grain here in cellars underneath the street.

It was on April 25th that I offered my ex-voto.

The trip from Rome to Loreto, which took us four days and a half, cost me six crowns in coin, which are fifty sous apiece, per horse, and the man who rented us the horses fed them and us. The bargain is disadvantageous, inasmuch as they hurry your daily journeys because of the expense they have, and then have you treated as stingily as they can.

On the 26th I went to see the port three miles beyond, which is handsome; and there is a fort that belongs to the community of Recanati.

Don Luca Giovanni, the beneficiary, and Giovanni Gregorio da Cagli, custodian of the sacristy, gave me their names, so that if I had business with them either for myself or for others, I might write to them; these men did many courteous things for me. The former is in charge of this little chapel, and would not take anything from me. I am obliged to them for what they did for me and for their courteous words.

On the said Wednesday after dinner I followed along a road through fertile, open, and varied countryside, and came for supper to

ANCONA, fifteen miles. This is the chief town of the Marches; to the Latins the Marches were Picoenum. It is thickly populated, especially with Greeks, Turks, and Sclavonians; very mercantile, well built, flanked by two big headlands that run down into the sea, on one of which there is a large fort, by way of which we arrived. On the other, which is very near, there is a church. Between these two headlands and on their slopes, on either side, this city is set; but the main part is situated at the bottom of the valley and along the sea, where there is a very fine port in which there is still to be seen a great arch in honor of the Emperor Trajan, his wife, and his sister.

They say that one may often cross to Sclavonia in eight, ten, or twelve hours. I believe that for six crowns or a little more I could have found a bark that would have taken me to Venice. I gave thirty-three demi-pistoles for the hire of eight horses as far as Lucca, which is about eight days' journey. The driver has to feed the horses, and in case I am on the road four or five days more than the eight, I have the horses free for that time, and need only pay the expenses of the horses and the boys.

This country is full of excellent setters, and for six crowns there would be found some for sale. There were never so many quails to eat, but very lean.

I stayed on the 27th until after dinner, to see the beauty and the configuration of this town. At San Ciriaco, which is the church on one of the two headlands, there are more famous relics than in any other church in the world, and they were shown to us.

We verified the fact that the quails come over here from Sclavonia in great abundance, and that every night people stretch the nets on the shore on this side, and call them with a counterfeit call of theirs; and they call them back down from way up in the air, where they are in passage; and they say that around the month of September they go back across the sea to Sclavonia.

In the night I heard a cannon shot. From the Abruzzi on, in the kingdom of Naples and beyond the city, at every league there is a tower; the first one that discovers a corsair galley makes a signal with fire to the second watchtower, the second to the third, with such rapidity that they have found that in an hour the warning runs from the end of Italy as far as Venice.

Ancona was so called in ancient times from the Greek word, because of the angle that the sea forms in this place;[5] for its two horns advance and make a deep cove, where the town is protected in front by these two headlands and the sea, and also behind by a high rise, where formerly there used to be a fortress. There is also a Greek church, and over the door, on an old stone, some letters that I think are Sclavonian. The women here are generally beautiful, and there are many fine men and good artisans.

After dinner we followed the seacoast, which is gentler and more accessible than our ocean coast, and cultivated all the way to the water, and came to sleep at

SINIGAGLIA, twenty miles, a beautiful little town situated in a very beautiful plain right next to the sea, and it makes a fine port; for a river coming down from the mountains washes it on one side. They are making it into a channel studded and lined with large wooden piles on either side, where boats take shelter; and the entry to it is closed. I saw no antiquities here; besides, we stayed outside of town in a handsome hostelry which is the only one in this place. They formerly called it Senogallia, from our ancestors who settled here after Camillus had beaten them; it is in the jurisdiction of the duke of Urbino.

I did not feel very well. The day I left Rome, as Monsieur d'Ossat was walking with me, I tried to salute another gentleman, with such heedlessness that with my right thumb I wounded the corner of my right eye so that the blood immediately came out, and it has been very red for a long time. Then it got better; and "then there was pain in that sinister thumbnail."[6]

I was forgetting to say that at Ancona, in the Church of San Ciriaco, there is a low tombstone of one "Antonia, a Rocamoro on her father's side, a Valletta on her mother's, a Frenchwoman from Guienne, married to Paciotto of Urbino, a Portuguese,"[7] who has been buried ten or twelve years.

We left here early in the morning and followed the seashore by a very pleasant road. Near our dinnertime we crossed the river Metro, Metaurus, over a large wooden bridge, and dined at

FANO, fifteen miles, a little town in a beautiful and very fertile plain next to the sea, rather badly built, heavily walled. We were very well treated here as for bread, wine, and fish; the lodging is not worth much. It has this advantage over the other towns on this coast, like Sinigaglia, Pesaro, and others, that it has an abundance of fresh water, many public fountains and private wells, whereas the others have to go as far as the mountains to fetch their water. Here we saw a big ancient arch on which there is an inscription under the name of Augustus, "who had given walls to the city." The town used to be called Fanum, and was Fanum Fortunae.[8]

---

[5] Ἀγκών, elbow, or bend. It was founded by Doric Greeks from Syracuse.

[6] This remark in Latin, seemingly a quotation, plays on the two meanings of *sinistrum*: left (hand), and sinister. Thus his right nail became left (sinister).

[7] Montaigne quotes the inscription in Latin.

[8] The Temple of Fortune.

Almost everywhere in Italy they sift their flour with wheels, whereby a baker does more work in an hour than we do in four.

You find rhymers at almost all the hostelries who make rhymes on the spot, suitable for the persons present. There are instruments in all the shops, even those of the clothes menders at the street corners.

This town is famous above all those in Italy for beautiful women; we saw none but very ugly ones; and when I inquired of a good man of the town, he told me that that time had passed.

On this route you pay about ten sous per meal, twenty sous a day per man; the horse, for hire and expenses, about thirty sous; which makes fifty sous.

This town belongs to the Church.

We abandoned the idea of going a little farther on this same road to see Pesaro, a beautiful town and worth seeing, and then Rimini, and then ancient Ravenna; and especially, at Pesaro, a handsome building, strangely situated, which the duke of Urbino is having built, so I was told. That is the road down to Venice.

We left the coast and took our left, following a broad plain through which the Metaurus passes. You discover everywhere, on either hand, very beautiful hillsides, and the aspect of this countryside is not unlike the plain of Blaignac at Castillon. In this plain, on the other side of this river, the battle took place which Salinator and Claudius Nero fought against Hasdrubal, in which Hasdrubal was killed. At the entrance to the mountains which you encounter at the end of this plain, right at the entrance, is

FOSSOMBRONE, fifteen miles, belonging to the duke of Urbino, a town lying against the slope of a mountain, having at the base one or two beautiful streets, very straight, level, and well located; however, they say that the people of Fano are much richer than themselves. Here in the square is a large marble pedestal with a very long inscription, which is of the time of Trajan, in honor of a private inhabitant of this place, and another inscription against the wall which bears no indication of the time. This was in ancient times the Forum Sempronii; but they hold that their first town was farther over toward the plain and that the ruins are still there in a much more beautiful site. This town has a stone bridge to cross the Metaurus, toward Rome, by the Via Flaminia.

Because I arrived here early (for the miles are short and our days' journeys were of only seven or eight hours' riding), I talked to several worthy men who told me what they knew about their town and the environs. Here we saw a garden of the cardinal of Urbino, and lots of vines grafted onto other stocks. I talked with a good man who makes books, named Vincentius Castellani, who is from here.

I left here the next morning, and after riding three miles I turned off to the left and crossed a bridge over the Candigliano, the river that flows into the Metaurus, and went three miles along some wild mountains and rocks, by a narrow and rather difficult road, at the end of which we saw a passage a good fifty paces long which has been cut through one of these high rocks. And because this is a big job, to which Augustus first set his hand, there was an inscription in his name, which time has effaced; and another is to be seen at the other end in honor of Vespasian.[9]

Around here you see plenty of big walls rising from the bed of the river, which is extremely deep; below the road, cut and leveled rocks of tremendous thickness; and all along this road, which is the Via Flaminia, by which you go to Rome, traces of their big paving blocks, which are for the most part buried; and their road, which was forty feet wide, is now not even four.

I had turned out of my way to see this, and I retraced my steps to my road, which I followed along the base of some accessible and fertile mountains. Toward the end of our stage, we began to go up and down hill, and came to

URBINO, sixteen miles, a town of little distinction, on the top of a mountain of medium height, but lying in all directions according to the slopes of the place, so that there is nothing level about it, and everywhere you have to go up and down. The market was being held, for it was Saturday.

Here we saw the palace, which is very famous for its beauty. It is a great mass, for it stretches right to the foot of the mountain. The view extends to a thousand other neighboring mountains and has not much charm, nor is there anything very attractive about this whole building either inside or around it, and it has only a tiny little garden of twenty-five paces or thereabouts. They boast that it has as many bedrooms as there are days in the year. In truth, there are a very great number of them, and, in the manner of Tivoli and other palaces of Italy, through one door you often see twenty other doors in succession in one direction and as many or more in the other direction. There is something ancient about it, but the main part of it was built in 1476 by Federigo Maria della Rovere,[10] who inscribed inside many of his titles and his great offices and exploits in war, with which his walls are thickly covered, as well as an inscription saying that this is the most beautiful house in the world. It is of brick, and all built with arches, without any wooden flooring, like most of the buildings in Italy.

The present duke is his grandnephew. He descends from a line of good princes, who are loved by their subjects. They are all men of letters, from father to son, and have a fine library in this palace, but the key was not to be found. They incline to Spain. The arms of the king of Spain are seen in rank and favor, and the Order of England and that of the Golden Fleece, and nothing of ours.

They themselves show a painting of the first duke of Urbino, a young man who was killed by his subjects for his injustice; he was not of this line. The present one married the sister of the duke of Ferrara, ten years older than he. They are on bad terms, and separated, purely because of her jealousy, so they say. What with this and her age, which is forty-

---

[9] The Furlo Pass, where the Via Flaminia passes through a tunnel about forty yards long.

[10] This should be Federigo da Montefeltro.

five, they have little hope of children, the lack of which they say will cause this duchy to revert to the Church, and they are unhappy about it.

I saw here a portrait from life of Pico della Mirandola: a pale, very handsome face, beardless, seeming about seventeen or eighteen, a longish nose, gentle eyes, rather thin face, blond hair falling down to his shoulders, and a strange costume.

In many places in Italy they have a fashion of making winding staircases, even very steep and narrow ones, so that you can mount to the top of them on horseback; this is also the fashion here, with tiles set on a slant. It is a cold place, they say, and the duke makes it a habit to be here only in summer. To provide against this cold, in two of their bedrooms there are to be seen other square rooms in a corner, closed in on all sides except for a window or so which lets in light from the room; within these shelters is the master's bed.

After dinner I turned out of my way another five miles to see a place that the people from time immemorial have called Hasdrubal's Tomb, on a very high and steep hill which they call Monte d'Elce. Here there are four or five wretched little houses and a little church, and you see also a building of large bricks or tiles, twenty-five paces round or thereabouts, and twenty-five feet high. All around it there are supports of the same brick at every three paces. I do not know what the masons call these pieces, which they make for support like beaks.[11] We climbed up it, for there is no entry from below. We found a vault there, nothing inside, no cut stone, nothing inscribed. The inhabitants say that there used to be a piece of marble on which there were a few marks, but that it has been taken away in our time. Why this name was given it I do not know, and I scarcely believe that it is really what they say. To be sure, it is certain that he was defeated and killed rather near here.

Afterward we followed a very mountainous road, which became muddy merely because it had rained for an hour, and we crossed the Metaurus again—by a ford, since it is nothing but a torrent that will not bear a boat—which we had crossed another time since dinner; and toward the end of the day we came by a low and easy road to

CASTEL-DURANTE,[12] fifteen miles, a little town situated in the plain along the Metaurus, belonging to the duke of Urbino. The people here were making a bonfire and celebrating the birth of a male child to the princess of Bisignano, sister of their duke.

Our drivers unsaddle their horses whenever they unbridle them, whatever state they are in, and have them drink anyway. Here and at Urbino we drank wines that had been sophisticated to make them milder.

On Sunday morning we came along a rather fertile plain surrounded by hills, and passed first through a beautiful little town, Sant' Angelo, belonging to the said duke, along the Metaurus, with very beautiful approaches. We found in the town some little girls dressed up for May

[11] Presumably flying buttresses.
[12] Modern Urbania.

Day like queens of mid-Lent, for it was the eve of the first of May. From here, following this plain, we went through still another little town in the same jurisdiction, named Marcatello, and, by a road that already was beginning to smack of the Apennine mountains, we came to dine at

BORGO-PACE, ten miles, a little village and a wretched inn for a meager meal, in a corner of the mountains.

After dinner, we followed first a narrow, wild, and stony road, and then had to climb a high mountain, two miles up and four miles downward slope; the road shaly and annoying, but not frightening or dangerous, the precipices not being so steeply cut that the eye does not have something to rest on. We followed the Metaurus right to its lair, which is in this mountain; thus we have seen its birth and its end, having seen it fall into the sea at Sinigaglia. On descending this mountain we perceived a very beautiful and large plain, in which runs the Tiber, only eight miles or so from its source, and other mountains beyond: a prospect rather resembling that which is offered in the Limagne of Auvergne to those who descend the Puy de Dôme to Clermont-Ferrand. On the top of our mountain ends the jurisdiction of the duke of Urbino, and that of the duke of Florence begins, with that of the Pope on the left hand. We came to sup at

BORGO SAN SEPOLCRO, thirteen miles, a little town in this plain, belonging to the said duke of Florence, having nothing singular about it; we left it on the first day of May.

A mile from this town we crossed a stone bridge over the river Tiber, which still has its clear, beautiful waters—a sign that that dirty reddish color, *flavum Tiberim*,[13] which you see in it at Rome, comes from the admixture of some other river. We crossed this four-mile plain, and at the first hill found a little town on top. Several girls, both here and elsewhere on the road, came to meet us and seized our horses' bridles, and there asked for some liberality for the day's festival, singing a certain song to that effect.

From this hill we went back down into a very stony bottom, which we followed a long time along the bed of a torrent, and then we had a barren and very stony mountain to climb, three miles for the ascent and descent, from which we descried another large plain, in which we crossed the river Chiassa over a stone bridge, and afterward the river Arno over a very big, handsome stone bridge, on the hither side of which we lodged at

PONTE BORIANO, a tiny little house, eighteen miles. A bad inn, like the three preceding ones and most of those on this route. It would be great folly to bring good horses this way, for there is no hay.

After dinner we followed a long plain all split by horrible crevices which the waters make in a strange fashion, and I believe it must be very ugly in winter; but then, they are repairing the road. On our left, very soon after dinner, we passed the town of Arezzo in this same plain, two miles or so away. Its site, however, seems to be a little raised. We

---

[13] "The yellow Tiber." An expression used by Horace in his *Odes*.

crossed the river Ambra on a handsome stone bridge of great height, and came for supper to

LEVANELLA, ten miles. The hostelry is a mile or so short of the said village, and is famous; indeed it is held to be the best in Tuscany, and with reason; for by the standard of the hostelries of Italy it is one of the best. It is so highly thought of that they say the nobility of the region often gather there, as at Le More's in Paris or Guillot's in Amiens. They serve on pewter plates there, which is a great rarity. It is a house by itself, very beautifully situated in a plain, and has a spring at its service.

We left there in the morning and followed a very fine straight road across this plain, and on it passed through four little towns or walled villages, Montevarchi, San Giovanni, Figline, and Ancisa, and came to dine at

PIAN DELLA FONTE, twelve miles, a pretty poor inn, where there is also a spring, a little above the said village of Ancisa, which is situated in the valley of the Arno. They maintain that Petrarch, who speaks of it, was born at the said Ancisa, at least in a nearby house a mile from there, of which you no longer find anything but very unimpressive ruins; however, they do point out the place. They were then sowing melons there among the others that were already sown, and they expected to gather them in August.

This morning I had a heaviness in the head and trouble with my vision, as from my old migraines, which I had not felt for ten years.

This valley through which we passed was once all marshes, and Livy maintains that Hannibal was forced to cross them on an elephant, and lost an eye there because of the bad weather. It is in truth a very flat, low area, and subject to floods from the Arno.

I would not eat any dinner there, and was sorry for it, for that would have helped me to vomit, which is my promptest cure; otherwise I carry about this heavy-headedness for a day or two, as happened to me then. We found this road full of people of the region, bringing various kinds of foods to Florence. We arrived at

FLORENCE, twelve miles, by one of the four stone bridges which are there over the Arno.

The next day, after having heard Mass, we left there, and turning a bit off the straight road, went to see Castello, of which I have spoken elsewhere;[14] but because the duke's daughters were there, and at this very hour were going through the garden to hear Mass, we were asked to be good enough to wait, which I did not wish to do.

On the road we met many processions. The banner goes ahead, the women after, most of them very beautiful, with straw hats, which they make better in this region than anywhere else in the world, and well dressed for village women, their slippers and pumps white. After the women walks the curate, and after him come the men. The day before, we had seen a procession of monks, almost all wearing these straw hats.

We followed a very beautiful, very wide plain, and to tell the truth

[14] *Travel Journal*, pp. 931–32.

I was virtually forced to confess that neither Orléans, nor Tours, nor Paris itself, is surrounded by so great a number of houses and villages, and so far out, as Florence; as for beautiful houses and palaces, that is beyond doubt. Along this route we came to dine at

PRATO, ten miles, a little town belonging to the said duke, situated on the river Bisenzio, which we crossed by a stone bridge at the gate of the said town.

There is no other region so well supplied, among other things, with bridges, and such solid ones; and indeed along the roads everywhere you come across big cut stones on which is written what piece of road each district has to keep up and be responsible for. In the palace of the said place we saw the arms and name of the legate da Prato, who they say was a native of here. Over the door of this palace is a large crowned statue, holding the world in its hand, and at its feet, *Rex Robertus*.[15] Here they say that this town was formerly ours; the fleurs-de-lys are everywhere; but the town's own arms bear gules powdered with fleurs-de-lys or. The cathedral here is beautiful and enriched with much black and white marble.

On leaving here we took another side road, a detour of a good four miles, to go to the Poggio, a house about which they make much ado, belonging to the duke, situated on the river Ombrone; the form of this building is the model of Pratolino. It is a marvel that in such a small mass there can be contained a hundred very beautiful rooms. Here I saw among other things a great number of beds of very beautiful stuff that is not expensive: they are some of those light varicolored materials which are nothing but very fine wool, and they line it with four-thread taffeta of the same color as the material. Here we saw the duke's distillery and his workroom fitted with a lathe and other instruments; for he is a great mechanic.

From here, by a very straight road through extremely fertile country, the road enclosed by trees with vines attached which form a hedge, a thing of great beauty, we came for supper to

PISTOIA, fourteen miles, a big town on the river Ombrone; the streets very wide, paved, like Florence, Prato, Lucca, and others, with big and very wide stone slabs. I was forgetting to say that from the table in the rooms at Poggio you see Florence, Prato, and Pistoia. In the said Pistoia there are very few people; the churches are beautiful, and there are many beautiful houses. I inquired about the sale of straw hats, which they made for fifteen sous. It seems to me that they would be worth quite as many francs[16] in France. Near this town and in its territory Catiline was defeated long ago.

At Poggio there are some tapestries representing every kind of hunting; among others, I noticed one hanging that showed the hunting of ostriches, which they show being pursued by men on horseback, and speared with javelins.

---

[15] Robert of Anjou, king of Naples, to whom the town surrendered in 1313.

[16] The franc was worth one livre, or, as now, twenty sous.

The Latins called Pistoia Pistorium; it belongs to the duke of Florence. The say that the ancient feuds of the houses of the Cancellieri and the Panciatici, which existed formerly, made it as it is now, as it were uninhabited, so that it numbers only eight thousand souls in all; and Lucca, which is no bigger, has twenty-five thousand inhabitants and more.

Messer Taddeo Rospigliosi, who had had a letter of recommendation from Rome on my behalf from Giovanni Franchini, invited me to dinner the next day, with all the others who were in our company. The palace is very ornate, the service a little strange in the order of dishes; little meat, few servants; the wine served again after the meal, as in Germany.

We saw the churches: at the elevation in the principal church they blew trumpets. Among the choirboys there were some priests in their vestments who played on sackbuts.

This poor town compensates for its lost liberty by a vain image of its ancient constitution. They have nine Priors and a Gonfalonier, whom they elect every two months. These have charge of keeping order, and are maintained by the duke, as they formerly were by the public; they are lodged in the palace, and hardly ever leave it except all together, being perpetually confined there. The Gonfalonier marches in front of the podestà whom the duke sends there, which podestà has in fact all the power; and the said Gonfalonier salutes no one, imitating the petty royalty they imagine themselves to be. I felt pity to see them feed on this monkey business; and meanwhile the grand duke has increased the taxes by ten times over what they formerly were.

In most of the big gardens in Italy they grow grass in the principal walks, and mow it.

About this time the cherries were beginning to ripen; and on the road from Pistoia to Lucca we found village people who offered us bunches of strawberries for sale.

We left here on Thursday, Ascension Day, after dinner, and first followed that plain for a while, and then a slightly hilly road, and afterward a very beautiful wide plain. In the wheat fields they have many trees, well arranged, and covered and linked to one another by vines: these fields seem like gardens. The mountains that are seen on this route are heavily covered with trees, chiefly olive and chestnut trees and mulberry trees for their silkworms. In this plain you come upon

LUCCA, twenty miles, a city one-third smaller than Bordeaux, free, except that because of its weakness it has cast itself under the protection of the Emperor and the house of Austria. It is well enclosed and flanked; the moats not deep, with a little channel of water flowing in them, and full of green plants; flat and broad at the bottom. All around the wall, on the raised walk on the inside, two or three rows of trees are planted which serve for shade, and, they say, for faggots in case of need. From the outside you see only a wood that hides the houses. They always have a guard of three hundred foreign soldiers.

The city is thickly populated, notably with silk workers; the streets narrow but handsome, and almost everywhere beautiful big houses.

They are running a little channel through it from the river Serchio; they are building a palace at an expense of a hundred and thirty thousand crowns, and it is well advanced.

They say they have six-score thousand souls as subjects, not counting the city. They have a few small fortified places, but no town under their subjection. Their gentlemen and men-at-arms all make a profession of trade. The Buonvisi are the richest here. Strangers enter only by one gate, where there is a heavy guard.

It is one of the most pleasant sites for a town that I ever saw, surrounded by two full leagues of plain, of superlative beauty at the narrowest point, and then beautiful mountains and hills, where most of them have country lodgings.

The wines here are moderately good; the cost of living twenty sous a day; the hostelries in the manner of this country, pretty unimpressive. I received many courtesies from several private persons, and wines and fruits and offers of money.

I was here Friday and Saturday, and left on Sunday after dinner— dinner for the others, not for me, since I was fasting. The hills nearest the city are studded with plenty of pleasant houses very close together. Most of the trip was by a low road, rather easy, between the mountains, almost all very shady and inhabitable, all the way along the river Serchio. We passed several ordinary villages and two very large walled villages, Decimo and Borgo, on this side of the said river, which we had on our right hand, and then crossed over a bridge of unusual height, with one arch embracing a great width of the said river; and we saw three or four bridges of this kind.

Italy: First Stay at La Villa (May 7-June 21, 1581)

We came about two o'clock in the afternoon to the

BATH OF LA VILLA, sixteen miles. It is a thoroughly hilly country. In front of the bath, along the river, there is a plain of three or four hundred paces, above which the bath is on the side of a medium-sized mountain, part way up, about as high up as the spring of Bagnères, where they drink near the town.

The site of the bath is fairly level, and there are thirty or forty houses very well fitted for this purpose; the rooms pretty, quite private, and as free as you like, each with a toilet, and each with a door to an adjacent room and another for private use. I inspected almost all the houses before making a bargain, and settled on the finest, especially for the view, which overlooks (at least the room I chose) all this little valley, and the river Lima, and the mountains that shelter the said valley, all well cultivated and green all the way to the summit, full of chestnut and olive trees, and elsewhere of vines, which they plant around the mountains, girding the mountains with terraces. The edge of the terrace toward the outside, a little raised, is vine; the hollow of the terrace is wheat. All night from my room I heard, very soft, the sound of the river.

Between these houses is a place to walk, open on one side in the form of a terrace, from which you look down on that small plain below the walk through a public trellis, and you see along the river in that small plain, two hundred paces below you, a handsome little village which also serves for these baths when there is a crowd. Most of the houses new; a fine road to go there; and a handsome square in the said village. Most of the inhabitants of this place stay here in the winter and have their shops here, especially apothecaries' shops; for almost all are apothecaries.

My landlord is named Captain Paulino, and he is an apothecary. He gave me a dining room, three bedrooms, a kitchen, and also a garret for our men, and in them eight beds, for two of which there was a canopy; furnished salt, a napkin every day, a tablecloth every third day, all the iron utensils for the kitchen, and candlesticks, for eleven crowns, a few sous more than ten pistolets, for a fortnight. The pots, dishes, and plates, which are of earthenware, we bought, as well as the glasses and knives; they have meat, as much as you want, veal and kid; not much else. At each inn they offer to do your marketing for you, and I think you could have it done for twenty sous a man per day; and if you want to do it yourself, you find in every inn some man or woman capable of doing your cooking. The wine is not very good; but anyone who wants can have it brought from either Pescia or Lucca.

I was the first to arrive here, except for two Bolognese gentlemen who did not have any big retinue. Thus I had a choice and, from what they say, a better bargain than I would have had in the crowd, which they say is very great here. But their practice is not to begin to come until June, and to stay here until September; for by October they are gone; and they very often have gatherings here solely for recreation. Any visiting that they do earlier—as we found some who were returning home after being here a month already—or in October, is extraordinary.

In this place there is a house belonging to the lords of Buonvisi, much more magnificent than the others, and assuredly very handsome; they call it the Palace. It has a beautiful live spring in the dining room, and many other conveniences. It was offered to me, at least a four-room apartment that I wanted, and the whole thing if I needed it. The four rooms, furnished as above, they would have let me have for twenty crowns of the country[1] for a fortnight; I was willing to give a crown a day. In consideration of the season and the price, which changes, my landlord is bound to our bargain only for the month of May; we will have to make a new one if I want to stay longer.

---

[1] Italian scudi, not French écus. One écu was worth about 1.2 scudi.

There is water to drink here and also to bathe in; a covered bath, vaulted and rather dark, half as wide as my dining room at Montaigne. There is also a certain dripping apparatus that they call *la doccia*:[2] this consists of pipes by which you receive hot water on various parts of the body, and especially on the head, the water coming down on you in steady streams and warming the part of your body that they are beating down on; and then the water is received in a wooden trough, like that of washerwomen, along which it flows away. There is another bath, vaulted in the same way, and dark, for the women; the whole thing coming from a spring from which one drinks, rather unattractively situated, in a hollow to which one has to go down several steps.

On Monday morning, May 8th, with great difficulty, I took some cassia which my landlord offered me, not with the grace of the man in Rome, and I took it with my own hands. I dined two hours later and could not finish my dinner; the operation of the cassia made me throw up what I had taken, and vomit again later. I had three or four stools from it, with great pain in the belly because of the flatulence, which tormented me for almost twenty-four hours, and I have promised myself not to take any more of it. I would rather have a fit of colic than have my belly thus upset, my taste altered, and my health disturbed by this cassia; for I had come here in good condition; so that on Sunday after supper, which was the only meal I had that day, I went very blithely to see the bath of Corsena, which is a good half mile from here, on the other side of this same mountain; you have to go up and then come down again to about the same height as the baths on this side. This other bath is more famous for the bathing and *la doccia*; for ours has no generally accepted use, either according to the doctors or by usage, except for drinking; and they say that the other has a more ancient reputation. However, for all this age, which goes back to the times of the Romans, there is no trace of antiquity at either bath.

There are three or four large baths there, vaulted except for a hole in the middle of the vault like a vent hole; they are dark and unattractive. There is another hot spring two or three hundred paces from there, a little higher up on this same mountain, called Monte San Giovanni; and there they have made a hut with three baths, also covered; no house nearby, but room to place a mattress to rest on for an hour or so in the day. At Corsena they do not drink at all. Moreover, they diversify the operation of its waters: one cools, one warms, one for this malady, one for another; and on this subject a thousand miracles; but in short, there is no sort of malady that does not find its cure there.

There is one handsome inn with many rooms, and about a score of others not very handsome. In the matter of convenience they cannot compare with ours, nor in the beauty of the view, although they have our river at their feet and their view extends farther into a valley; and yet they are much more expensive. Many drink here, and then go to bathe there. For the moment Corsena has the reputation.

2 The shower.

On Tuesday, May 9th, 1581, early in the morning before sunrise, I
went to drink right from the spout of our hot spring, and drank seven
glasses right in a row, which hold three pounds and a half: that is the
way they measure.[3] I think that would be about twelve glasses, or our
quart. It is a very moderately hot water, like that of Aigues-Caudes or
Barbotan, having less taste and savor than any other I have ever drunk.
I could perceive nothing of it but its tepidness and a little sweetness.
For that day it had no effect on me, and yet I was five hours from drinking it until dinner, and I did not pass a single drop of it. Some said I had
taken too little, for here they order a *flask*, that is, two *jars*, which is eight
pounds, or sixteen or seventeen of my glasses. I myself think that it found
me so empty because of my medicine that it found room to serve me for
food.

This same day I had a visit from a Bolognese gentleman, a colonel
of twelve hundred foot, in the pay of the signory of Lucca, who is staying four miles from the baths; and he came and did me many civilities,
and was with me about two hours; he ordered my landlord and others
in the place to favor me to the extent of their power.

This signory has a rule to use foreign officers, and distributes its men
in the villages by number and according to the country, and gives them
a colonel to command them: one has a larger, another a smaller command. The colonels are paid; the captains, who are inhabitants of the
country, are paid only in wartime, and command the individual companies when there is need. My colonel had sixteen crowns a month in
wages, and has no responsibility but to keep himself ready.

They live more by rule in these baths than in ours, and especially
keep strict fast as regards drinking. I found myself better lodged here
than at any other baths, even at Bagneres. The situation of the country
is quite as beautiful at Bagnères, but not at any other bath; the places for
bathing at Baden surpass all others by far in magnificence and convenience; the inn at Baden bears comparison with any other, except for the
view from here.

Wednesday morning early I again drank of this water; and being
pretty disturbed over the little effect I had felt from it the day before
(for I had indeed had a stool immediately after taking it, but I attributed
that to the medicine of the preceding day, not having passed one drop
of water that resembled that of the bath), I took on Wednesday seven
glasses measured by the pound, which was at least double what I had
taken the other day, and I believe I have never taken so much at one
time. I felt from it a great desire to sweat, which I would not indulge
at all, having often heard that this was not the effect I needed; and, as
on the first day, I kept to my room, now walking around, now at rest.
The water proceeded mostly through the rear, and made me have several loose, light stools, without any effort.

I hold that it did me harm to take this purge of cassia, for the water,
finding nature moving to the rear and provoked, followed that course;
whereas, because of my kidneys, I would have liked it better to the

---

[3] The Italian pound was only twelve ounces; see below, p. 991.

front; and I am thinking, at the first baths I take, of preparing only by some fasting the day before. Also I believe this water is very weak and of little effect, and consequently safe and without risk: apprentices and delicate people would be well off with it. They take it to cool the liver and get rid of red pimples on the face, a fact I carefully note as a service I owe to a very virtuous lady in France.[4]

The water of San Giovanni they use a lot for cosmetics, for it is extremely oily. I saw that they exported it in barrelfuls to foreign countries, and still more of that which I was drinking, on many donkeys and mules, to Reggio, Modena, Lombardy, to drink. Some take it here in bed, and their principal instructions are to keep their stomach and feet warm, and not to move around much. The people in the neighborhood have it brought three or four miles to their houses. To show that it is not very aperient, they have the custom of having water brought here from a bath near Pistoia, which has an acrid taste and is very hot at its source; and the apothecaries here keep it to drink before the water from here, one glassful, and hold that it helps it along, being active and aperient.

The second day I passed some water that was clear, but not without some alteration of color, as elsewhere, and voided a lot of gravel; but it was helped along by the cassia, for I passed a lot of it on the day I took the cassia.

Here I learned of a memorable incident. An inhabitant of this place, a soldier named Giuseppe, who is still alive and commands [the oarsmen on] one of the galleys of the Genoese as a convict, and several of whose near relations I saw, was captured by the Turks in a battle at sea. To regain his liberty he became a Turk (and there are many of this condition, and especially in the mountains near this place, still alive), was circumcised, and married in their territory. Coming to pillage this coast, he went so far from his base that there he was, with a few other Turks, caught by the people, who had risen up. He had the presence of mind to say that he had come to surrender deliberately, that he was a Christian. He was set at liberty a few days later, came to this place, and to the house opposite the one I am lodging in; he entered and encountered his mother. She asked him roughly who he was and what he wanted; for he still had on his sailor's clothes, and it was strange to see him there. Finally he made himself known, for he had been lost for ten or twelve years, and embraced his mother. She uttered one cry and fell quite distracted; until the next day they did not see much sign of life in her, and the doctors were entirely without hope. She finally came back to herself but she did not live long afterward, and everyone judged that this shock shortened her life. Our Giuseppe was feted by one and all, was received into the Church to abjure his error, and received the Sacrament from the bishop of Lucca, with several other ceremonies. It was just humbug: he was a Turk at heart. To return to the Turks he steals away from here, goes to Venice, and mixes with them again. Resuming his travels, here he falls into our hands again; and because he is a man

[4] Quite possibly Montaigne's wife.

of unusual strength and a soldier well versed in naval matters, the Genoese still keep him and use him, well bound and fettered.

This nation has many soldiers, inhabitants of the country, who are all registered for the service of the signory. The colonels have no other responsibility than to drill them often in marksmanship, skirmishing, and such things. The men receive no pay, but they may bear arms, chain mail, harquebuses, and whatever they please; and then they cannot be seized in person for any debt, and in war they receive pay. Among them are the captains, ensigns, sergeants. Only the colonel must necessarily be a foreigner and be paid. The colonel from the Borgo, the one who had come to visit me the day before, sent me from the said place (which is four miles from the bath) a man with sixteen lemons and sixteen artichokes.

The mildness and weakness of this water is further argued by the fact that it turns so easily into food; for it is immediately colored and digested, and does not stimulate the desire to urinate the way the others do, as I observed by my own experience and that of others at the same time.

Although I was pleasantly and very comfortably lodged, in such a way as to rival my lodging in Rome, still I had neither window frame nor fireplace, and still less windowpanes, in my room. This shows that in Italy they do not have as frequent storms as we do; for if they did, it would be an intolerable discomfort to have no other than wooden windows in nearly all the houses. Except for that, I was very well bedded.

Their beds are wretched little trestles on which they throw planks, according to the length and width of the bed; on top of these a straw mattress and a regular mattress, and there you are very well lodged, if you have a canopy. And to keep your trestles and planks from showing, three remedies: one, to have strips of the same stuff as the canopy, as I had in Rome; another, to have your canopy long enough to hang down to the ground and cover everything, which is the best way; the third, for the covering, which is fastened at the corners with buttons, to hang down to the ground; it should be of some light stuff, such as white fustian, with another covering underneath for warmth. At least I am learning this economy for my retinue, and for general use at home, and I have no need for bedsteads. One is very comfortable, and then it is a recipe against bedbugs.

The same day after dinner I bathed, contrary to the rules of this region, where they say that one operation impedes the other, and want to keep them distinct: drink for one spell, and then bathe for another. They drink eight days and bathe thirty: drink in this bath, and bathe in the other. The bath is very mild and pleasant. I was in it for half an hour, and it made me sweat only a little; it was about suppertime. I went to bed on leaving there, and supped on a salad of sugared lemon, without anything to drink; for that day I did not drink a pound, and I think that if the whole count had been kept until the next day, it would be clear that I had voided by this means almost all the water I had taken.

It is a stupid habit to keep count of what you piss.

I did not feel bad, but lively, as at the other baths; and yet I was greatly concerned to see that my water did not pass. Perhaps the same had happened to me elsewhere; but here they make a tragedy of this, and from the first day, if you fail to void at least two-thirds, they advise you to give up drinking or to take medicine.

For my part, if I judge rightly about these waters, they are not such as to do either much harm or much good; there is nothing but mildness and weakness in them, and it is to be feared that they warm up the kidneys more than they purge them; and I think I need hotter and more aperient waters.

On Thursday morning I again drank five pounds, fearing to be ill served by them and not to void them. They made me have one stool and urinate very little.

This same morning, writing to Monsieur d'Ossat, I was overcome by such painful thoughts about Monsieur de La Boétie,[5] and I was in this mood so long, without recovering, that it did me much harm.

The bottom of this bath is all red and rusty, as is the channel through which it passes: this, added to its insipidity, makes me believe that it contains much iron, and that it is binding. On Thursday, in five hours that I waited to dine, I voided only the fifth part of what I had drunk.

What a vain thing medicine is! I chanced to say that I repented of having purged myself so much, and that this made the water, finding me empty, serve as food and stay in me. I have just seen a doctor named Donati in print speaking of these waters, who says he advises dining little and supping better. I think my conjecture backs him up. His colleague Franciotti is of the contrary view, as in many other things.

That day I had some feelings of heaviness in the kidneys which I feared that the waters themselves caused me, and I was afraid that they were stagnating there; yet on counting up everything I passed in twenty-four hours, I came about up to my point, seeing how little I drank at meals.

Friday I did not drink, and instead of drinking went to bathe in the morning and wash my head, contrary to the common practice of the place.

It is a custom of the country to help along one's water by some drug mixed in, such as sugar candy, or manna, or still stronger medicine, which they mix with the first glass of their water; and most ordinarily they use the water of the Tettuccio, which I tasted; it is salty. I have some suspicion that the apothecaries, instead of sending to get it near Pistoia, where they say it is, sophisticate some natural water; for I found its taste extraordinary, besides the saltiness. They have it heated up and start by drinking one, two, or three glasses. I have seen it drunk in my presence without any effect. Some put salt in the water for the first and second glasses or more. They consider sweating virtually fatal, and also sleeping after drinking. I felt that the operation of this water strongly inclined me to sweat.

[5] Montaigne's dear friend, who died eighteen years earlier. See, for example, *Essays* I: 28; *Letters,* No. 2.

[THE JOURNAL BY MONTAIGNE IN ITALIAN]

Let us try to speak this other language[6] a little, especially since I am in this region where I seem to hear the most perfect Tuscan speech, particularly among those natives who have not corrupted and altered it with that of their neighbors.

On Saturday morning early I went to take the water of Bernabò. This is one spring among all the others on this mountain; and it is a marvel how many there are, both hot and cold. The mountain is not very high. It is perhaps three miles around. People drink only from this one principal spring, and from one other that has been used for a few years. One Bernabò, a leper, had tried both waters and baths from all the other springs, and, giving up, resolved on this one; here he was cured. Thereby it came into repute.

There are no houses around, and only a small covered shed and stone seats around the duct, which, although it is of iron and has not been there long, is mostly eaten away underneath. They say it is the strength of the water that consumes it, and this is very likely. This water is a little hotter than the other, and in the general opinion heavier and more violent. It has a little more odor of sulphur, but only a little; and where it falls, it whitens the spot with an ashen color, like ours, but less. It is a little less than a mile from my lodging around the foot of the mountain; its site is a good deal lower than all the other hot springs. It is about a pike's length or two from the river.

I took five pounds of this water, with some discomfort, because I was none too well that morning. The day before, I had taken a long walk of three miles after dinner in the heat; and after supper I felt the effect of this water somewhat more; I began to get rid of it in half an hour. I took a big detour of about two miles to return to my house. I do not know whether this unusual exercise did me good, because on the other days I returned immediately to my room so as not to be chilled by the morning air; and the houses are not thirty paces from the spring. The first water that I voided was natural and pretty gravelly, the rest white and undigested. Broke wind endlessly. About the third pound that I got rid of began to recover a sort of reddish color. I had discharged more than half of it before dinner.

Going around this mountain in all directions I found many hot springs. And furthermore, the peasants say that in certain places in winter the mountain smokes: a proof that there are still others. They seem to me of about the same heat, without smell, without taste, without fumes, compared with ours.

I saw another place at Corsena much lower than the baths, where there are a large number of shower baths, more comfortable than the others. They say there are still more springs that feed these pipes, some eight or ten; and they have different names inscribed over each tap, indicating their effects: the Savory, the Gentle, the Enamored, the

---

[6] Tuscan. For Montaigne's comment on this experience, see *Essays* III:5, p. 665.

Crown, the Desperate, etc. In truth, some of the channels are hotter than others.

The mountains around are almost all fertile in wheat and grapes, whereas fifty years ago they were covered with woods and chestnuts. You see a few bare mountains with snow on top, but very distant. The people eat "wooden bread": so they proverbially call the bread made of chestnuts, which is their principal crop; and it is prepared like what they call *pain d'épice*[7] in France. I never saw so many toads and snakes. And for fear of the snakes the boys often do not dare to pick the strawberries, of which there is a very great abundance on the mountains and in the hedges.

Some people take three or four grains of candied coriander with each glass of water to get rid of the wind.

On Whitsunday, May 14th, I took five pounds and more of the water of Bernabò, because my glass held more than one pound. The four principal holidays of the year they call *Pasqua*.[8] I voided a lot of gravel the first time, and in less than two hours I had got rid of more than two-thirds of the water, having taken it with a desire to urinate and with my usual appetite as at the other baths. It made my bowels loose and purged me thoroughly in that respect. The Italian pound is only twelve ounces.

You live here very cheaply. A pound of meat, veal, very good and very tender, is about three French sous. Plenty of trout, but small. There are good workmen at making parasols, which in these parts they carry everywhere. The country is hilly, and there are few level roads. However, there are some very pleasant ones, and even the approaches to the mountains are mostly paved.

After dinner I gave a dance for the peasant girls, and danced in it myself so as not to appear too reserved. In certain parts of Italy, including all of Tuscany and Urbino, the women curtsy French style, at the knees.

Near the channel of the spring at La Villa there is a square marble that was put there just 110 years ago, on these Calends of May, on which are inscribed the virtues of this spring. I omit it, because it is found in many printed books which deal with the baths of Lucca. At all the baths you find a good many small clocks[9] for public use. I always had two on my table, which were lent to me.

This evening I ate nothing but three slices of bread, toasted, with butter and sugar, without drinking.

On Monday, judging that this water had sufficiently opened the way, I went back to drinking that of the ordinary spring, and took five pounds of it. It did not induce me to sweat, as it used to do. The first time I

---

[7] Gingerbread.

[8] In this neighborhood these would seem to be Easter (*Pasqua d'uove*, of eggs), Whitsunday (*Pasqua di rose*, of roses), Christmas (*Pasqua di ceppo*, of the log), and Ascension Day (with no special name).

[9] Presumably hourglasses.

passed some of the water I discharged some gravel, which seemed in fact to be broken up stones. This water seemed to me almost cold in comparison with that of Bernabò, although that of Bernabò had a very moderate warmth; it is very far from coming up to that of Plombières and the ordinary water of Bagnères. It had a good effect in both directions; and so it was lucky that I did not believe those doctors who ordered me to give up drinking if it did not succeed on the first day.

On Tuesday, May 16th, as is the custom in these parts (and I like it), I discontinued drinking, and stayed in the bath an hour and more, under the spout, because the water everywhere else seems cold to me. Since I still felt that wind remaining in the lower bowels and intestines, without pain, and a little in the stomach, I was afraid that the water was the particular cause of this; wherefore I discontinued it. I enjoyed the bath so much that I would gladly have gone to sleep in it. It did not make me sweat, but it moved my bowels. I dried myself well and stayed in bed for a while.

Every month they hold a review of the soldiers of each vicariate. The colonel, our man, from whom I had received a world of courtesies, held his. There were two hundred soldiers, pikesmen and musketeers. He had them fight. They are extremely well trained for peasants. But this is his principal responsibility, to keep them in order and teach them military discipline.

The people are all divided among themselves into the French faction and the Spanish faction; and in this strife serious quarrels are always arising. They make public demonstrations of their feelings. The women and men of our side wear over their right ear bunches of flowers, a biretta, locks of hair, and all that kind of thing; the Spaniards wear them on the other side.

These peasants and their wives are dressed like gentlefolk. You never see a peasant woman who does not wear white shoes, fine thread stockings, a colored apron of light silk taffeta; and they dance, capriole, and pirouette very well.

When they speak of the "Prince" in this signory, they mean the Council of One Hundred and Twenty. The colonel cannot take a wife without the permission of the "Prince," and he has great difficulty in obtaining it, because they do not want him to acquire friends and family relationships in the region; and moreover he cannot buy any property. No soldier leaves the country without permission; and there are many who through poverty go begging through these mountains, and buy their arms with what they gain.

On Wednesday I was at the bath and stayed there more than an hour, sweated a little, and bathed my head.

We see here that the German custom of warming clothes and everything else in winter by their stoves is convenient; for our bath attendant, by holding a little charcoal under a *focone*, and raising the mouth of it with a brick, so that it gets air to feed the fire, warms the clothes very well and quickly, and indeed more conveniently than do our fires. A *focone* is one of our warming pans.

Here they call unmarried girls and girls of marriageable age *bambe*; and boys, until they have a beard, *putti*.

On Thursday I was a little more prompt and took my bath earlier. I sweated a little in the bath and bathed my head under the spout. I felt my strength a little weakened by the bath, and a little heaviness in the kidneys; I was still discharging gravel as I did from drinking, and a lot of phlegm. Indeed it seemed to me that this had the same effect on me as drinking. I continued on Friday.

Every day they sold unlimited quantities of water from this spring and from the other at Corsena, for various parts of Italy. It seemed to me that these baths cleared up my complexion. I was still bothered by that wind around the groin, without pain, which made me discharge in my urine a lot of foam, and bubbles that did not burst for some time. Sometimes there were also black hairs, but not many. I had noticed at other times that I discharged many of them. My urine was usually cloudy and charged with matter. The urine had something greasy on its surface.

This nation is not in the habit of eating as much meat as we do. Only ordinary meat is sold. They hardly know the price of it. A very fine young hare was sold me in this season at the very first word, so to speak, for six of our sous. They do not hunt them, they do not breed them, because no one buys them.

On Saturday, because the weather was cloudy and there was such a wind as made you feel the lack of shutters and windows, I stayed quiet without bathing or drinking. I perceived one great effect of these waters: that my brother,[10] who had never noticed voiding any gravel by himself or at the other baths where he had drunk with me, yet discharged an infinite amount of it here.

On the Sunday morning I bathed, but not my head; and after dinner I gave a dance with public prizes, as is the custom at these baths; and I wanted to give the first one of this year. First, five or six days beforehand, I had the party announced in all the neighboring places. The day before, I sent special invitations to all the gentlemen and ladies who were staying at the two baths. I invited them to the ball and to supper afterward.

I sent to Lucca for the prizes. The custom is to give several of these, so as not to appear to select just one woman out of them all, and so as to avoid jealousy and suspicion. There are always eight or ten for the women; for the men, two or three. I was asked by many women not to forget themselves, or a niece, or a daughter. On the day before, Messer Giovanni da Vincenzo Saminiati, a great friend of mine, sent me from Lucca a leather belt and a biretta of black cloth for the men, as I had written asking him to do. For the women, two taffeta aprons, one green, the other violet (for it must be noted that there is always some more honorable prize for the one or two you want to favor), two aprons of

---

[10] Presumably Bertrand de Mattecoulon, whom the party had left in Rome but who had apparently rejoined them there.

coarse muslin, four papers of pins, four pairs of pumps (but I gave one of these to a pretty girl, not at the dance); a pair of slippers (to which I added a pair of pumps, and made a single prize of the two); three crystal nets and three tresses of hair, which made three prizes; four little necklaces. There were nineteen prizes for the women. It all came to six crowns, little more. I had five fife players. I gave them food for the whole day and a crown for the lot; which was my good luck, for they do not normally do it for that price. These prizes are hung from a sort of hoop, heavily decorated all over, and are displayed for everyone to see.

We began the dance in the square with the women of the neighborhood, and at first I was afraid that we would be left alone. Soon there came much company from all directions, and particularly a good many gentlemen and ladies of this signory, whom I received and entertained to the best of my ability. At all events, it seemed to me that they were satisfied. Since it was a bit warm, we went to the hall of the Buonvisi palace, which was very suitable.

As day was beginning to fall, a little after five in the afternoon, I addressed myself to the most important ladies, saying that since I lacked sufficient skill and boldness to judge such beauties and graces and nice manners as I saw in these girls, I begged them to assume this charge of judging and to distribute the prizes to the company according to their merits. We were held up on ceremony for a bit because they refused to assume this charge, which they took to be too much courtesy to them. Finally I added this condition, that if they would be good enough to take me into their counsel, I would give my opinion. And this was the result, that I picked out with my eyes now this one, now that; wherein I did not fail to have some regard for beauty and grace, pointing out that the charm of the dance depended not only on the movement of the feet, but also on the carriage and grace and charm and elegance of the whole person. Thus the presents were distributed, more to one, less to another, according to their merit, this lady offering them to the dancers on my behalf, and I on the contrary referring all the obligation to her. The thing went off in a very orderly and regular manner, except that one of the girls refused the prize. She sent to beg me that for her sake I should give it to another girl; which I did not consent to do. The other was not one of the most attractive.

They were called up one by one from their places, and came before that lady and me, who were seated side by side. I would give the present that seemed right to me to the lady, kissing it, and she, taking it, would give it to the girl, saying graciously: "Here is this lord knight who is giving you this fine present: thank him." "On the contrary, you are obliged to her ladyship, who out of so many others has judged you worthy to receive a prize. I am very sorry that the present is not more worthy of such-and-such a quality of yours"—and I named these according to what they were. The same thing was promptly done with the men. The gentlemen and ladies are not included in this competition, although they take part in the dancing.

In truth it is a beautiful thing, and a rare one to us French, to see these peasant girls, so elegant, and dressed like ladies, dance so well: they are a match for the rarest of our ladies in that ability, but they dance differently.

I invited them all to supper, for the banquets in Italy are nothing but a very light meal by French standards—a few cuts of veal and one or two brace of chicken is all. There stayed to supper Signor Francesco Gambarini, the colonel of this vicariate, a gentleman of Bologna who is like a brother to me; one French gentleman; and no others; except that I had Divizia sit at the table. She is a poor peasant woman of the neighborhood, living about two miles from the baths, who, like her husband, has no other way of earning a living except by the work of her own hands; ugly, thirty-seven years old, with a swollen neck. She can neither write nor read. But in her tender youth there was an uncle in her father's house who was always reading Ariosto and other poets in her presence, and her mind was found to be so born to poetry that she not only composes verses with the most wonderful readiness possible, but also brings into them ancient fables, names of the gods, countries, sciences, famous men, as if she had been brought up to study. She delivered a number of verses in my honor. To tell the truth, they are nothing but verses and rhymes. Her delivery is elegant and very rapid.

The company at the ball amounted to a hundred visitors and more, although the season was unfavorable; for at that time the great and most important harvest of the whole year takes place, that of silk; and these days they tire themselves out with work, without regard for any holiday, morning and evening, collecting the mulberry leaves for their silkworms; and all these girls are employed in this labor.

On Monday morning I went to the bath a little later, because I got a shave and a haircut. I bathed my head and gave it a shower for more than a quarter of an hour under the main tap.

Among others at my dance was the Lord Vicar, who administers justice. Thus they call a magistrate appointed for six months, whom the signory sends to each vicariate to judge civil cases in the first instance, and he decides them up to a certain small sum. There is another officer for criminal cases. I gave him to understand that it seemed reasonable to me that the signory should make some rule (which would be very easy; and I suggested to him the ways that seemed most appropriate to me) obliging the innumerable dealers who come here to take these waters and carry them all over Italy to show a certificate of the amount of water they carry, so as to deprive them of the opportunity of perpetrating a fraud. Whereof I gave him an experience of my own, which was this: One of these muleteers came to my landlord, a private person, and begged him to give him a statement in writing that he was taking away twenty-four loads of this water; and he had only four. The landlord at first refused, for that reason; but the other added that in four to six days he would be returning to get the twenty loads. I said that this muleteer had not returned. The Lord Vicar received this advice of mine very well; but he did all he could to find out who that witness was and who was that muleteer, what he looked like, what horses he had. I never would tell him either one, never.

I also told him that I wanted to initiate the custom observed in all the famous baths of Europe, that persons above a certain rank leave their coat of arms there as a token of the obligation they have to those waters; for which he thanked me very much on behalf of the signory.

In these days they were beginning to mow the hay in some places.

On Tuesday I stayed two hours in the bath and gave my head a shower for a little more than a quarter of an hour.

There came to the baths in these days a merchant from Cremona, living in Rome. He was suffering from many extraordinary infirmities. Nevertheless he talked and walked, and led quite a jolly life, as far as I could see. His principal failing, he said, was a weak head: he had lost his memory so completely that when eating he never remembered what had been put before him at table. If he left the house to go on some business of his, he had to go back to the house ten times to ask where he was to go. He could hardly finish the paternoster: from the end he went a hundred times to the beginning, never noticing at the end that he had begun, or, on beginning again, that he had ended. He had been deaf and blind, and had suffered from toothache. He felt so much heat in the kidneys that he always had to have a strip of lead around them. He had been living under doctors' orders for many years, and observing them most religiously.

It was an amusing thing to see the various prescriptions of the doctors from various parts of Italy, so contradictory, and particularly on the matter of these baths and showers, that out of twenty consulted there were not two in agreement; on the contrary, they almost all condemned one another and accused one another of homicide.

This man was subject to an amazing accident because of the flatulence: the wind rushed out of his ears with such fury that many times it would not let him sleep. Instead, whenever he yawned he immediately felt great winds coming out of his ears. He said that for getting the bowels moving the best remedy he had was to put four big candied coriander seeds in his mouth for a bit, and after moistening and smoothing them a little, to put them up the anus; which had a very apparent and prompt effect.

On him I first saw one of those big hats made of peacock feathers, covered with light taffeta, the crown a good hand's-breadth high, and big; and inside it a coarse muslin cap of the size of the head to keep out the sun; and around it wings a foot and a half wide, in place of our parasols, which in truth are a nuisance to carry on horseback.

Since at other times I have repented of not having written more in detail on the subject of the other baths, so that I could derive rules and examples for those I used later, this time I want to expatiate.

On Wednesday I went to the bath. I felt a heat in my body, more sweat than usual, a little weakness, dryness and bitterness in my mouth, and an indescribable dizziness on getting out of the bath, as happened to me on account of the heat of the waters at all the other baths: Plombières, Bagnères, Préchacq. At that of Barbotan and at this one never, except this Wednesday; whether because I had gone there much earlier than on the other days, and before discharging my bowels, or because I found the water much hotter than usual. I was there for an hour and a half, and showered my head for about a quarter of an hour.

I did many things contrary to the common rule: taking a shower in the bath, for the custom is to do one separately, and then the other; taking a shower with this water, whereas there are few who do not go to the other bath for a shower, and take it from this tap or that, some at the first, some at the second, some at the third, according to the doctor's prescription; drinking and then bathing and then drinking, thus mixing up the days for one or the other, whereas the others drink for certain days and then use the baths for a stretch; not observing the appropriate periods, for the others drink for ten days at the most, and bathe at least twenty-five days in succession; bathing only once a day, whereas they always bathe twice; taking such a short shower, whereas they always stay in it at least an hour in the morning and the same in the evening. As for getting tonsured, as they all do, and then putting on the bald place a little piece of satin with a sort of net to keep it on the head, my polished head had no need of it.

This same day, in the morning, the Lord Vicar came to visit me—one of the principal gentlemen of this signory, coming specially from the other baths, where he was staying. Among other things he told me an amazing story about himself, that the bite of a beetle on the fleshy tip of his thumb a few years ago had brought him to such an extremity that he nearly died of exceeding faintness; and from that he fell into such misery that he was five months in bed without moving, lying constantly on his loins, thus heating them so immoderately that they engendered the renal calculus, from which he suffered a great deal for over a year, as well as from colic. Finally his father, governor of Velletri, sent him a certain green stone which had come into his hands through a monk who had been in India. As long as he had this stone against his back he never felt either pain or flow of gravel. And he had been in this state for two years. As for the sting, his thumb and almost his whole hand had remained useless, and even his arm so weakened that every year he comes to the baths of Corsena to shower that arm and hand, as he was doing then.

The common people here are very poor. At this time they were eating green mulberries, which they picked from the trees as they stripped them of their leaves for the silkworms.

Since our terms for renting the house for the month of June had been left undecided, I wanted to clear this up with my landlord, who, realizing how much I was in demand with all his neighbors, and particularly with the steward of the Buonvisi palace, who had offered it to me for a gold crown a day, made up his mind to let me have my rooms for as long as I liked at the rate of twenty-five gold crowns a month; this agreement beginning on the first of June, and the first bargain being in force until then.

The inhabitants of this place are very full of envy and of secret deadly enmities, although they are all related.

A woman here told me this proverb:

> To make your wife conceive, the surest way
> Is: send her to the bath, and stay away.

Among other very pleasant things in my house was this, that I could go from the bath to bed by a level path only thirty paces long.

I did not like to see these mulberry trees stripped of their leaves, looking like winter in the middle of summer.

The gravel I was continually voiding seemed to me much rougher than usual, and left me with an indescribable stinging in my prick.

Every day you could see being brought to this place from all sides samples of various wines in tiny little bottles, so that the visitors there who liked them might order some; and there were very few good wines. There were light, rather bitter, and raw whites, or really coarse, rough reds, unless you sent to Lucca or Pescia for the white Trebbiano, very mature, though not too delicate for all that.

On Thursday, the feast of Corpus Christi, I took a temperate bath for an hour or more; I sweated very little, and came out of it without any alteration. I showered my head for half of a quarter hour, and on going back to bed went to sleep for a while. I found this bathing and showering pleasurable rather than otherwise. I felt on my hands and other parts of the body a rash, and moreover I noticed that many of the peasants around here had the itch, and many children suffered from milk crust.

It happens here as elsewhere, that what we seek with so much difficulty is held in contempt by the people of the country: and I saw many of them who had never tasted these waters and had a low opinion of them. Withal there are few old people.

With the phlegm that I voided in my urine (which happens to me continually) there was gravel enveloped and suspended. I seemed to feel this effect from the bath when I put my groin under the spout, that it drove the winds out of me. And certainly I have felt my right testicle suddenly and clearly be reduced in size at times, if it had chanced to swell up, as happens to me fairly often. From this I almost conclude that this swelling is caused by the effect of the wind enclosed inside it.

On Friday I bathed as usual and showered my head a bit more. The extraordinary quantity of gravel that I continually voided made me suppose that it had not been enclosed in the kidneys, because you could have made a big ball of it by squeezing it; and that what the water did was rather to make it conceive and gradually give birth.

On Saturday I bathed for two hours and took a shower for more than a quarter of an hour. On Sunday I kept quiet. On this day a gentleman from Bologna treated us to another ball.

The lack of clocks in this place and in most of Italy seemed to me very inconvenient.

In the bathhouse there is a Madonna, and these verses:

> Pray grant to all who enter, Goddess kind,
> To leave here sound in body and in mind.

One cannot praise too highly, both for beauty and for utility, this way of cultivating the mountains right up to the summit, forming terraces in a circle around them, and supporting the tops of these terraces now with stones, now with other ramparts, if the ground does not hold them of itself; filling with wheat the flat part of the terrace, wider or narrower as it happens to be; bordering with vines the outside of the flat part toward the valley, that is to say the circumference and edge; and where they cannot find or form a flat surface, as for example near the summit, putting vines all over.

At this ball[11] a woman began to dance with a pitcher full of water on her head, keeping it steady and firm, with no lack of lively movements.

The doctors were stupefied to see most of our Frenchmen drink in the morning and then bathe on the same day.

Monday morning I stayed in the bath two hours. I did not give myself a shower because I took three pounds of water on a whim, which made my bowels move. I used to bathe my eyes every morning, holding them open in the water. I felt no effect from it, either good or bad. I believe that I got rid of those three pounds of water in the bath—where I urinated a good many times and then sweated a little more than usual—and in my stool. Having felt more constipated than usual for the last few days, I used the aforementioned three grains of candied coriander, which drove out a lot of wind, of which I was very full, but little matter. Although I purged my kidneys wonderfully, I did not stop feeling some pricking there; and I judged that it was due rather to wind than to anything else.

Tuesday I stayed two hours in the bath, showered myself for half an hour, and did not drink. Wednesday I stayed in the bath an hour and a half and showered myself about half an hour.

Up to now, to tell the truth, from the little dealing and familiarity I have had with the people of this country, I have not noted those miracles of wit and reason with which rumor credits them. I have seen no extraordinary ability: indeed they have marveled at and made too much of that little power of ours.[12] Thus today certain doctors who had to hold an important consultation for a young lord, Signor Paolo Cesi (nephew of Cardinal Cesi), who was at these baths, came to ask me, at his behest, to be good enough to hear their opinions and arguments, because he was resolved to rely wholly on my judgment. I laughed

---

[11] The one referred to four paragraphs earlier, given by the gentleman from Bologna.

[12] Presumably in the sense of *mine*.

about this to myself. Many other similar things have happened to me, both here and in Rome.

My eyes still sometimes felt dazzled when I had grown tired either from reading or from fixing them steadily on some bright and brilliant object; and I have been very worried to feel this weakness continuing ever since the day I had a migraine recently near Florence: that is to say, a heaviness in the head around the forehead, without pain, a certain clouding of the eyes that did not shorten my sight but somehow troubled it at times. After this the migraine came upon me again two or three times; and on those occasions it lasted longer, without, however, interfering with my activities. But since this showering of my head it has attacked me again every day, and my eyes have begun to run, as before, without pain or redness; and it has been more than ten years from the time I last had this headache until I got this migraine.

Fearing also that this water might weaken my head, on Thursday I would not take a shower, but bathed for an hour. During Friday, Saturday, and Sunday I discontinued the cure in every form, for that reason and because I felt a good deal less cheerful, since I was still discharging gravel furiously; but my head, still the same, was not restored to its former good condition. At certain times I felt this alteration, which was increased by the working of the imagination.

On Monday morning I drank, in thirteen glasses, six pounds and a half of water from the ordinary spring. I passed about three pounds of this, white and undigested, before dinner; the rest little by little. This headache, although it was not continuous or very troublesome, made my complexion much worse. I did not feel any failing or weakness in my head, as sometimes formerly, but only a weight on the eyes accompanied by rather cloudy vision.

On this day they began to cut the rye on our plain.

On Tuesday at daybreak I went to the Bernabò spring and there drank six pounds, one at a time. It was raining a bit. I sweated a little. It gave me a movement and washed out my bowels lustily. For that reason I could not judge how much I had given out. I did not urinate much, but in two hours my urine had taken on some color.

They take boarders here for six gold crowns a month, or a little more, for lodging in a private room, as comfortable as you please; with a valet, as much again. If you have no valet, you will still be furnished by the landlord with many provisions for eating suitably.

Before the natural day was over I had passed all the water, and more than I had drunk of all kinds of drink. I had only one little drink at dinner, half a pound. I ate little supper.

On Wednesday, a rainy day, I took seven pounds, one at a time, from the ordinary spring, and passed them, as well as what I had drunk besides.

On Thursday I took nine pounds: seven in a row at first, and then, when I had begun to discharge it, I sent for two more pounds. I discharged it in both ways. I drank very little at dinner. On Friday and Saturday I did the same. On Sunday I stayed quiet.

On Monday I took seven glasses, seven pounds. I was still voiding gravel, but a little less than after a bath; I saw examples of this effect of the baths in a good many other people at the same time. On this day I felt a pain in my groin as from the descent of stones, and I passed a small one.

On Tuesday, another. And I can say, and almost affirm, that I have observed that this water has the power to break them up, because I could feel the large size of some of them as they were coming down, and then I discharged them in smaller pieces. This Tuesday I drank eight pounds in eight times.

If Calvin had known that the Preaching Friars hereabouts call themselves Ministers, he would no doubt have given another name to his.

Wednesday I took eight pounds, eight glasses. I almost always passed the first half of it, undigested and natural, in three hours; then about a half a pound, reddish and colored; the rest after dinner and at night.

In this season people were gathering at the bath. And from those examples that I saw, and from the opinion of the doctors, especially of Donati, who has written about these waters, I had made no great mistake in bathing my head in this bath; for they too have the custom, when they are in the bath, of giving their stomach a shower with a long pipe, attaching one end to the tap and the other to their body in the bath; and since ordinarily they took their head shower with this same water, they bathed on the same day that they took the shower. So I cannot have made a great mistake in mixing the two together, or in having taken the water from the channel of the spring itself instead of the pipe. And perhaps I was wrong not to continue. And the feeling I have about it up to now seems to be that I have stirred up the humors which in time would have been driven out and purged.

This Donati permitted drinking and bathing on the same day. And I am sorry I did not have the boldness, as I had the desire, and with some reason, to drink in the bath in the morning. He greatly praised Bernabò, but with those reasons and arguments that the medicos use.

The effect of these waters on the gravel, which continued in me all the time, was not to be seen in a number of others who were free from this infirmity. Which I say because I cannot make up my mind to believe that they produced the gravel that I discharged.

Thursday morning I was in the bath for an hour without bathing my head, and before daybreak, in order to have the first place. For that reason, I believe, and because I slept afterward in bed, I felt bad: my mouth, dry and thirsty, and so hot that in the evening, on going to bed, I drank two big glasses of that water, cooled; from which I felt no other change.

On Friday I stayed quiet. The Minister Friar of Saint Francis (so they call the provincials),[13] a worthy man and courteous and learned, who was at the bath with many other friars of various orders, sent me

---

[13] A provincial is the superior of all the Franciscan monasteries in one province.

a handsome present of very good wine, marzipan, and other things to eat.

On Saturday I did not take the cure, and went to dine at Menabbio, a handsome large village at the top of one of these mountains. I took some fish along, and was received into the house of a rich soldier who has traveled much in France and other places, and took a wife and got rich in Flanders. He is called Signor Santo. There are vast numbers of peasant soldiers here, a beautiful church, and few who have not traveled much; everyone is strongly divided into these Spanish and French factions. Without thinking about it I put a flower at my left ear. The French faction took it as an insult.

After dinner I climbed up to the fort, which is a place protected by high walls right at the top of the hill, very steep, but thoroughly cultivated everywhere. And here among the ever-present crags, among the rocky precipices and steep places and rugged hills, you find not only vines and wheat, but also meadows; and in the plain they have no grass. I then came straight down by another side of the mountain.

On Sunday morning I went to the bath with several other gentlemen. I stayed there half an hour. There came to me from Signor Ludovico Pinitesi a beautiful present of a horse laden with very beautiful fruit, and among other things some early figs, of which none had yet been seen at the bath, and twelve bottles of very sweet wine. And at the same time the aforesaid friar sent me other kinds of fruit in great quantity; so that I too was able to exercise liberality to the country people.

After dinner was the ball, where a number of gentlewomen gathered, well dressed, but of ordinary beauty, although they were among the most beautiful of Lucca.

In the evening Signor Ludovico di Ferrari, of Cremona, whom I knew very well, sent me a present of some boxes of very good quince jelly, scented, and some lemons, and some oranges of extraordinary size.

At night, a little before daybreak, I was seized by a cramp in the calf of the right leg, with very great pain, not continuous but intermittent. I remained in that discomfort for half an hour. I had felt one not long before, but it passed in a flash.

On Monday I went to the bath and was there for an hour with my stomach under the tap. That vein in my leg still pricked me a little.

Just at this time we began to feel the heat and to hear the grasshoppers, though no more than in France; until then the seasons had seemed cooler to me than at home.

Free nations do not have the same distinction between people's ranks as do the others; and even those of the lowest class have something lordly in their manner. When they ask for alms they always mix in some authoritative word: "Give me alms, will you?" or "Give me alms, understand!" As they say in Rome: "Do good for your own sake."[14]

On Tuesday I stayed in the bath for an hour.

[14] Montaigne quotes this again in the *Essays* (III: 5, p. 682).

Italy: Florence—Pisa—Lucca (June 21-August 13, 1581)

On Wednesday, June 21st, early, I left La Villa, after receiving, when I took leave of the company of men and women who were there, all the indications of friendliness that I could desire. I came through steep, but pleasant and wooded mountains, to

Pescia, twelve miles, a little walled village on the river Pescia, in Florentine territory. Handsome houses, open streets, the famous wines of Trebbiano; situated among very thick olive trees; the people most affectionate toward France: and for this reason, they say, the city bears a dolphin as its arms.[1]

After dinner we came upon a beautiful plain, heavily populated with châteaux and houses. And through absent-mindedness, despite my intention and settled plans, I forgot to see Montecatini, where they have the hot salt water of the Tettuccio, which I left a mile off my road on the right, about seven miles from Pescia; and I did not realize this until I had nearly reached

Pistoia, eleven miles. I was lodged outside the city, where the son of Rospigliosi[2] came to see me.

Anyone who goes through Italy with other than hired horses does not know what he is doing. And it seems to me more convenient to change them from place to place than to put yourself in the hands of the drivers for a long trip. From Pistoia to Florence, which is twenty miles, the horses cost only four giulii.

From here, passing through the town of Prato, I came to dine at

Castello, in a hostelry opposite the grand duke's palace, where we went after dinner to examine the garden more minutely. And it happened to me here as in many other things: imagination transcended the reality. I had seen it in the winter bare and stripped. I had thought more of its future beauty in the milder season than appeared to me in actuality. Castello, seventeen miles. After dinner I came to

Florence, three miles.

On Friday I saw the public procession, and the grand duke in his coach. Among other displays one saw a car in the form of a theater, gilt on top, in which there were four little boys and a friar dressed up to represent Saint Francis, standing up, holding his hands as you see them in the pictures, with a crown on his cowl—either a friar or a man dressed as a friar, with a false beard. There were some armed boys of

---

[1] The French for dolphin, *dauphin*, also means the eldest son of the king. The Pescian dolphin appears to owe its place on their coat of arms to another pun, on *pesce* (fish).

[2] Taddeo Rospigliosi had entertained Montaigne at Pistoia before. See *Travel Journal*, p. 982.

the city, and among them one as Saint George. There came to meet him
in the square a big dragon, supported pretty clumsily and carried by
men, spouting fire noisily from his mouth. The boy gave him one with
the lance and the sword, and cut his throat.

I was warmly entertained by a Gondi who lives at Lyons and who
sent me some excellent wines, that is to say, Trebbiano.

It was so hot as to astonish even the natives.

This morning at daybreak I had the colic in my right side. It afflicted
me for about three hours. Then I ate my first melon. Cucumbers and
almonds are eaten in Florence from the beginning of June.

About the 23rd they had the chariot race in a beautiful large square,[3]
rectangular, longer than it is wide, surrounded on all sides by beautiful
houses. At each end was placed a square wooden obelisk, and a long
rope was attached from one to the other, so that people could not cross
the square; and some men placed themselves across to reinforce the
said rope. All the balconies crowded with ladies, and in one palace the
grand duke, his wife, and his court. The populace along the square,
and on a kind of grandstand, as I was too.

Five empty coaches raced. They were assigned their places by lot
at one side of one pyramid. And some said that the outside one had
the advantage, because it could make the turns more easily. They
started at the sound of trumpets. The third turn around the pyramid
they started from is the one that gives the victory. The grand duke's
coach was ahead all the way until the third lap. Here Strozzi's coach,
which had been second all the way, with the horses given free rein, putting on greater speed than before and closing in, placed the victory in
doubt. I noticed that the silence of the people was broken when they
saw Strozzi coming close, and with shouts and applause they gave him
all the encouragement possible under the eyes of the prince. And then,
when this dispute and altercation came to be judged by certain gentlemen, and those favoring Strozzi referred it to the opinion of the populace present, there immediately arose from the people a universal shout
and a public consensus in favor of Strozzi, who finally had it—contrary
to justice, in my opinion. The prize would be worth a hundred crowns.
I enjoyed this spectacle more than any other I had seen in Italy for its
resemblance to the ancient type of race.

Because today was Saint John's Eve, certain little fires were placed
at the top of the cathedral in a circle in two or three rows, from which
rockets were launched into the air. They say that it is not the custom
in Italy, as in France, to make Saint John's fires.

Saturday, Saint John's Day, which is the principal holiday in Florence, and the one they celebrate most; so that at this feast even the
young girls are seen in public; however, I saw no great beauty. In the
morning, in the palace square, the grand duke appeared on a stand
(under a canopy, along the walls of his palace) decked with very rich

[3] The Piazza di Santa Maria Novella.

tapestry, having on his left side the Pope's nuncio, and much further away the ambassador of Ferrara. There passed before him all his villages and fortified places, as they were called by a herald. So, for Siena, a young man came forward dressed in black and white velvet, carrying in his hand a kind of large silver vessel and the figure of the she-wolf of Siena. Thus dressed and laden, this man made an offering to the grand duke and a little speech. When he had finished, there came forward as they were called some badly dressed boys on very wretched horses and mules, carrying one a silver cup, another a torn and dilapidated banner. These in great numbers passed along their way without saying a word, without respect and without ceremony, more as if for a joke than otherwise; and they were the fortified places depending on the State of Siena. Every year this is repeated as a matter of form.

There also passed by there a car carrying a large square wooden pyramid, and on certain steps around it some little boys dressed some in one way, some in another, as angels or saints; and at the top, at the height of the tallest houses, a Saint John, a man dressed up in his guise, bound to an iron bar. The officials, and particularly those of the mint, followed this car.

At the end came another car, on which were certain young men bearing three prizes for the different races, having at their side the Barbary horses that were to race that day, and the boys who were to ride them, with the colors of their masters, who are among the highest lords. The horses are small and handsome.

The heat did not seem to me more violent than in France. However, to escape it in these hotel rooms, I was forced to sleep at night on the dining room table, putting mattresses and sheets on it; not having found here any comfortable lodging to rent, for this city is not a good one for strangers; also to escape the bugs, with which the beds are most thickly infested.

There is not much fish, and no trout or other fish is eaten except what comes from elsewhere and is marinated. I saw that the grand duke sent to Giovanni Marliani, a Milanese lodging in the same hotel where I was, a present of wine, bread, fruit, and fish; but the fish alive, small, in earthenware coolers.

I had a dry and arid mouth all day and felt parched not from thirst, but from an internal heat which I have experienced at other times in our hot spells. I ate nothing but fruit and salad with sugar. In short, I was not well.

Those open-air recreations that are practiced in France after supper here come before it. And on the longest days they often sup at night. Day breaks in the morning between seven and eight.

After dinner the Barbary horses ran for the prize. The Cardinal de' Medici's horse won it. This prize was worth two hundred crowns. It is not a very entertaining sight, because, being in the street, you see nothing but these horses going furiously past.

On Sunday I saw the Pitti Palace, and among other things a marble mule representing an actual mule that is still alive, because of its long service carrying materials for building this palace. So the Latin verses say.[4]

At this palace we saw the chimaera, which has between the shoulders a nascent head with horns and ears, and a body in the form of a little lion.

On the Saturday the grand duke's palace was open and full of country people, to whom everything was open, and the great hall was full of groups of dancers, some here, some there. To these people I believe this is a kind of symbol of their lost liberty, which is refreshed at this main festival of the city.

On Monday I went to dine at the house of Signor Silvio Piccolomini, well known for his valor and in particular for his mastery in fencing. Many topics were brought up, for there was a good company of other gentlemen. He utterly despises the fencing technique of the Italian masters, the Venetian, the Bolognese, that of Patinostrato, and others. And in this respect he praises only a pupil of his own who is at Brescia, where he teaches this art to certain gentlemen. He says that there is no rule or art in the usual teaching; and he particularly condemns the practice of thrusting the sword forward and putting it at the power of the enemy, and then the *botta passada*[5] to make another assault and stop; for he says that this is completely different from what is actually seen among combatants. He was about to publish a book on this subject. As for matters of war, he has great contempt for artillery; and I was very pleased with him on this account.[6] He praises Machiavelli's book *On the Art of War* and follows his opinions. He says that of the sort of men who plan fortifications the most outstanding is now in Florence in the service of the most serene grand duke.[7]

It is customary here to put snow into the wine glasses. I put only a little in, not being too well in body, having pain in the sides many times, and all the time ejecting an incredible amount of gravel; besides this, I could not restore my head to its original condition. Dizziness and a kind of heaviness on the eyes, the forehead, the cheeks, teeth, nose, and face. It came into my mind that it was the sweet, heady white wines, because at the time the migraine first seized me again I had drunk a great quantity of Trebbiano, when heated by traveling and by the season, and when its sweetness did not quench my thirst.

I finally confessed that Florence is rightly called "the beautiful."

On this day I went alone for fun to see the women who let themselves be seen by anyone who wants. I saw the most famous: nothing exceptional. The lodgings are gathered in one particular part of town, and are therefore contemptible, and wretched besides, and they do not approach in any way those of the Roman or Venetian prostitutes; nor do

---

[4] The bedding, stones, wood, columns, all that store
   It carried hither, brought, conveyed, and bore.
[5] Thrust in which one foot crosses over the other.
[6] For Montaigne's similar views see *Essays* I: 48, p. 211.
[7] Francesco Pacciotto of Urbino.

they themselves in beauty or grace or dignity. If one of them wants to live outside these limits, she must be of little account and must perform some other trade for concealment.

I saw the shops of the silk spinners; they have certain machines, by turning which one single woman can twist and turn five hundred spindles at once.

Tuesday morning I ejected a little red stone.

Wednesday I saw the grand duke's casino. What seemed most important to me was a rocky structure in the form of a pyramid, composed and fabricated of all kinds of natural minerals, one piece of each, joined together. This structure later spouted water, by which many objects inside it were seen to be set in motion, water mills and windmills, little church bells, soldiers of the guard, animals, hunts, and a thousand such things.

Thursday I would not wait to see another horse race. I went after dinner to Pratolino, which I studied again very minutely. And being asked by the caretaker of the palace to give my opinion of these beauties and of those of Tivoli, I talked about this, not comparing these places in general, but part by part, with the various advantages of the one and the other, each one alternately being the victor.

Friday at the Giunti's shop I bought a number of comedies, eleven of them, and certain other little books. And here I saw Boccaccio's will printed together with certain treatises on the *Decameron*. This will shows an amazing poverty and lowliness of fortune in that great man. He leaves some sheets and then certain parts of beds to his female relatives and his sisters; the books to a certain friar, whom he orders to communicate them to anyone who asks for them. He takes account even of vessels and the meanest pieces of furniture. He gives orders for Masses and for his burial. It is printed as it was recovered, on a very tattered and ruined sheet of parchment.

As the Roman and Venetian prostitutes come to the windows for their lovers, so these come to the doors of their houses, where they stand in the public view at the convenient hours; and there you see them in groups, some with more company, some with less, chatting and singing in the street.

On Sunday, July 2nd, I left Florence after dinner, and after crossing the Arno on the bridge, we left it on our right hand but followed its course. We passed some beautiful fertile plains in which are the most famous melon beds in Tuscany. The good melons are not ripe until the 15th of July. The place in particular where the most excellent ones are grown is called Legnaia, three miles this side of Florence.

We went along a road through country mostly level and fertile, and very thickly built up throughout—almost without a break—with houses, small walled towns, and villages. We passed through, among others, one pretty town named Empoli. The sound of this name has something ancient about it. A most pleasant site. I did not discover here any vestige of antiquity except a ruined bridge on the road nearby, which has something old about the look of it.

I noted three things worth considering: to see the people of these parts working, some in threshing wheat or stacking it, some at sewing or spinning, on the Sunday holiday. The second, to see these country people lute in hand, and even the shepherd girls with Ariosto in their mouth; this is to be seen throughout Italy. The third is to see how they leave the reaped wheat on the fields for ten or fifteen days or more, without fear of their neighbor.

Toward dark we arrived at

LA SCALA, twenty miles: one single lodging house, pretty good. I did not eat supper, and slept little, troubled by a toothache on the right side, which I felt many times with my headache. It bothered me most when eating, and I was not able to touch a thing without very great pain.

On Monday morning, July 3rd, we followed the level road along the Arno, and, toward the end, a plain abounding with wheat. We arrived about noon at

PISA, twenty miles, a city belonging to the duke of Florence, situated in this plain on the Arno, which passes through the middle of it and six miles from here pours into the sea, and brings to this city a good many kinds of craft.

At this time the school[8] was closing, as is the custom, for three months of the great heat.

Here we came across the excellent company of the Desiosi, actors.

Because I was not satisfied with the hostelry, I rented a house with four bedrooms and a dining room. The landlord was to do the cooking and supply the furniture. A fine house. The whole thing for eight crowns a month. Because what he had promised by way of tablecloths and napkins was too skimpy (seeing that in Italy the custom is to change the napkins very little except when they change the tablecloths, and the tablecloths twice a week), we left the servants to board themselves, and we ate at the hostelry at four giulii a day.

The house was in a most beautiful location, with a pleasant view, overlooking the channel through which the Arno passes and crosses the city. This bed is very wide and more than five hundred paces long, bending and curving a bit, making a pleasant sight, revealing more easily by its curve both ends of this channel, with three bridges which there cross the Arno, full of vessels and merchandise. Both banks of this channel are built up with handsome walls with parapets at the top, like the Quai des Augustins in Paris. And then broad streets on both sides, and on the edge of the streets a row of houses. Ours was located there.

On Wednesday, July 5th, I saw the cathedral, where the palace of the Emperor Hadrian used to be. There are countless numbers of marble columns, varied in workmanship and form; very handsome metal doors. It is decorated with various spoils from Greece and Egypt, and built of ancient ruins, so that you see inscriptions upside down, others half cut off, and in certain places unknown characters, which they say are ancient Etruscan.

[8] The University.

I saw the bell tower, of extraordinary appearance, leaning by seven arm's-lengths, like that other one at Bologna, and others; surrounded on all sides by pilasters and open galleries.

I saw the neighboring Church of Saint John,[9] itself also very rich in famous works of sculpture and painting—among others, a marble pulpit with thickly crowded figures, so rare that the Lorenzo who killed Duke Alessandro is said to have taken off the heads of some of these statuettes and made a present of them to the queen.[10] The shape of the church resembles that of the Rotunda in Rome.

The natural son of the duke lives here, and I saw him, an old man. He lives comfortably on the liberality of the duke, and nothing else matters to him. There is wonderful hunting and fishing here. He makes this his business.

Of holy relics, rare works, and marbles and stones wonderful for their rarity, size, and workmanship, you find as many here as in any other city of Italy.

I took inordinate pleasure in the cemetery building that is called the Campo Santo, of unusual size, rectangular, three hundred paces long and one hundred wide. An inner corridor goes all around, forty paces wide, roofed with lead, paved with marble. The walls are covered with ancient paintings.

The nobles of this city have their tombs indoors under this corridor. There are the names and arms of the families to the number of four hundred—among others that of Gondi of Florence, founder of that house—of whom there are now barely four that have survived the wars and the ruin of this most ancient city; of the people just as few: it is inhabited and possessed by foreigners. Of these noble families there are several marquises, counts, and grandees in other parts of Christendom to which they have moved.

In the middle of this building there is an uncovered place where they are continually performing burials. It is stated positively by all that the bodies which are put here swell in eight hours so much that you can see the ground rise; in the following eight it goes down and subsides; in the final eight the flesh is so utterly consumed that before twenty-four hours are up there is nothing left but the bare bones. This miracle is similar to that other at the cemetery in Rome, where if you put in the body of a Roman, the earth promptly ejects it. This place is paved beneath with marble like the corridor, and earth is laid over it to the height of one or two yards. They say that this earth was brought from Jerusalem, because the Pisans took part in that enterprise with a large army.[11] With the bishop's permission, a little of this earth is taken away and sprinkled on other graves, with the idea that the bodies will be promptly consumed. This seems likely, because for a cemetery of a

---

[9] The Battisterio or Baptistry.

[10] Catherine de' Medici.

[11] On the order of Archbishop Ubaldo (1188–1200), fifty-three Pisan ships in Frederick Barbarossa's crusade brought back loads of earth for this cemetery from the Mount of Calvary.

city of this size you see very few bones, almost none, and no place where they are gathered together and enclosed, as in other cities.

The neighboring mountains produce very beautiful marble, for which this city has many renowned workmen. At this time they were working on a very richly wrought theater for the king of Fez, in Barbary, which he plans to build with fifty very high marble columns.

In this city our arms may be seen in countless places, and also a column that King Charles VIII gave to the cathedral. And in one house, on the wall toward the street, the said king is represented life-size, on his knees before the Madonna, who appears to be giving him counsel. The inscription says that when the said king was supping in this house it came into his mind to give the Pisans their ancient freedom, whereby he surpassed the greatness of Alexander. The titles of the said king are there: king of Jerusalem, of Sicily, etc. The words concerning that matter of the granting of freedom have been purposely disfigured and half effaced. Other private houses still have these arms as a decoration, to show the nobility that this king gave them.

There are not many vestiges of ancient buildings here. There is a handsome brick ruin where the palace of Nero was, and it retains his name; and the Church of Saint Michael, which used to be a temple of Mars.

Thursday, which was the feast of Saint Peter, I was told that formerly it was the custom for the bishop to go in procession to the Church of Saint Peter, four miles outside the city, and from there to the sea, where he threw in a ring and "married" the sea; for this city used to have a very powerful navy. Now only a schoolmaster goes there. But the priests in procession go to the church, where there is a great granting of indulgences. The Pope's bull of a little less than four hundred years ago (if I take as authority a book that dates it after 1200)[12] says that this church was built by Saint Peter, and that as Saint Clement was performing the service at a marble table, three little drops of blood fell on it from the nose of the said saint. These three drops seem as though they had been imprinted there for only three days. The Genoese broke this table and carried away one of these drops. Therefore the Pisans removed the rest of the said table from the said church and carried it into their city. But every year they carry it back in procession to its place on the said Saint Peter's Day. The people go there all night in boats.

On Friday, the 7th of July, I went early to see the dairy farms of Don Pietro de' Medici, two miles distant from the town. He has a world of possessions there which he holds in his own name; every five years he rents to new tenants; and he takes half of the produce. A soil most abundant with wheat; pastures where he keeps all sorts of animals. I dismounted to see the particularities of the house. There are a great number of people working at making curds, butter, and cheeses, and divers implements for that work.

[12] The bull is actually of Innocent VI and dated 1354 in Avignon.

From there, following the plain, I arrived at the shore of the Tyrrhenian Sea, where I saw Lerici on the right hand; on the other, Leghorn; nearer, a fortified town standing in the sea. From there when it is clear you can make out the island of Gorgona, and beyond that Capraia, and beyond that Corsica. I turned to the left along the shore until we reached the mouth of the Arno, which is difficult to enter for ships, seeing that from various little streams which flow together into the Arno come earth and mud, which accumulate there and raise the bottom of the said mouth.

I bought some fish there, which I then sent to the actresses.[13]

Along this river you see many tamarisk thickets.

On Saturday I bought a barrel for six giulii, which I have had hooped with silver. It cost three crowns at the artificer's. I bought, besides, a bamboo cane to lean on, six giulii; a little vase and a cup of Indian nut, which has the same effect on the spleen and on the gravel as the tamarisk, eight giulii. The artisan, an able man and famous for making fine mathematical instruments, taught me that all trees bear as many circles and rings as they have lasted years; and showed this to me in all the woods he had in his shop; for he is a cabinet maker. And the part that faces north is narrower and has its rings closer and denser than the other. Therefore he boasts that whatever wood is brought him, he can judge how old the tree was, and in what position it stood.

At this time the trouble in my head was still with me, always remaining the same; together with such constipation that my bowels would not move without artificial help in the form of sweetmeats—a feeble help. The kidneys in good condition, considering.

This city was not long ago blamed for its bad air; but since Duke Cosimo has drained the marshes that are all around, it is good. And it was so bad that when people wanted to confine someone and get him out of the way, they confined him in Pisa, where in a few months it finished him.

This place produces no partridges, for all the trouble the princes have gone to.

Girolamo Borro,[14] a physician, doctor of the University of Rome, came to see me several times at my house. And when I went to visit him on the 14th of July he made me a present of his book on the ebb and flow of the sea, in the vulgar tongue; and he showed me another book he had written, in Latin, on the diseases of the body.

This same day, near my house, twenty-one Turkish slaves escaped from the arsenal, having found a frigate fully equipped, which Signor Alessandro di Piombino had left while he went fishing.

Except for the Arno and the beautiful way in which it flows through the town, these churches and vestiges of antiquity, and its private works, Pisa has little distinction and charm. It seems deserted. And in this re-

---

[13] Of the Desiosi troupe. See above, p. 1008.

[14] Borro is the man whom Montaigne describes (*Essays* I: 26, p. 111) as having got in trouble with the Inquisition in Rome for being too perfect an Aristotelian.

spect, in the shape of its buildings, its size, and the width of its streets, it is a lot like Pistoia. It is extremely short of water, and the water is bad, for it all has a marshy taste.

The men are very poor, and no less haughty, hostile, and discourteous toward foreigners, especially toward the French since the death of a bishop of theirs, Pietro Paolo Bourbon,[15] who said he was of the house of our princes; and there is a family of that name here. He was so affectionate toward our nation and so liberal that he had given orders that every Frenchman arriving here should immediately be brought to his house. He has left to the Pisans a most honored memory of his good life and liberality. It is only five or six years since he died.

On July 17th I joined twenty-five others in playing raffle at a crown apiece, for some belongings of Fargnocolo, one of the comedians. First they drew lots to see who should play first, second, and so on to the last. They follow this order. Then, there being various things to play for, they made two equal parts of them. The man who made the most points won the one, he who made the least the other. It fell to my lot to come out second.

On the 18th, at the Church of Saint Francis, there arose a great squabble between the priests of the cathedral and the friars. A Pisan gentleman had been buried at the aforementioned church the day before, and the priests wanted to say Mass. They came there with their equipment and paraphernalia. They alleged their ancient custom and privilege. The friars, on the contrary, alleged that it was their business and no one else's to say Mass in their own church. One priest, approaching the high altar, tried to seize the marble table. A friar attempted to drag him away. The vicar, patron of this church of priests, slapped this friar. One thing leading to another, gradually the matter came to fighting with fists, sticks, candlesticks, torches, and the like; they used everything. The end of it was that Mass was said by neither party. This angry combat caused a great scandal. As soon as the news of it spread, I went there; and the whole thing was related to me.

On the 22nd at dawn three galleys of Turkish corsairs landed on the coast nearby and carried off fifteen or twenty fishermen and poor shepherds as prisoners.

On the 25th I went to visit Cornacchini, a famous doctor and lecturer of Pisa. He lives in his own way, which is very different from the rules of his art. He sleeps immediately after dining, drinks a hundred times a day, and so on. He recited to me some of his verse, pleasant and in rustic patois. He does not set much store by the baths in the near vicinity of Pisa, but thinks well of those at Bagno-Acqua,[16] sixteen miles from Pisa. He says they are wonderful for getting rid of liver ailments (and he told me a great many miracles about them) as well as for the stone and the colic; but his advice is, before using them, to drink the waters of La Villa. He has become convinced that except for bloodletting,

15 Pietro Jacopo Bourbon del Monte, archbishop of Pisa from 1574 to 1575.
16 Now Casciana.

medicine is nothing compared to the baths, for a man who knows how to use them and avail himself of them well. He said further that at these baths of Bagno-Acqua there are good lodgings, and that you are comfortable and at your ease there.

On the 26th in the morning I passed some turbid and black urine, more so than I had ever seen it before, with one small stone; and this did not stop the pain which I had already suffered for about twenty hours, below the navel and in the member; it was easy to bear, however, and caused no alteration in the loins and the side. A little later I passed another little stone, and my pain subsided.

On Thursday, July 27th, we left Pisa early, I feeling very satisfied with the courtesy and kindness I had received from Signor Vintavinti, from Lorenzo Conti, from San Miniato (in whose house lives the knight Camillo Gatani; he offered to have his brother come to France with me), from Borro, and others, artisans and tradesmen, with whom I had dealt. And I hold for certain that I would not have lacked even money if I had needed it, although this city is considered very uncivil and the inhabitants haughty. But at any rate a man who is courteous makes others so.

Among other things, this town is most abundant in pigeons, hazelnuts, and mushrooms.

For a while we crossed the plain, and at the foot of a hill we came upon the so-called "Baths of Pisa." There are several of them, and an inscription on marble which I could not quite decipher. It consists of Latin verses in rhyme, which testify to the virtues of these waters; and the inscription was dated 1300, as far as I could make out.

The largest and most respectable of these baths is square, and, except for one side, very well arranged, with a marble staircase. Each side is thirty paces long. In one corner you see the tap of the spring. I drank some water to judge it. It seemed to me tasteless and without any odor. I felt only a little sharpness on the tongue. Very moderate heat; very easy to drink. I noticed at this tap that in this water there were again those white corpuscles or atoms that I cursed in the baths of Baden, and judged to be filth and dirt coming from outside. Now I think rather that it comes from some quality of the mines; the more so because these particles appear thicker at the tap and where the water springs from, and where in reason it should be purer and cleaner, as I experienced more clearly at Baden. A solitary place; wretched lodgings. These waters are almost abandoned, and those who use them go there in the morning from Pisa, four miles, and return home. This big bath is uncovered, and it alone bears any sign of antiquity: they call it Nero's Bath. Public rumor says that this emperor conducted this water by means of aqueducts into his palace in Pisa.

There is another covered bath of common workmanship, which the common people use, with clear and very pure water. They say it is good for the liver and for the itch produced by the heat of the liver. They take the same quantity of the drink as at the other baths, and they walk around after drinking, and they follow Nature, whether she makes you sweat or operates in other ways.

As soon as I had climbed this hill,[17] there appeared a most beautiful view looking over that great plain, the sea, the islands, Leghorn, Pisa. When I had come down, we entered the plain on this side, in which stands

Lucca, ten miles. This morning I ejected another much bigger stone, which clearly seemed to be detached from a larger body. God knows! His will be done!

We were at the hostelry on the same terms as at Pisa, at four giulii per master and three per servant, per day. On the 28th, being almost forced to it by the most courteous offers of Signor Ludovico Pinitesi, I took a ground-floor apartment in his house, very cool and nobly furnished, with five bedrooms, a dining room, and a kitchen; and I was provided with all sorts of furniture, most honorably and delicately, according to Italian custom, which in many matters not only compares with but surpasses the French.

A very great ornament indeed to the buildings in Italy is the very high, beautiful, and broad vaults. They make the entrances to the houses pleasant and dignified, because all the lower part is built with that construction, with wide and high doors. In summer the gentlemen of Lucca eat in public under these entryways, in sight of anyone passing along the street.

To tell the truth, wherever I have stayed in Italy, except Florence (because there I did not leave the hotel, in spite of the discomforts you find in that sort of house, especially when it is hot) and Venice (where we put up in a house too public, and in bad condition, since we were to stay there only a short time), I have always had not only good but even delightful lodgings. My room was secluded; I lacked nothing; there was no hindrance or disturbance at all. Since courtesies are sometimes tiresome and annoying, it very seldom happened that I was visited by the local people. I slept and studied as I pleased, and when I wanted to go out I could talk anywhere with women or men, with whom I could pleasantly pass an hour or two of the day; and then shops, churches, squares. And, continually changing the scene, I did not lack matter to feed my curiosity. In the meantime I enjoyed a tranquil mind, as far as my infirmities and old age allow; for very few occasions came along from outside to disturb it. I felt only one lack, that of company that I liked, being forced to enjoy these good things alone and without communication.

The Lucchesi play *pallone*[18] very well, and you often see some beautiful games. It is not their custom for the men to go along the street on horseback, or very little; and still less in coaches. The ladies, yes, but on mules; and they go with a servant on foot. Houses to let are very hard to find for foreigners, for very few come here, and this city in itself is

[17] The Monte San Giuliano, which keeps the Pisans from seeing Lucca, as Dante noted (*Inferno* XXXIII. 30).

[18] A game somewhat like court tennis, but played with a wooden armlet instead of a racket.

well populated. For an ordinary house with four furnished bedrooms and one dining room and kitchen, I was asked seventy crowns a month rent.

You cannot enjoy the company of the Lucchesi because they are all, even the children, continually occupied at their business and in acquiring goods by means of trade. Therefore the city is somewhat tiresome and disagreeable for strangers.

On the 10th of August we went outside the town for a pleasure trip with some other gentlemen of Lucca, from whom I had borrowed horses. I saw some very pleasant villas around the town at three or four miles' distance, with porticoes and loggias, which are a great ornament to them. Among others, a big loggia, all vaulted inside, covered with branches and tendrils of vines planted all around it, and supported on some props: a living and natural arbor.

My headache at times left me for five or six days or more, but I could not quite get rid of it.

I had an impulse to learn the Florentine language by methodical study. I put a lot of time and concentration into it, but got very little benefit out of it.

In this season we felt a much greater heat than is commonly felt.

On the 12th I also went outside of Lucca to visit the villa of Signor Benedetto Buonvisi: moderately attractive. Among other things I saw there formations of certain little thickets that they make in steep places. In an area of about fifty paces they plant various trees, of those that stay green all year round. This place they encircle with little ditches, and inside it they construct certain little covered alleys. In the middle is a place for the fowler, who, with a silver whistle and a number of thrushes caught for the purpose and tied down, having arranged on all sides a number of birdlime snares, at a certain season of the year, say about November, will in one morning make a catch of two hundred thrushes; and this is done only in a certain area on a certain side of the city.

On Sunday the 13th I left Lucca, having ordered that the said Messer Ludovico Pinitesi be offered fifteen crowns for the use of his house. This reckoning came to one crown a day, with which he was very satisfied.

We went on this day to visit a great many of the villas of gentlemen of Lucca, which are clean, nice, and handsome. They have lots of water, but artificial—that is to say, not running, not natural or continuous. It is a marvel to see so great a rarity of springs in so hilly a place. They draw certain waters from streams, and for the sake of beauty they arrange them in the manner of fountains with vases, grottoes, and other works of similar service.

We came to supper this evening in a villa of the said Messer Ludovico, having still in our company his son Messer Orazio, who received us very comfortably in this villa and gave us a very good supper, by night, under a large portico, very cool, and open on all sides, and then had us sleep in good separate rooms, with very white clean linen sheets, such as we had enjoyed in Lucca at the father's house.

Italy: Second Stay at La Villa
(August 14-September 12, 1581)

Monday early we left there. And along the road, without dismounting, after stopping a while to visit the villa of the bishop, who was there (and we were made much of by his men, and invited to stay there to dinner), we came to dine at

THE BATHS OF LA VILLA, fifteen miles. I received a warm welcome and greetings from all those people. In truth it seemed that I had come back to my own home. I went back to the same room I had the first time, at the price of twenty crowns a month, and on the same conditions.

Tuesday August 15th I went to the bath early and stayed there a little less than an hour. I again found it rather cold than otherwise. It did not start me sweating at all. I arrived at these baths not only healthy, but I may further say in all-round good spirits. After bathing, I passed some cloudy urine; and in the evening, after walking a good bit over alpine and not at all easy roads, I passed some that was quite bloody; and in bed I felt something indefinably wrong with the kidneys.

On the 16th I continued the bathing, and I went to the women's bath, where I had not yet been, in order to be separate and alone. I found it too hot, either because it was really so or indeed because my pores, being opened from the bathing of the day before, had made me get hot easily. At all events I stayed there an hour at most and sweated moderately. My urine was natural; no gravel at all. After dinner my urine again came turbid and red, and at sunset it was bloody.

On the 17th I found this same bath more temperate. I sweated very little. The urine rather turbid, with a little gravel; my color a sort of yellow pallor.

On the 18th I stayed two hours in the aforesaid bath. I felt I know not what heaviness in the kidneys. My bowels were reasonably loose. From the very first day I felt full of wind, and my bowels rumbling. I can easily believe that this effect is characteristic of these waters, because the other time I bathed I clearly perceived that they brought on the flatulence in this way.

On the 19th I went to the bath a little later to give way to a lady of Lucca who wanted to bathe, and did bathe, before me; for this rule is observed, and reasonably so, that the ladies may enjoy their own bath when they please. I again stayed there two hours. There came over me a little heaviness in my head, which had been in the best of condition for several days. My urine was still turbid, but in different ways, and it carried off a lot of gravel. I also noticed some sort of commotion in the kidneys. And if my feelings are correct, these baths can do much in that particular; and not only do they dilate and open up the passages and conduits, but furthermore they drive out the matter, dissipate and scatter it. I voided gravel that seemed really to be stones broken up into pieces.

In the night I felt in the left side the beginning of a very violent and painful colic, which tore me for a good while and yet did not run its ordinary course: it did not reach the belly and the groin, and ended in a way that made me believe it was wind.

On the 20th I was two hours in the bath. The wind in my lower intestines gave me much annoyance and discomfort all day. I continually voided very turbid, red, thick urine with some little gravel. I felt bad in my head. My bowels were rather livelier than usual.

Feast days are not observed here as religiously as we observe them, especially Sunday. The women do most of their work after dinner.

On the 21st I continued my bathing. After taking my bath I had a lot of pain in my kidneys. My urine was very turbid. I voided gravel, but not much. The pain I suffered then in the kidneys, as far as I could judge, was caused by wind, which was stirring all over. From the turbidity of the urine I guessed that some large stone was about to descend. I guessed only too well.

After writing this up in the morning, I came to be greatly afflicted with colicky pains immediately after dinner. And in order not to leave me too relaxed, one of these spasms attacked me together with a very acute toothache in the left jaw, which I had not felt before. Not being able to endure this discomfort, after two or three hours I went to bed, where in a short time this pain in the jaw left me.

Since the colic still tormented me, and I finally sensed (from feeling it move from place to place and occupy different parts of my body) that it was rather wind than a stone, I was forced to ask for an enema, which was administered to me at nightfall very comfortably, made of oil, camomile, and anise, and nothing else, by the prescription of the apothecary alone. Captain Paulino served me with it artfully in this way: feeling the wind rushing out against it, he stopped and drew back; and then continued very gently, so that I took in the whole thing without trouble. He did not need to remind me to retain it as long as I could, for it did not give me any desire to move my bowels. I stayed this way for as long as three hours, and then I tried to void it by myself. Being out of bed, I took a mouthful of marzipan with great difficulty, and four drops of wine. After going back to bed and sleeping a bit, I felt an inclination to go to the toilet; and by daybreak I had gone four times, though still keeping some part of the said enema that was not voided.

In the morning I felt much relieved, having got rid of an infinite amount of wind. I was left very tired, but with no pain. I ate a little dinner, without appetite; I drank without relish, although I felt very thirsty. After dinner that pain in my left jaw attacked me once again, from which I suffered very much from dinner to supper time. Considering it certain that this flatulence was caused by the bath, I let the bath alone. I got through the night with a good sleep.

In the morning on waking I found myself again weary and short of breath, my mouth dry, with a sharp bad taste, and my breath as if I had a fever. I did not feel any pain, but I continued passing this extraordinary and very turbid urine, which all the time carried with it sand and reddish gravel, but not in great quantity.

On the 24th, in the morning, I pushed down a stone that stopped in the passage. I remained from that moment until dinnertime without urinating, in order to increase my desire to do so. Then I got my stone out, not without pain and bleeding, both before and after: as big and long as a pine nut, but as thick as a bean at one end, and having, to tell the truth, exactly the shape of a prick. It was a very fortunate thing for me to be able to get it out. I have never ejected one comparable in size to this one. I had guessed only too truly from the quality of my urines that this would be the result. I shall see what is to follow.

There would be too much weakness and cowardice on my part if, finding myself every day in a position to die in this manner, and with every hour bringing death nearer, I did not make every effort toward being able to bear death lightly as soon as it surprises me. And in the meantime it will be wise to accept joyously the good that it pleases God to send us. There is no other medicine, no other rule or science, for avoiding the ills, whatever they may be and however great, that besiege men from all sides and at every hour, than to make up our minds to suffer them humanly, or to end them courageously and promptly.

On August 25th my urine regained its usual color, and I found my body in the same condition as before; except that many times, both day and night, I suffered in my left cheek; but it was a sort of pain that did not last at all. I remember that this pain bothered me at other times in my home.

On Saturday the 26th I was in the bath for an hour in the morning.

On the 27th after dinner I was cruelly tormented by a very acute toothache, so that I sent for the doctor, who, when he had come and considered everything, and especially that my pain had left me in his presence, judged that this defluxion had no body unless a very subtle one, and that it was wind and flatulence that mounted from the stomach to the head and, mingling with a little humor, gave me that discomfort. This indeed seemed to me very likely, considering that I had suffered similar accidents in other parts of the body.

On Monday, August 28th, at dawn, I went to drink at Bernabò's spring, and drank seven pounds four ounces of the water, at twelve ounces to the pound. It made my bowels move once. I voided a little less than half of it before dinner. I clearly felt that it sent vapors to my head and made it heavy.

On Tuesday the 29th I drank at the ordinary spring nine glasses, which each contained one ounce less than a pound. Immediately my head felt bad. To tell the truth, my head was of itself in bad condition, and it had never fully recovered from the bad state it had fallen into in my first season of bathing. I was troubled by it more rarely and in a little different way than a month before, because my eyes were not weakened or dazzled. I suffered more in the back, and never in the head without the pain passing immediately to the left cheek, affecting the whole of it, the teeth, even the lower ones, the ear, part of the nose. The pain was brief, but most of the time very acute, and seized me very many times, day and night. Such was the condition of my head this season.

I do believe that the fumes of this water, from drinking and also from bathing (though more so in the former case than in the latter), are very bad for the head, and, I can say with assurance, even worse for the stomach. And therefore their custom is generally to take medicine to provide against this.

During that whole day and night I passed all but a pound of the water, counting what I drank at table, which was very little, and less than a pound. After dinner, toward sunset, I went to the bath and stayed there three-quarters of an hour. I sweated a little.

On Wednesday, August 30th, I drank nine glasses, eighty-one ounces. I passed half of it before dinner.

On Thursday I discontinued the drinking, and in the morning went on horseback to see Controne, a very populous municipality in these mountains. There are many beautiful fertile plains, and pastures at the top of the mountains. This municipality has many little villas, comfortable stone lodgings, their roofs covered with stone. I made a long tour around these hills before returning home.

I did not like the way I had got rid of the water I had taken lately. Therefore I thought of giving up drinking it. I was displeased because I did not pass it all, and the count of what I urinated did not match with what I had drunk. More than three glasses of the water of the bath must have remained inside me. Besides, I had an attack of constipation, in contrast with my ordinary state.

Friday, September 1st, 1581, I bathed for an hour in the morning. I sweated some in the bath, and voided with the urine a large quantity of red gravel. When drinking, I had voided none, or little. My head remained still in the same state, that is to say bad.

I began to find these baths unpleasant. And if news had come from France, which I was expecting, having been four months without receiving any, I would have been ready to leave at the first opportunity, and do my autumn cure at any other baths whatever. If I went toward Rome, I would come across at a short distance from the main road the baths of Bagno-Acqua, and those of Siena and Viterbo; if I went toward Venice, those of Bologna, and then those of Padua.

I had my coat of arms made in Pisa, gilt, and in handsome vivid colors, for a French crown and a half, and then pasted on a board (for it was on canvas) at the bath, and this board I had very carefully nailed up on the wall of the room I stayed in, with this condition: that it was to be considered as given to the room, not to Captain Paulino the landlord, and that on no account was it to be removed, whatever might happen to the house in the future. And this he promised and swore.

On Sunday, September 3rd, I went to bathe and stayed there an hour and a little more. I felt a quantity of wind, but without pain.

That night and the morning of Monday the 4th, I was cruelly tormented by a toothache, and I continued to suspect that it was some decayed tooth. I chewed mastic in the morning without any relief. From the change that this very acute pain brought me there also followed constipation, because of which I did not dare to resume drinking at the bath; and thus I did very little by way of a cure. Toward dinnertime and for three or four hours after dinner it gave me some peace. Toward two in the afternoon it attacked me with such fury in the head and both jaws that I could not stay on my feet. The sharpness of the pain made me want to vomit. Now I was all in a sweat, now chilled. This pain that attacked me on every side led me to believe that the trouble was not caused by a bad tooth. For although the left side was in much greater torment, nevertheless in both temples, and the chin, and even in the shoulders and the throat, in every part, I felt at times the greatest pain; so that I passed the cruelest night that I remember ever having passed. It was really rage and fury.

In the night I sent for an apothecary, who gave me some brandy to put on the side of my mouth that tormented me most. I received wonderful help from it, for at the very instant that I put it into my mouth, all my pain subsided. But as soon as I had spat it out, the pain seized me again as before; so that I had the glass continually to my mouth. I could not keep the brandy in my mouth, because as soon as the pain left me, weariness sent me fast asleep, and as soon as I was asleep a drop of this brandy would go down my throat, and so I had to spray it again. At daybreak my pain passed.

I was visited Tuesday morning in bed by all the gentlemen who were at the baths. I had a small mastic plaster applied to my left temple over the pulse. On this day I felt little pain. At night they put hot tow on my cheek and on the left side of my head. I slept without pain, but a troubled sleep.

On Wednesday I still felt the pain in the teeth and the left eye. I voided some gravel with my urine, but not in the great quantity that I voided it the first time I was here. I passed certain solid grains of it, like millet, and red.

On Thursday, September 7th, in the morning I was an hour in the big bath.

This same morning they delivered into my hands, by way of Rome, letters from Monsieur de Tausin, written in Bordeaux on August 2nd, by which he advised me that the day before, by general consent, I had been made mayor of that city; and he urged me to accept this charge for the love of my country.[19]

On Sunday, September 10th, I bathed for an hour in the morning in the women's bath; and since it was a bit warm, I sweated some.

After dinner I went alone on horseback to see some other places in the neighborhood, and a little villa called Granajolo, which stands on the top of one of the highest mountains in these parts. As I passed over these heights, they seemed to me the most beautiful, fertile, and pleasant inhabited slopes that could possibly be seen.

---

[19] For Montaigne's mayoralty, see especially *Essays* III: 10, "Of Husbanding Your Will."

Talking with the natives, I asked one very elderly man whether they used our baths, and he replied that it worked out with them as it did with the people who live near Our Lady of Loreto: that those people rarely go there on a pilgrimage, and that there is little use of the baths except for the benefit of foreigners and those who live far away.[20] He said he was very sorry about one thing, that for a number of years he had observed that the baths did more harm than good to those who used them. He said that the cause of it was this: that whereas in times past there was not a single apothecary in these parts, and you never saw a doctor except rarely, now you see the contrary; for those people who consider their own profit have spread the notion that the baths are of no value unless you take medicine, not only after and before the bath, but even mixing it with the operation of the waters; and they would not readily consent to your taking the waters pure. From this, he said, there followed this very evident result, that more people died from these baths than were cured by them. And he held it for certain that in a little while they would fall into universal disrepute and be abandoned.

Monday, September 11th, in the morning, I voided a good quantity of gravel, most of it looking like millet, solid, red on the surface and gray inside.

Italy: Return to Rome (September 12-October 15, 1581)

On September 12th, 1581, we left the baths of La Villa early in the morning and came to dine at

LUCCA, fourteen miles. These days they were beginning to gather the grapes.

The Feast of the Holy Cross is one of the principal ones in this city; and for a week around it freedom is given to anyone who wants it and who has been banished on account of a civil debt, to return in security to his house, to give him opportunity to attend to his devotions.

I have not found in Italy a single good barber to shave my beard and cut my hair.

On Wednesday evening we went to hear vespers in the cathedral, where there was a gathering of the whole city, and processions. The relic of the Holy Face[1] was to be seen uncovered; it is held in great veneration by them, inasmuch as it is very ancient and famous for sev-

---

[20] Compare *Essays* II: 15, p. 464: "The people of the March of Ancona prefer to make their vows to Saint James [of Compostela in Galicia], and those of Galicia to Our Lady of Loreto [in the March of Ancona]. At Liége they make much ado about the baths of Lucca, and in Tuscany about those of Spa."

[1] A cedar crucifix supposedly carved by Saint Nicomedes and brought miraculously from the Orient in 782. The chapel for it was built in 1484.

eral miracles. For its service the cathedral was built; thus the little chapel in which this relic is kept still stands in the middle of this great church, in an undesirable place, and against every rule of architecture. When vespers were over, the whole procession moved to another church, which in times past was the cathedral.

Thursday I heard Mass in the choir of the said cathedral, along with all the officials of the signory. In Lucca they take great delight in music, and they all join in the singing. It is apparent, however, that they have very few good voices. This Mass was sung with all possible effort, and yet it was not much. They had built for the occasion a big, very high altar of wood and cardboard, covered with images and big silver candlesticks and many silver vessels placed in this order, a basin in the middle and four plates around it; and, adorned in this manner from top to bottom, it produced a notable and beautiful effect.

Every time the bishop says Mass, as he said it today, at the point where he says the *Gloria in excelsis* they set fire to a certain bundle of tow fixed to an iron grating that hangs in the middle of the church for this purpose.

In this region the weather was already much colder and humid.

On Friday the 15th of September I had almost a flux of urine—that is to say, I passed nearly twice as much water as I had drunk. If some part of the water from the bath had remained in my body, I believe I voided it.

On Sunday morning I passed a rough little stone, without any difficulty. I had felt it slightly during the night in the groin and the base of the penis.

On Sunday, September 17th, the ceremony of the changing of the city's Gonfalonier took place. I went to see it at the palace.

They work here almost without regard to Sundays, and there are many shops open.

On Wednesday, September 20th, after dinner, I left Lucca, having first had two bales of stuff made up to send to France. We followed a fast and level road. The country is barren like the Landes of Gascony. We crossed a big stream over a bridge built by Duke Cosimo. In this place are mills for making iron, belonging to the grand duke, and a handsome lodging. There are also three fishponds, or places separated like enclosed ponds, and paved with bricks on the bottom, in which are kept an infinite number of eels, which are easy to see, there being little water. Then we crossed the Arno at Fucecchio and arrived at dusk at

LA SCALA, twenty miles. I left La Scala at sunrise and passed along a fine and almost level road. The country was hilly, with small and very fertile hills like the hills of France. We passed through the middle of Castel-Fiorentino, a little walled-in place, and then passed by the foot of and near Certaldo, Boccaccio's native place, a pretty country seat on a hill. We came to dine at

POGGIBONSI, eighteen miles, a little village. From there to supper at

SIENA, twelve miles. It seems to me that the weather was colder at this season in Italy than in France.

The square in Siena is the most beautiful that is to be seen in any city. Mass is said there every day in public, at an altar in view of all the houses and shops round about, so that the artisans and all these people can hear it without leaving their place and abandoning their work. And when the elevation takes place a trumpet sounds to give notice to all.

On Sunday, September 24th, after dinner, we left Siena, and after following a fast though slightly uneven road (this country being hilly with fertile hills and mountains unlike the Alps), we reached

SAN CHIRICO, twenty miles, a little stronghold. We lodged outside the walls. Since the pack horse had lain down in a little stream that we crossed at a ford, all my things, and particularly my books, were ruined, and it took time to dry them. On the neighboring hills to the left stood Montepulciano, Montichiello, and Castiglioncello.

Early on Monday I went to see a bath two miles away, which is called Vignone, from the name of a little château that is near it. The bath is situated in a rather high place, at the foot of which passes the river Orcia. In this place there are a dozen little houses, or thereabouts, uncomfortable and disgusting, located around it. It looks verminous and wretched. A large pond surrounded by walls and steps, in the middle of which you see bubbling up several springs of that hot water, which, having no odor of sulphur, little vapor, and a reddish sediment, seems to be rather ferruginous than anything else. It is not drunk. The length of this pond is sixty paces, the width thirty-five. In certain places around this pond there are four or five spots set apart and covered, where it is usual to bathe. This bath is rather well-known.

They do not drink this water, but they do drink that of San Cassiano, which has a bigger reputation, near the said San Chirico, eighteen miles toward Rome, on the left-hand side of the main road.

Considering the cleanliness of these earthenware vessels, which are so white and neat that they seem like porcelain, and are so cheap, they really seemed to me more pleasant for eating than the pewter of France, especially when it is dirty, as you find it in the hostelries.

These days I felt a little headache, from which I had thought I was fully freed. And, as before, there came around the eyes, the forehead, and other parts of the front of the head, a heaviness, weakness, and disturbance, which greatly troubled my mind. Tuesday we came to dine at

LA PAGLIA, thirteen miles, and to sleep at

SAN LORENZO, sixteen miles: wretched inns. The vintage was beginning in these parts.

On Wednesday morning there arose a dispute between our men and the drivers from Siena: considering that we had been longer on this journey than usual and that they had to meet the expenses for the horses, they said they would not pay this expense for that evening. The thing went so far that it was necessary to speak to the mayor, who, after hearing me, ruled in my favor, and put one of the drivers in prison. I stated that the horse's falling into the water, which had ruined most of my things, had been the cause of our delay.

Near the main road six miles from Montefiascone, or thereabouts, a few paces away on the right, is a bath named [Naviso],[2] situated in a very large plain, and three or four miles from the nearest mountain. It consists of a little lake, at one end of which you see a big spring bubbling lustily and spouting scalding water. It stinks strongly of sulphur, and forms a white scum and sediment. From this spring on one side a conduit branches off, which leads the water to two baths that are in a nearby house; which house stands alone, with a good many little rooms, but wretched ones. I do not believe that much of a crowd comes here. They drink for seven days, ten pounds each time; but they have to let the water cool a little first to take away that great heat, as is done at the baths of Préchacq. They take their baths the same number of days. This house and the baths are in the domain of a certain church.[3] It rents for fifty crowns. But besides this profit from the sick people who go there in the spring, the man who leases the house sells a certain mud which is drawn from the said lake; and this mud is good for humans when dissolved in warm oil to soothe the itch, or indeed for scabby sheep and dogs, when dissolved in water. This mud sells in its crude form for two giulii a load, in dried balls for seven quattrini apiece. Here we came across a large number of Cardinal Farnese's dogs, which were brought here to be bathed. About three miles from here we reached

VITERBO, sixteen miles. It was so late that we had to make one meal of dinner and supper. I was then very hoarse and chilled, and had slept fully dressed on a table at San Lorenzo because of the bugs; which I had not had to do except there and in Florence. At Viterbo I ate some sort of acorn called *gensole*. These are found in many places in Italy. They are tasty. There are still so many starlings here that you can get one for one baiocco.[4]

On Thursday, September 28th, in the morning, I went to see some other baths near this town, situated in the plain a good way off, and far from the mountain. First you see buildings in two different places where not long ago there used to be baths, which have been ruined by neglect.[5] The ground, however, gives off a great stench. There is also a wretched little hovel in which a tiny little spring of hot water makes a little lake to bathe in.[6] This water has no smell and an insipid taste; it is moderately hot. I judged that it had a lot of iron in it. This water is drunk. Farther on is the palace that is called the Pope's, because it is believed that Pope Nicholas[7] built it or rebuilt it. At the foot of this palace and in the ground, in a very low spot, there are three different springs of hot water. One of these serves for drinking. It is of moderate and temperate heat; no stink, no odor. In taste, it has a little tang and sharpness. I think it contains much niter. I had gone with the intention

---

[2] Montaigne left the name blank.
[3] The Church of Sant' Angelo in Spata, in Viterbo.
[4] About a half a sou.
[5] The baths of San Paolo and Almadiani.
[6] The bath of the Madonna.
[7] Nicholas V.

of drinking for three days. It is drunk as in other places in regard to quantity. You take a walk afterward, and it is a good thing to sweat.

This water has a very great reputation, and is carried in loads all over Italy. And this is the water which the doctor[8] who has written about baths in general says is the best for drinking of all the waters of Italy. In particular they attribute to it great virtue for kidney troubles. It is drunk most commonly in May. It was a bad omen for me to read an inscription on the wall by one who cursed the doctors for having sent him there, and who had got much worse; and besides, the bath-keeper said the season was too far advanced, and was cool in encouraging me to drink.

There is only one lodging, though it is large and respectably comfortable, a mile and a half from Viterbo. I went there on foot. There are three or four baths, varying in their effect, and also a place for showers. These waters form a very white scum, which readily hardens and becomes solid as ice, making a hard crust on the water. The whole place appears whitened and encrusted in this way. Put a piece of linen on it, and immediately you see it loaded with this scum, and as solid as if it were frozen. This stuff[9] is useful for cleaning your teeth, and is exported and sold. When you chew it, the only taste you get is of earth or sand. It is said to be the same substance as marble. Who knows whether it might not also become petrified in the kidneys? They say, however, that this water, which is carried in bottles, forms no sediment and keeps clear and very pure. I believe it may be drunk with pleasure, and that it gets some taste from its sharpness that makes it easy to drink.

Returning from there, in this same plain, which is very long and eight miles wide, I went to see the place where the inhabitants of Viterbo (among whom there is not a single gentleman; they are all laborers and merchants) collect the flax and hemp, which is a great industry of theirs. The men do this work; there are no women among them. There was a great quantity of it and many laborers around a certain lake of water which is equally hot and boiling at every season.[10] They say that this lake has no bottom. From it they draw off water to form other little tepid lakes, in which they put the hemp and flax to steep.

Back at the house, having made this trip going on foot and returning on horseback, I ejected a small, red, solid stone, as big as a big grain of wheat. I had felt its descent a little around the groin the day before. It stopped in the passage. In order to ease it out it is good to hold the urine from passing and squeeze the prick a little, so that it may come out more vigorously. The seigneur de Langon showed me this remedy at Arsac.

On Saturday, the Feast of Saint Michael, after dinner, I went to

---

[8] Andrea Bacci, author of *De Thermis* (Venice, 1571).
[9] Calcium carbonate.
[10] The Bulicame, which Dante mentions in the *Inferno* (xiv.79–80).

the Madonna della Quercia, a mile out of the town. You go by a very fine big road, level and straight, bordered with trees from one end to the other, built with great care by Pope Farnese [Paul III]. The church is beautiful, most religious, and full of innumerable votive tablets. The Latin inscription states that a hundred years ago or thereabouts a man, attacked by robbers and half dead, took refuge by an oak on which was this image of the Madonna, and after praying to her became miraculously invisible to the robbers and thus escaped a most certain danger. This miracle gave rise to this local cult of the Madonna. Around this oak was built this very beautiful church. The trunk of the oak is now seen cut at the base, and the part where the image is placed is attached to the wall, and the branches around it are cut away.

On Saturday, the last day of September, in the morning, I left Viterbo and took the road to Bagnaia, a place belonging to Cardinal Gambara, very ornate, and provided among other things with fountains. And in this respect it seems not only to equal but to surpass both Pratolino and Tivoli. In the first place it has running spring water, which Tivoli has not; and this is so abundant (as it is not at Pratolino) that it suffices for an infinite number of purposes. The same Messer Tomaso da Siena who directed the work at Tivoli, or most of it, is also in charge of this, which is not finished; and thus, always adding new inventions to the old, he has put into this, his latest work, much more art, beauty, and grace. Among a thousand other members of this excellent body you see a high pyramid which spouts water in many different ways: one jet rises, another falls. Around this pyramid are four beautiful little lakes, clear, clean, full of water. In the middle of each is a little stone ship with two musketeers which draw water and shoot it against the pyramid, and in each a trumpeter which also draws water. You go around these lakes and the pyramid by very beautiful alleys with balustrades of fine stone, most artfully carved. The others liked other parts more. The palace is small but clean and pretty. Certainly, if I know anything about it, this place easily takes the prize for the use and service of water. The cardinal was not there. But since he is French at heart, his men showed us all the courtesy and friendliness that could be desired.

From here, following the straight road, we came upon Caprarola, a palace of Cardinal Farnese, which is very greatly renowned in Italy. I have seen none in Italy that may be compared with it. It has a great moat around it, cut out of the tufa. The building is above, in the manner of a terrace; you do not see the tiles. The form is pentagonal, but to the eye it appears distinctly square. Inside, however, it is perfectly round, with wide corridors going around it, all vaulted and painted on all sides. The rooms are all square; the building, very large; very beautiful public rooms. One of these is wonderful: on its vaulted ceiling (for the building is vaulted throughout) you see the celestial sphere, with all the constellations; around it on the walls, the terrestrial globe, the regions and the whole world, everything painted very richly directly on the wall itself.

In various other places you see depicted the noblest actions of Pope Paul III and of the house of Farnese. The persons are portrayed so true to life that where you see portrayed our Constable, or the Queen Mother, or her sons Charles, Henry, and the duke of Alençon, and the queen of Navarre,[11] they are immediately recognized by those who have seen them; likewise King Francis, Henry II, Pietro Strozzi, and others. In one and the same room, you see the effigy of King Henry II at one end and in the place of honor, under which the inscription says "Preserver of the House of Farnese," and at the other end King Philip,[12] whose inscription says "For the many benefits received from him."

Outside there are also many noteworthy and beautiful things, among others a grotto, which, spraying water artfully into a little lake, gives the appearance to the eye and the ear of the most natural rainfall. The location is barren and alpine. And the cardinal has to draw the water for his fountain all the way from Viterbo, eight miles away.

From here, following a level road and a large plain, we came upon some very big meadows, in the middle of which, in certain dry and grassless spots, you see springs bubbling up of pure cold water, but stinking so much of sulphur that the odor of it is perceived from a great distance.[13] We came to sleep at

MONTEROSSI, twenty-three miles. On Sunday, October 1st, to

ROME, twenty-two miles. We felt at this season an extreme cold and an icy north wind from the mountains.

On Monday and for some days after, I had indigestion in my stomach. And for this reason I took some meals apart in order to eat less; and my bowels were loose, so that I felt physically pretty sprightly, except for my head, which has never completely recovered.

On the day I arrived in Rome I received the letters from the jurats of Bordeaux,[14] who wrote me very courteously about the fact that they had elected me mayor of their city, and urgently requested me to join them.

On Sunday, October 8th, 1581, I went to the Baths of Diocletian on Monte Cavallo to see an Italian who had been for a long time a slave of the Turks, and had learned a thousand rare tricks in riding.[15] For example, while riding at full speed he would stand up straight on the saddle, hurl a javelin with all his might, and then suddenly drop back into the saddle. Galloping furiously and holding the saddlebow with one hand, he would get off his horse and touch the ground with

---

[11] These personages are respectively the Constable Anne de Montmorency, Catherine de' Medici, Charles IX, Henry III, Duke Francis of Alençon, and Margaret of Valois, queen of Navarre.

[12] Philip II of Spain.

[13] La Solfatara, near Ronciglione.

[14] The municipal council.

[15] Compare *Essays* I: 48, p. 215.

his right foot while the left remained in the stirrup; and many times in this way he dismounted and jumped into the saddle again. He would turn his body around in the saddle several times, galloping all the while. He shot a Turkish bow forward and backward with great ease. Leaning his head and shoulders on the horse's neck and holding his feet straight up in the air, he let the horse go at full speed. He took a club and threw it in the air and caught it again on the run. Standing up on the saddle, he aimed a lance at a glove and pierced it, as people tilt at the ring. On foot he made a pike revolve around his neck, in front and behind, having first given it a hard push with his hand.

On October 10th, after dinner, the French ambassador sent a footman to tell me that if I wished, he was coming to pick me up in his coach to take me to see the furniture of Cardinal Orsini, which was being sold, since he had died this summer in Naples and had left as heir to all his vast property a niece of his, a little girl. Among other rare things was a taffeta coverlet lined with swans' feathers. In Siena you see a good many of these swans' skins complete with feathers, and I was asked no more than a crown and a half for one, all prepared. They are the size of a sheepskin, and a few of them would be enough to make a coverlet of this sort. I also saw an ostrich egg, decorated all over and painted with pretty pictures. Also a square box to put jewels in, which contained a certain quantity of them; but since the box was most artfully arranged with mirrors all around, when it was opened it appeared much wider and deeper in every direction, and seemed to hold ten times as many jewels as were in it, since one and the same thing was seen many times by the reflection of the mirrors, and the mirrors were not easy to detect.

On Thursday, October 12th, the cardinal of Sens took me alone with him in his coach to see the Church of Saints John and Paul, of which he is the patron, as he is of those friars who make the waters and perfumes I spoke of above;[16] it is situated on Mount Celio. And this lofty site seems to be made artificially, since underneath it is all vaulted, with great corridors and underground rooms. It is said that the Forum Hostilium[17] was there. The gardens and vineyards of these friars are so placed as to give a beautiful view of Rome, old and new, from a place set apart by its steep and precipitous height, and almost inaccessible on every side.

This same day I gave a well-filled wooden case to a carrier to send to Milan. The muleteers ordinarily take twenty days on the road there. The whole thing weighed 150 pounds, and you pay four baiocchi, which comes to two French sous, per pound. There were many things of value in it, above all a very handsome Agnus Dei necklace, which had not its like in Rome, having been made especially for the Empress's ambassador, who had it blessed by the Pope; and also a *cavalliere*.[18]

[16] The Jesuates. See above, pp. 917–19.
[17] Montaigne presumably has in mind the Cura Hostilia, where at one time the Senate met. It was located on the Forum, some distance away.
[18] A kind of chaplet.

Italy and France: The Return Home
(October 15-November 30, 1581)

On Sunday morning, October 15th, I started out from Rome and left my brother[1] there with forty-three gold crowns, with which, he had decided, he could stay there and learn fencing for five months. Before I left he had rented a nice little room for twenty giulii a month. Messieurs d'Estissac, de Monluc, de Chasai, Morens, and several others accompanied me for the first stage. And if I had not started early in order to save these gentlemen the trouble, there would have been a good many others ready to come, who had already hired horses, Messieurs du Bellai, d'Ambres, d'Alègre, and others. I came to sleep at

RONCIGLIONE, thirty miles, having hired the horses for as far as Lucca at twenty giulii each, the driver paying the expenses of the said horses.

On Monday morning I was astonished to feel such a piercing cold that it seemed to me I had never experienced such a cold winter, and to see the vintage and vine harvest not yet finished in these parts. I came to dine at

VITERBO, where I put on my furs and all my winter trappings; and from there to sup at

SAN LORENZO, twenty-nine miles. From there I came to sleep at

SAN CHIRICO, thirty-two miles. All these roads have been repaired this year by order of the duke of Tuscany; which work is very fine and serves the public to great advantage. May God reward him for it! For the most difficult roads have by this means become as fast and comfortable as the streets of a city.

It was an astounding thing to see the great multitude of people who were going to Rome. On this account it was to be observed that horses for hire to go to Rome were beyond all price for their scarcity, and to return from Rome they let you have them for nothing. Near Siena, as in innumerable other places, there is a double bridge, that is to say a bridge above which another stream crosses over an aqueduct. We arrived in the evening at

SIENA, twenty miles. Tonight I felt some colic for about two hours, and it seemed to me I felt the stone descending.

Early on Thursday Guglielmo Felice, a Hebrew doctor, came to see me and gave me a long lecture on the regimen I should follow for my kidneys and gravel. In this condition I left Siena; and the colic seized me again, and lasted three or four hours. At the end of this time I clearly perceived, from an extreme pain in the groin, the prick, and the ass, that the stone had descended. I came for supper to

PONTE A ELSA, twenty-eight miles. Here I voided a stone bigger

[1] Bertrand de Mattecoulon, who was later to be involved in a duel in Rome (see *Essays* II:27, p. 526).

than a grain of millet, with some red gravel, without pain or difficulty in the passage. I left here Friday morning and stopped on the road at

ALTO PASCIO, sixteen miles. I stayed here an hour to have the animals fed. Here, without much pain, I passed with a good deal of gravel a long stone, partly solid and partly soft, of the size of a big grain, and bigger. On the road we came upon a number of country people who were picking the vine leaves, which they keep as fodder for the animals in the winter; others were gathering ferns to make their litter. We came to sleep at

LUCCA, eight miles. Here a number of gentlemen and artisans came to visit me.

On Saturday morning, October 21st, I ejected another stone, which stopped a while in the passage but nevertheless came out without pain or difficulty. This one was rather round than otherwise, hard and massive, but harsh and rough, white inside and red outside, much bigger than a grain. Meanwhile I voided gravel all the time. From this we see that nature sometimes purges itself, and you feel a sort of flux of this stuff. God be thanked that it comes out without serious pain and does not disturb my actions!

As soon as I had eaten a grape (for on this trip I ate very little or nothing in the morning), I left Lucca without waiting for certain gentlemen who were getting ready to come and accompany me. I had a fine road, mostly level, with the hills covered with numberless olive trees on my right, on my left some marshes, and the sea not far off.

In one place in the state of Lucca I came across a machine that is half ruined owing to the negligence of the said lords; and this lack does great harm to the surrounding country. This machine was made for the purpose of draining the soil in these marshes and making them fertile. A great ditch had been dug, at the end of which three wheels were kept continually in motion by means of a stream of running water which came falling down from the mountain onto them. These wheels, with certain vessels attached to them, drew the water from one side of this ditch, and on the other side poured it into another, higher ditch and channel; which ditch, made for this purpose and provided with walls on each side, carried this water into the sea. Thus the whole country around was drained.

I passed through the middle of Pietrasanta, a fairly large fortress town of the duke of Florence, with many houses but empty of people, because, from what they say, the air is so bad that you cannot live there, and most of them die or barely exist. We came for supper to

MASSA DI CARRARA, twenty-two miles, a town belonging to the prince of Massa, of the house of Cibo. You see a fine castle on the top of a hill. About midway up this hill, around the said castle and below it, are the streets and houses, surrounded by good walls. And further down, outside the said walls, is a large suburb in the plain, surrounded by other new walls. The place is handsome: handsome streets, handsome painted houses.

I was forced to drink new wines—they drink no others in these parts—which, with a certain kind of wood and the whites of eggs, are made so clear that they lack none of the color of the old wines; but they have an indefinable unnatural taste.

On Sunday, October 22nd, I first followed a very level road, having the Tyrrhenian Sea still on my left, a harquebus-shot away. And on this road, between us and the sea, we saw some ruins, not very big, which the people of the country say used to be a great city called Luna.[2]

Then we came to Sarzana, a town belonging to the Republic of Genoa; and you see their coat of arms there, a Saint George on horseback. They keep a guard of Swiss soldiers, since the town once belonged to the duke of Florence. And if the prince of Massa were not in between them, there is no doubt that Pietrasanta and Sarzana, the frontier towns of the two states, would be continually at grips.

We passed Sarzana, where we were forced to pay four giulii per horse for one stage, and where a great artillery celebration was being held for the passage of Don Giovanni de' Medici, natural brother of the duke of Florence, who was returning from Genoa from seeing the Empress,[3] on whom many other princes of Italy had also gone to call, on behalf of his said brother. And among other things there was much ado about the sumptuosity of the duke of Ferrara, who had come to meet her at Padua with four hundred carriages. He had asked permission of the Signory of Venice to pass through their territory with six hundred horse, and upon their replying to his request that they would allow him to come with a certain somewhat smaller number, he put all his people into carriages and thus brought them all, but diminished the number of horses. I came across this prince Don Giovanni on the way, a young man very handsome in person, accompanied by twenty men in good harness but on hired horses; a way of traveling which is not considered unbecoming in Italy, even for a prince. After passing Sarzana, we left the road to Genoa on our left.

To get to Milan it makes little difference whether you go by way of Genoa or by the other way; it comes to the same thing. I wanted to see that city, and the Empress, who was there. What bothered me was that there are two routes to go there, one three days' journey from Sarzana, which has forty miles of very bad and very alpine road, of rocks and precipices and bad inns; this road is little frequented. The other is through Lerici, three miles from Sarzana, where you embark on the sea and in twelve hours cross over to Genoa. Since I cannot endure the water because of the weakness of my stomach, and feared the discomfort of this route even less than the difficulty of getting lodgings, because of the great crowd of people in Genoa; and moreover, since it was said that the road from Genoa to Milan was none too

---

[2] An ancient Etruscan town, already decayed in Roman times, and demolished by the Arabs in 1016.

[3] Maria, widow of Maximilian II.

safe from robbers; and since I had nothing but my return home on my mind; I decided to pass up Genoa, and followed the road on the right through many mountains, always keeping to the bottoms and the valley along the river Magra. And having this river on our left, we passed now through the state of Genoa, now through that of the duke of Florence, now that of the lords of the house of Malespina. Finally, by a road that was reasonably good, except for a few steep and precipitous spots, we came to sleep at

PONTREMOLI, thirty miles, a very long town, full of ancient buildings which are not very attractive. There are a few ruins, and they say that the town was called Appua[4] by the ancients. It now belongs to the state of Milan, and recently the Fieschi family held it.

At table the first thing they gave me was cheese, as they do around Milan and in the country around Piacenza. Following the Genoese practice, they gave me olives without pits, prepared with oil and vinegar like a salad—very good.

The site of this town is among the mountains and at the foot of them.

To wash your hands they furnished a basin full of water placed on a stool. Everyone had to wash his hands in the same water.

I left here Monday morning, the 23rd, and on leaving the house climbed the Apennines—very high, but the road not at all hard or dangerous. All day we were climbing and coming down mountains, mostly alpine and barren. In the evening we came to sleep at

FORNOVO, in the state of the count of San Secondo, thirty miles. It was a pleasure to find myself out of the hands of those scoundrels of the mountains, who practice every sort of cruelty imaginable on travelers in charging for food and horses.

They put on the table for me an assortment of condiments in the form of excellent relishes of various kinds. One of these was made with quinces.

In these parts you find that horses for hire are extremely scarce. You are in the hands of people who have no rules and who do not keep their word to foreigners. Others paid two giulii per horse for each stage; they demanded of me three, four, and five giulii for each stage, so that every day it came to more than a crown to hire one horse, because they also counted two stages where there was only one.

Here I was two stages away from Parma; and to Piacenza from Parma it was the same distance as from Fornovo, so that by going to Parma I would have lengthened the trip by only two stages. I decided not to go there so as not to upset my trip home, having put aside all other plans. This place is a tiny village of six or seven little houses, situated on a plain along the flooded river Taro—I think that is the name of it—which we followed for a time on Tuesday morning, coming to dine at

---

[4] In ancient times there was a people of Liguria called the Appuans, but no town of Appua is believed to have existed.

BORGO SAN DONNINO, twelve miles, a little stronghold which the duke of Parma is beginning to surround with fine walls, well-flanked. Here they put on the table a mustard-like relish made with apples and oranges cut in pieces, like half-cooked quince marmalade.

From here, leaving on our right Cremona at the same distance as Piacenza, we followed a very fine level road in a countryside where as far as the horizon you see no mountains or unevenness, with very fertile soil; changing horses at every stage. I took these two stages at a gallop to test the strength of my loins, and felt neither pain nor fatigue from it; my urine was natural.

Near Piacenza there are two big columns, one on either side of the road, with about forty paces between them. At the foot of these columns are Latin inscriptions which forbid building or planting trees or vines between them. I do not know whether they merely wanted to preserve the width of the road, or indeed to keep the esplanade open, as we see it to be, from these columns to the town, which is half a mile away. We came to sleep at

PIACENZA, twenty miles, a very big city. Having arrived very early, I went all around in it for three hours. Muddy, unpaved streets, small houses. And in the square, which is its most beautiful spot, is the Palace of Justice, and the prisons, surrounded by shops of no account and the crowd of citizens from all around.

I saw the castle, which is in the hands of King Philip, who keeps here a guard of three hundred Spaniards, badly paid, so I understood from them. The dian[5] is sounded morning and evening with the instruments that we call oboes and they call *pifferi*; and it is sounded for an hour. There are many people in the castle, and handsome pieces of artillery. The duke of Parma never goes there. He for his part (and he was in the city at that time) is lodged in the citadel, which is a castle in another place; and he never goes to the castle that King Philip holds.

In short, I saw nothing here worth seeing except the new Monastery of Saint Augustine, built with money that King Philip has used here, in exchange for another Church of Saint Augustine, from the materials of which he has made this castle; for he holds part of the revenue of the church itself. The church remains to be built, and is well begun. But the lodgings of the friars, who are seventy in number, and the double cloisters, are finished. In corridors, dormitories, wine cellars, and other facilities, this building seems to me the most sumptuous and magnificent that I have seen anywhere, if I remember rightly, for the service of the Church.

At table here they put on the salt in a lump, the cheese in a big piece without a dish.

The duke of Parma was expecting the arrival in Piacenza of the first-born son of the archduke of Austria, which son I saw at Innsbruck; and now it was said that he was going to Rome to be crowned king of the Romans.

[5] Normally, the reveille.

They offer water for the hands, and for mixing with the wine, with a big brass spoon. The cheese they eat here is exactly like the Piacentini cheeses that are sold all over.

Piacenza is exactly halfway between Rome and Lyons. In order to go more directly to Milan I would have had to go and sleep at Marignano, thirty miles, and from there to Milan it is ten miles. I lengthened my trip by ten miles in order to see Pavia. I left early on Wednesday, October 25th, following a fine road, in which I urinated one soft little stone and a lot of gravel.

We passed through the middle of a walled village of Count Santafiore. Toward the end of the trip we crossed the Po on a ferry made of scaffolding placed on two boats and surmounted by a little cabin, with a long rope resting in various places on some small boats arranged in order on the river. Near this place the Ticino joins the Po. We came early to

PAVIA, thirty short miles. Immediately I set about seeing the principal sights of the city: the bridge over the Ticino, the cathedral, the churches of the Carmelites, Saint Thomas, Saint Augustine, in which is the shrine of Saint Augustine, a rich sepulcher of white marble with many statues.

In a certain square in the city may be seen a brick column, on top of which is a statue which seems to be a copy of the one of Antoninus Pius[6] on horseback in front of the Capitol. This one is smaller and not at all comparable in beauty. But what makes me more doubtful is that this statue has two stirrups and a saddle with saddlebows in front and behind, whereas the other does not have these; and this is all the more in agreement with the opinion of the learned, that stirrups, and saddles of this kind, were invented later. Perhaps some ignorant sculptor thought that these were lacking. I also saw the beginning of Cardinal Borromeo's building for the use of the students.

The city is large and rather beautiful, comfortably populated, and there is no lack of artisans of many kinds. There are few beautiful houses; and the one in which the Empress stayed these past days is not much. I saw the arms of France, but the lilies had been effaced. In short, there is nothing rare here.

In these parts horses are hired for two giulii per stage. The best hostelry, or, to be more precise, the best hotel in which I have stayed from Rome to here was the Post at Piacenza; and I believe it is the best in Italy, after that of Verona. The worst on this journey was the Falcon in Pavia. Here and in Milan you pay extra for firewood, and the beds lack mattresses.

I left Pavia on Thursday, October 26th. I took the road to the right, half a mile off the direct route, to see the spot where they say the shattering of King Francis' army occurred,[7] which is a level place; and also to see the Charterhouse, which with good reason has the reputation

6 Not Antoninus Pius, but Marcus Aurelius.

7 The battle of Pavia, in which Francis I was defeated and taken prisoner by Charles V in 1525.

of being a very beautiful church. The façade of the entrance, all of marble, with numberless carvings, is really something stupendous. There is also an altar decoration in ivory, on which are carved the Old and the New Testament. Besides this there is the marble tomb of Gian Galeazzo Visconti, founder of the church; and then the choir, and the decorations of the high altar, and the cloisters, very beautiful and of unusual size. These are the finest things. The house is very large in area and gives the impression—not only in the size and number of its different buildings, but even more in the number of people, servants, horses, coaches, laborers, and artisans—of being the court of a very great prince. They are continually working on it at incredible expense, which the Fathers pay out of their revenues. The site is in the middle of a very beautiful meadow. From here we came to

MILAN, twenty miles. This city is the most populous in Italy, large, and full of all sorts of artisans and merchandise. It is not too much unlike Paris, and has much the appearance of a French city. It lacks the palaces of Rome, Naples, Genoa, Florence; but in size it beats them all, and in its crowds of people it comes up to Venice.

On Friday, October 27th, I went to see the castle from the outside, and went almost all around it. It is a very big building and wonderfully strong. The garrison in it consists of at least seven hundred Spaniards, excellently supplied with artillery; and they were adding more defenses all around. This day I stopped there because of the very heavy rain that suddenly caught us. Until then the weather and the roads had treated us very kindly.

On Saturday, October 28th, I left Milan in the morning. I set out on a fine level road, and although it rained continuously and the road was full of water, there was no mud, for the country is sandy. I came for dinner to

BUFFALORA, eighteen miles. Here we crossed the bridge over the river Naviglio, which is narrow, but deep enough to carry big boats to Milan. And a little farther on we crossed the Ticino by boat and came to sleep at

NOVARA, twelve miles, a little town, not very attractive, standing in a plain, with vineyards and groves and fertile land around it. We left there in the morning and came and stopped a bit to feed our animals at

VERCELLI, ten miles, a town belonging to the duke of Savoy, also in a plain and along the river Sesia, which we crossed by boat. The said duke has built in this place, in a great hurry and with a world of people, a fortress—a handsome one, as far as I could see from outside— and has thereby aroused the suspicion of the Spaniards near these parts.

From here we passed through the middle of San German and then Santhià, two little walled villages. And, always following a beautiful plain, fertile mainly in walnuts (for in this region there are no olives, and no oil except from walnuts), we came to sleep at

LIVORNO, twenty miles, a little village with a good many houses. We left Monday early, and following a level road came to dine at

CHIVASSO, ten miles; and from here, crossing a lot of rivers and streams by boat and at fords, we came to

TURIN, ten miles. We could easily have arrived here in time to dine. A small city in a very watery location, not very well built or attractive, although a little stream runs through the middle of the streets to clean away the dirt. In Turin I paid five and a half crowns per horse for my use as far as Lyons, six days, their expenses to be paid by the drivers.

Here they ordinarily speak French, and they all appear very devoted to France. The language of the people is a language that has almost nothing Italian about it but the pronunciation; the rest of it is French words.

We left here on Tuesday, the last of October, and came along a level road to dine at

SAN AMBROGIO, two stages. From there, following a narrow plain between the mountains, to sleep at

SUSA, two stages, a little walled place with a good many houses. Here I felt a great pain in my right knee, which pain had already bothered me a good many days, but kept increasing all the time. The hostelries are better here than in other parts of Italy—good wines, bad bread, much to eat, courteous innkeepers—and throughout Savoy. On All Saints' Day, after hearing Mass, I came to

NOVALESA, one stage. Here I hired eight *marroni*[8] to carry me in a chair to the top of Mont Cenis and take me down in a sledge on the other side.

[THE JOURNAL BY MONTAIGNE IN FRENCH]

Here they speak French; so I quit this foreign language, which I use easily but with very little sureness, not having had the time to learn it at all well, since I was always in the company of Frenchmen.

I made the ascent of Mont Cenis halfway on horseback, halfway on a litter carried by four men, with another four who relieved them. They carried me on their shoulders. The ascent takes two hours, stony and difficult for horses that are not accustomed to it, but otherwise without danger or difficulty; for since the mountain is broad and rises steadily, you find no precipices, and no danger except of a stumble.

From the top of the mountain you see beneath you a plain two leagues wide, many little houses, lakes, and fountains, and the post-house; no trees, but a lot of grass and meadows that are useful in the mild season. At that time everything was covered with snow. The descent is one league, steep and straight, and I was taken on a sledge by the same *marrons*. And for all their service, for the eight of them, I paid two crowns. The sledging alone costs only one teston. It is a pleasant sport, but without any risk.

We dined, without much appetite, at

LANSLEBOURG, two stages, which is a village at the foot of the mountain, where Savoy begins; and we came on to sleep in a little village[9]

8 French *marrons*: litter-carriers.
9 Possibly Termignon.

two leagues away. There are lots of trout all around here and excellent old and new wines. From here we came, by a hilly and stony road, to dine at

SAINT-MICHEL, five leagues, a village where the posthouse is. From here we came to rest, very late and very wet, at

LA CHAMBRE, five leagues, a little town from which the marquises de La Chambre take their title. On Friday, November 3rd, we came to dine at

AIGUEBELLE, four leagues, a little enclosed town, and to sleep at

MONTMÉLIAN, four leagues, a town with a fort which occupies the top of a low ridge that rises out of the middle of the plain between these high mountains. The said town is situated below the said fort on the river Isère, which goes on to Grenoble, seven leagues from the said place. Here I clearly felt the excellence of the Italian oils, for those over here began to give me a stomach-ache, whereas the others never gave me an aftertaste. We came to dine at

CHAMBÉRY, two leagues, the principal town of Savoy, small, handsome, and mercantile, set among the mountains, but in a place where they recede a long way and form a very big plain. From here we passed over the Mont du Chat, high, steep, and rocky, but not at all dangerous or hard, at the foot of which lies a big lake, and along this a castle called Bourdeau, where they make very renowned swords; and to rest at

YENNE, four leagues, a small town.

On Sunday morning we crossed the Rhone, which we had on our right, after passing a little fort on the river which the duke of Savoy has built between some rocks that are very close together; and along one of these rocks there is a little narrow path at the end of which is the said fort, not very unlike Chiusa, which the Venetians set at the end of the mountains of Tyrol. From here, still going along the low ground between the mountains, we came without a stop to

SAINT-RAMBERT, seven leagues, a tiny little town in the said valley. Most of the towns in Savoy have a stream in the middle that washes them; and the streets on both sides, as far as the said stream, are covered with big porch roofs, so that you are under cover and dry in all weather. It is true that the shops are the darker for it.

On Monday morning, November 6th, we left Saint-Rambert, where Monsieur Francesco Cenami, a banker from Lyons who had retired here because of the plague, sent his nephew to me with some of his wine and many very nice compliments. I left here Monday morning early, and after at last coming completely out of the mountains, I began to enter upon the really French plains. Here I crossed the river Ain in a boat at the harbor of Chazey, and came on without stopping to

MONTLUEL, six leagues, a small town on a much-traveled road, belonging to the duke of Savoy, and the last of his. On Tuesday after dinner I took the post and came to sleep at

LYONS, two stages, three leagues. I liked the sight of the city very much. On Friday I bought from Joseph de La Sone three unused little cropped horses to go in file, for two hundred crowns; and the day before I had bought from Malesieu one pacing horse for fifty crowns and another cropped one for thirty-three.

On Saturday, Saint Martin's Day, in the morning I had a bad stomach-ache, and stayed in bed until afternoon, when I had diarrhea; I ate no dinner and very little supper.

On Sunday, November 12th, Monsieur Alberto Giachinotti of Florence, who showed me many other courtesies, had me to dinner at his house, and offered to lend me money, though he had no knowledge of me until then.

On Wednesday, November 15th, I left Lyons after dinner, and by a hilly road came to sleep at

LA BOURDELLIÈRE, five leagues, a village in which there are only two houses. From here on Thursday morning we took a fine level road, and around the middle of it, near Feurs, a little village, we crossed the river Loire by boat and came on without stopping to

L'HÔPITAL, eight leagues, a little walled place. From here Friday morning we followed a hilly road in bitter, snowy weather with a cruel wind against us, and came on to

THIERS, six leagues, a small town on the river Allier, very mercantile, well-built, and populous. Their principal traffic is in paper, and they are renowned for carved knives and playing cards. It is equidistant from Lyons, Saint-Flour, Moulins, and Le Puy.

The closer I came to home, the more the length of the road seemed annoying; and indeed, counting the days, I was not halfway from Rome to my house until Chambéry at the earliest. This town is part of the appanages of the house of [Bourbon][10] belonging to the duke of Montpensier.

I went to Palmier's to see the cards made. There are as many workmen and as much to do in this as in any other worthy business. The common cards are sold at only one sou, and the fine ones at two caroli.

On Saturday we followed the rich plain of the Limagne, and, after crossing the Dore and then the Allier by boat, came to sleep at

PONT-DU-CHÂTEAU, four leagues. The plague has ravaged this place badly, and I heard many remarkable stories about it. The manor house, which is the ancestral home of Viscount de Canillac, was burned down as they were trying to purify it with fire. The said lord sent one of his men to me with many offers by word of mouth, and to ask me to write to Monsieur de Foix to recommend his son, whom he had just sent to Rome.

On Sunday, November 19th, I came to dine at

CLERMONT, two leagues, and stopped here for the sake of my young horses.

On Monday the 20th I left in the morning, and, at the top of the Puy de Dôme, I passed a rather large stone, broad and flat in shape, which had been in the passage since morning, and I had felt it the day before, only at the base of the penis; and at the time when it was about to descend into the bladder, I also felt it a bit in the kidneys. It was neither soft nor hard. I passed through

---

[10] Montaigne leaves the name blank.

PONTGIBAUD, where I went to greet Madame de La Fayette in passing, and I was half an hour in her parlor. This house has less beauty than reputation; the site of it is rather ugly than otherwise, the garden small, square, and the alleys in it raised a good four or five feet; the beds are at the bottom, with many fruit trees and few herbs in them, and the sides of these sunken beds are lined with freestone.

It was snowing so hard, and the weather was so bitter, with a cold wind, that you saw nothing of the country. I came to sleep at

PONTAUMUR, seven leagues, a little village. Monsieur and Madame du Lude were two leagues from there. The next day I came to sleep at

PONTCHARRAUD, a little village, six leagues. This road is studded with wretched hostelries as far as Limoges; they do not lack passable wines, however. No one passes but muleteers and messengers bound for Lyons.

My head was not in good shape; and if storms and cold winds and rain are bad for it, I gave it its fill of them on these roads, where they say the winter is more severe than anywhere else in France.

On Wednesday, November 22nd, in very bad weather, I left here, and having passed through Felletin, a little town that seems to be well built, situated in a valley bottom all surrounded by high slopes, and which was still half deserted because of the recent plague, I came to sleep at

CHATAIN, five leagues, a wretched little village. Here I drank some new and unpurified wine, for lack of old wine. On Thursday the 23rd, with my head still in the same condition, in rough weather, I came to sleep at

SAUVIAT, five leagues, a little village that belongs to Monsieur de Lauzun. From here I came the next day to sleep at

LIMOGES, six leagues, where I stayed all day Saturday, and bought a mule for ninety sun-crowns, and paid five crowns for a mule-load from Lyons to here, having been cheated in this of four livres; for all the other loads cost only three and two-thirds crowns. From Limoges to Bordeaux we paid one crown per hundredweight.

On Sunday, November 26th, I left Limoges after dinner and came to sleep at

LES CARS, five leagues, where there was no one but Madame des Cars. On Monday I came to sleep at

THIVIERS, six leagues. Tuesday to sleep at

PÉRIGUEUX, five leagues. Wednesday to sleep at

MAURIAC, five leagues. On Thursday, Saint Andrew's Day, the last of November, to sleep at

MONTAIGNE, seven leagues, which I had left on June 22nd, 1580, to go to La Fère. Thus my travels had lasted seventeen months and eight days.[11]

---

[11] On his copy of Beuther's *Ephemeris historica,* under the date November 30, Montaigne wrote this note: "1581, I arrived in my house, back from a trip I had made in Germany and Italy from June 22, 1579 [read 1580] until the said day; on which day the year before I had arrived in Rome."